HOME RUN

HOME RUN

EDITED BY

GEORGE PLIMPTON

A HARVEST ORIGINAL • HARCOURT, INC.

SAN DIEGO   NEW YORK   LONDON

www.harcourt.com

Library of Congress Cataloging-in-Publication Data
Home run/edited by George Plimpton.—1st ed.
p.   cm.
"A Harvest book."
ISBN 0-15-601154-9
1. Home runs (Baseball)—Anecdotes. 2. Baseball stories, American.
I. Plimpton, George.
GV868.4 .H64 2000
796.357'0973—dc21   2001016819

Designed by Linda Lockowitz
Text set in AGaramond
Printed in the United States of America
First edition
A B C D E F G H I J

Permissions acknowledgments appear on pages 277–78, which constitute a continuation
of the copyright page.

To Terry, Nick, and Tom

The scene is instant, whole and wonderful. In its beauty and design that vision of the soaring stands, the pattern of forty thousand empetalled faces, the velvet and unalterable geometry of the playing field, and the small lean figures of the players, set there, lonely, tense and waiting in their places, bright, desperate solitary atoms encircled by that huge wall of nameless faces, is incredible. And more than anything, it is the light, the miracle of light and shade and color—the crisp, blue light that swiftly slants out from the soaring stands and, deepening to violet, begins to march across the velvet field and towards the pitcher's box, that gives the thing its single and incomparable beauty.

The batter stands swinging his bat and grimly waiting at the plate, crouched, tense, the catcher, crouched, the umpire, bent, hands clasped behind his back, and peering forward. All of them are set now in the cold blue of that slanting shadow, except the pitcher who stands out there all alone, calm, desperate, and forsaken in his isolation, with the gold-red swiftly fading light upon him, his figure legible with all the resolution, despair and lonely dignity which that slanting, somehow fatal light can give him.

—THOMAS WOLFE, Of Time and the River

CONTENTS

• •

N OT LONG AGO, I was chatting with a fellow traveler on a long airplane flight who confessed that the most dramatic moment of his life was hitting a home run in a Little League game. Nothing could compare. Before he mentioned this, I had learned that he'd had a distinguished career as a newspaper correspondent before moving on to own a newspaper chain. He was a champion skier, an explorer who'd trekked through Nepal. But it was the home run that meant most to him. I had the feeling that he wanted to tell me everything about that magic moment, bending my ear as they say—he'd been quite loquacious—but he sat back in his seat, quite quiet now, as if it were best to recall what he'd done in reverent solitude.

I must confess to a personal home-run moment as well. During an early autumn game on a vast lawn in Dover, Massachusetts, in my college years, I can remember hitting a softball down the line over third base over the top of a distant pine tree into a rose garden. I can see the ball's flight in my mind's eye, seeming to hang forever in the late afternoon sky. Titanic! Sam Snead once advised President Eisenhower to "get his ass" into his golf swing, and I had done exactly that. The ball soared toward the pine, just grazing its upper branches. In fact, alas, the thing went *foul,* not more than a foot or so, and I knew this as I rounded the bases. The catcher never objected because she was standing four or five feet behind home plate—a slender girl in Pucci pants who worried about being swatted by a come-back foul ball and wasn't actually sure about what was foul and what wasn't. I have never fessed up about my foul home run until this very moment because somehow I knew at the time that I'd never "get my ass" into the ball quite the same way, never would be able to stand for that wonderful instant to relish the long flight of what I'd whacked, even if the thing went foul at the last. I feel much better for having confessed about this because the shame has nagged at me over the decades.

I would dare say as a weekend athlete that a home run stamps itself upon the memory like nothing else in sport except perhaps a hole in one. A home run is hardly a humdrum event even for major leaguers who hit a goodly number of them. Major league pitchers would rather talk about the single home run hit during the course of a career than their no-hitters. Bob Feller, a pitcher notoriously inept at the plate, once poked a ball barely into the right-field porch in Sportsman's Field in St. Louis in the first night game played there, but in his retelling, the length of the home run increased until his hit (by his account) was a deep smash over the pavilion.

A home run is by no means an easy thing to describe, no more or less than a military historian can wax fondly over the flight of a mortar shell. One of the best, if not the only, descriptions I know (at least from my reading) of what the sensation is like to hit a home run is from Sadaharu Oh, the Japanese home-run hitter who hit 868 of them in his lifetime: "No one can understand what it really is unless you have felt it in your own hands and body. It is different from seeing it or trying to describe it. There is nothing I know quite like meeting a ball in exactly the right spot. As the ball makes its high, long arc beyond the playing field, the diamond and the stands suddenly belong to one man. In that brief, brief time, you are free of all demands and complications. There is no one behind you, no obstruction ahead, as you follow this clear path around all the bases. This is the batsman's center stage, the one time that he may allow himself to freely accept the limelight, to enjoy the sensation of every eye in the stadium fixed on him, waiting for the moment when his foot will touch home plate. In this moment he is free."

Obviously, countless descriptions of important home runs have been written, but these are mostly described within seconds of the deed itself, tapped out on typewriters or computers up in the press box for consumption by sports fans who will read the copy in the next morning's papers. The text abounds with statistics: how far the ball was hit, the inning, who was on base at the time, how it affected the game, information essential to the reader at the breakfast table but which wears thin almost immediately. The present volume is composed of dramatic home runs observed in what William Wordsworth referred to as "reflection in tranquillity." It took John Updike five days to write his account of the Ted Williams home run that punctuated the end of his career; Paul Gallico's recounting of Babe Ruth's "called shot" home run was written many years after the event itself; similarly, Don DeLillo's great novel *Underworld*, written and published more than forty years after the event, uses the Bobby Thomson home run as the background for the opening chapter; only Red Smith's account of that same home run is included to show that great writing, pounded out in the press box, can come out of no period of reflection in tranquillity whatsoever.

In preparing this introduction, I took the opportunity to canvass a number of sportswriters, most of them members of the Baseball Writers Association of America ("BWAA"! an arresting acronym to shout out at a social gathering), to ask how they would rank historic, dramatic home runs. The Bobby Thomson home run ("the shot heard 'round the world") led the voting by a substantial margin over Bill Mazeroski's series-winning home run in 1960 (101 points to 77). Kirk Gibson came in next (55 points) for the home run that won the first game of the 1988 World Series, with Henry Aaron close behind (51 points) for breaking Babe Ruth's total home-run record. Babe Ruth was next (42 points), receiving points not only for the "called shot" home run off Charlie Root but for the three home runs he hit in a single game on behalf of the Boston Braves in 1935. He was forty at the time, and it was just a week before he retired. Ruth was followed by: Mark McGwire (39), Reggie Jackson (34), Bucky Dent (32), Carlton Fisk (25), Roger Maris (21), Ted Williams (20), Joe Carter (13), Griffey—*père et fils* (10), Mickey Mantle (10), Dave Henderson (8), Jimmy Piersall (6), Gabby Hartnett (4), Bo Jackson (2), Tony Perez (2), and one each for a half-dozen or so others.

Jimmy Piersall got one for running the bases backwards after hitting his 100th career home run off Dallas Green; Hank Greenberg got his for hitting a home run at his first at-bat on returning from his war service, and Bo Jackson one for hitting a home run in his first at-bat after hip surgery. Casey Stengel got a single vote for his inside-the-park home run against the Yankees in the 1923 World Series. He did it with two out in the ninth to win the first game— in fact the first World Series home run hit in the new Yankee Stadium. My friend Bill Francis, from the Baseball Hall of Fame in Cooperstown, polled some of his fellow curators and researchers, and they predictably came up with some interesting esoterica to add to all this. Tim Wiles, the Hall's director of research, recommended Ross Barnes for an obvious vote (he hit the first home run in major league history on May 2, 1876, for the Chicago White Stockings. His other choices would be less obvious: Justin "Nig" Clarke, an eighteen-year-old rookie who in 1902 hit eight home runs in a Texas minor league game which his team, the Corsicana Oil Citys, won 51–3 against a hapless organization from Texarkana; Tyrone Horne, a minor leaguer with the Arkansas Travelers, a St. Louis AAA farm club, who on July 27, 1998, hit four home runs in a game against the St. Antonio Missions—unique in that one was a solo shot, a second homer with one man aboard, a third with two, and then a grand slammer—a total of ten runs batted in. His bat, as might be expected, has its place in the Hall of Fame.

Wiles also mentioned Tom Lawless of the St. Louis Cardinals who in game four of the 1987 World Series against the Minnesota

Twins hit a pivotal three-run home run, only the second of his career, an act which so startled him that he ran the bases rather reluctantly, shrugging apologetically as if he had committed a grievous sin.

His reaction reminds me of my own experience with a major league home run ball back in the sixties—one that was hit during a post-season All-Star Game in Yankee Stadium off a pitch of mine in the first of my participatory journalistic stints. Frank Thomas of the Pittsburgh Pirates was the batter. I threw him my roundhouse curve ball (last thrown in my college years) and he parked it in the upper tier of the stadium, one of the longer drives hit there that year, I was told. It was hit so far that my own reaction was that I had assisted him in a considerable engineering feat. "Look what he and I have done *together!*" which (like Lawless's) was hardly a reaction suited to the occasion.

Eric Enders, who works at the reference desk at the Hall of Fame, had two recommendations—Josh Gibson for the home run supposedly hit out of Yankee Stadium (see page 26); and Jimmy Creighton, a star pitcher for the Brooklyn Excelsiors who in a game against the New York City Unions, "felt something pop" as he lunged at a pitch he hit for a home run; he was barely able to run the bases. It turned out he had ruptured his bladder hitting the home run and died very quickly thereafter. He was appoaching his twenty-first birthday.

Very sad. Though hardly of the same magnitude, I would like to add a single vote of sympathy for Stan Musial who hit five home runs against the Giants during a doubleheader and afterward reported that when he got home, he was greeted by his twelve-year-old son who said, "Boy, that's some crummy pitching staff they've got."

Along with their lists, many of the voters added comments. Bob Sherwin of the *Seattle Times,* who picked a game (September 14, 1990) in which Ken Griffey, Sr., and his son, Ken Griffey, Jr., hit back-to-back home runs off Kirk McCaskill, noted that the procedure of passing on the family business to the next generation had been speeded up to the ultimate. The writers gave Gibson's home run in the first game of the 1988 World Series a lot of attention—the outfielder came to bat against Dennis Eckersley, the game's dominant relief pitcher at the time, so crippled by a leg injury that it was a wonder Gibson could drag himself to the plate at all. He fell behind 0–2 before working the count full, and then hit the pitch out for a two-run home run to give the Dodgers a dramatic 5–4 victory, indeed setting the tone for the entire series. Afterward, as one of my correspondents wrote, it wasn't a question of whether Gibson could walk but whether he could walk on water!

A few correspondents had visual memories—more than one mentioned Carlton Fisk waving his arms to urge his home-run ball fair; McGwire's son waiting at home plate to be lifted high by his father coming down the third-base line after hitting the shortest (341-foot shot down the left-field line) home run of the season but the most important, being the 62nd, beating Roger Maris's long-standing record.

I should add that the polling was somewhat inconclusive since some writers voted for only one player's home run; thus casting what is known as a "bullet" vote since no one else in the competition benefits. Maury Allen was one of the "bullet" voters—picking only Mickey Mantle's home run that almost cleared the facade in Yankee Stadium—thus denying other candidates any supplementary votes. Maury was on hand in the stadium when Mantle hit it (off a high, fast ball thrown by a bald-headed Kansas A's reliever named Bill Fischer) so that may well be the reason for his single-mindedness. He described it for the *New York Post*: "The ball left the bat in a high arch, zooming toward the stands in right, continued to climb, and hit the facing of the third deck about two feet from the top. It was still on the rise when it hit the front at the very top of the stands and caromed back onto the field toward second base.

"Mantle jogged toward first base, stopping to stare at the flight of the ball. He stood still as it crashed against the facade, then continued jogging...

"After the game I asked him about the blast.

"'I think I got all of it,' he laughed.

"Then he was asked if that was the hardest home run he had ever hit. It was clearly the longest.

"'It hit the facade. It had to be.'"

Apparently Mantle in his Oklahoma accent pronounced the famous outer facing of the third deck as "fuh-card" rather than facade, and Maury mentioned this in his column. Then he added, "When you hit them as far as Mickey does it hardly matters how you pronounce them." That line and the fact that Mantle pronounced facade "fuh-card" was picked up by the Associated Press and reprinted around the country. "It was Mantle's favorite home run," Maury wrote me, "and mine too because it earned me a little extra attention."

My old friend Furman Bisher of the *Atlanta Constitution* took a different tack by demoting some of the more popular choices, specifically that he never believed the Babe Ruth "called-shot" home run; that, after all, Bobby Thomson's homer only decided a pennant race not a World Series; that Ted Williams's was only a signature to a great career; that surely Henry Aaron's was the most historic ("of course!"); and that the most dramatic was Bill Mazeroski's in 1960 with the score tied 9–9 in the ninth inning ("My God! that decided a World Series!").

My own favorites would conform pretty much along party lines. As a follower of baseball and a New York Giants fan, my most vivid memory was, of course, the Bobby Thomson home run. Studying at Cambridge University at the time, I was tuned in to the Armed Services broadcast of the game, the radio murmuring in a corner of the room to which I kept half an ear while playing an evening game of bridge with fellow classmates. When Thomson hit the home run and as Russ Hodges began shouting, "The Giants win the pennant! The Giants win the pennant!" I fell straight backwards in my chair with a loud cry; one foot flew up and hit up under the bridge table, sending the cards flying. Bewilderment, of course, from the others at the table who had to assume that I had suffered some violent form of spastic reaction, perhaps at the questionable play of my partner.

I remember getting a letter from my mother about a week later. She knows very little about baseball, but she happened to be standing in Grand Central Terminal when the ball was hit; all around her as the news spread men began shouting, hats thrown in the air, and she had to ask what on earth had happened. She wrote that if the Russian diplomatic corps had been in the terminal—it was at a particularly pesky time during the Cold War—they would have understood a lot about a seminal part of the American character.

It should be stated, of course, that in the case of a home run, one man's pleasure is often another's poison. Dodger fans in Grand Central were not throwing their hats in the air. If there were any throwing of hats, it would have been to the ground so they could be stomped upon. A hard-core old-time Brooklyn fan is not likely to dwell on anything written about Bobby Thomson's home run—better to turn quickly to *King Lear.*

Whatever a reader's reaction, my true pleasure in compiling this anthology is in the realization that whatever home run is under observation, it inspires words remarkable in that they reconstruct an event of a few seconds in astonishing and memorable detail; indeed, a far more difficult feat than the act of hitting a baseball over a fence. Possibly that is a bias too much in favor of the writer. Perhaps it would be preferable to say that here both writer and subject in perfect union have reached a very high level of inspired performance.

Let us then take our seats. The umpires have appeared on the field, moving slowly to home plate where they will meet the managers. In the dugouts the players move about, gazing on occasion at the bat rack (is there a bat among them like Roy Hobbs's Wonderboy?) and hoping this will be their day.

HOME RUN

A HOME-RUN CHRONOLOGY

On a spring afternoon, May 2, 1876, Ross Barnes of the Chicago White Stockings hit the first home run in major league history off the Cincinnati Red Stockings' Cherokee Fisher. The *Chicago Tribune* reported: "Barnes, coming to bat with two men out, made the finest hit of the game straight down the left field to the carriages, for a clean home run."

At the time, the home run did not play a prominent role in baseball. In 1901, the St. Louis Cardinals and the Boston Americans led the majors in home runs with team totals of 39 and 37, respectively. In 1906, the Chicago White Sox, known as the "Hitless Wonders," won 93 games, taking the pennant by three games with a team that had the lowest batting average on the circuit (.228) and only hit *seven* home runs. Most of the home runs during the game's so-called Dead Ball era were, in fact, hit inside the park. The ball was made of a loosely wound yarn that gave it a soft, somewhat squishy quality. Gavvy Cravath, a Philadelphia A's outfielder who won six home-run titles between 1913 and 1919, told the *Sporting News* in an interview in 1941, "The old ball we used was colored with tobacco juice or licorice and became as soft as squash toward the end of the game." In 1919, the A.J. Reach company introduced a yarn-winding machine that wound the yarn more tightly, which gave the ball a resilience, a bounce and distance it hadn't had before: it popped off the bat. Batting averages went up, so did attendance, and the home run achieved the same status as a shutout—thus an equalization of the two main properties of baseball: power and speed.

1919 In an exhibition game in Tampa against the New York Giants, Babe Ruth, a pitcher at the time, came to bat against a beanpole right hander named Columbia George Smith. Many years later a Red Sox outfielder named Harry Hooper described to the writer Donald Honig what happened—a ball hit so far that both dugouts emptied to watch it: "I came to attention with everybody else.... You watch the outfielder. He tells you how far it's going. I looked up once at that ball and then I watched the right fielder. It was Ross Youngs. He was running and running into right center. Getting smaller and smaller and smaller. There was no wall or grandstand out there, just a rail fence, way, way out. Youngs finally stopped at the fence and put his hands on his hips and stood there and watched that ball come down. Then he turned and looked back toward the infield."

1920 Capitalizing on the introduction of the more tightly wound "rabbit" ball, the banning of the spitball, and the practice of changing game balls more frequently, Babe Ruth christened the Live Ball era by hitting 54 home runs. The following season, the league players homered 937 times, an increase of more than 150 percent from 1910. The fans quickly became infatuated with the home run, though official circles weren't so sure. An article in the April 1926 issue of *Baseball Magazine* described the home run as a "growing problem. [The home run] has introduced a hazard into the average game that has proved a disquieting factor in team play.... Yes, the home run is under suspicion."

1922 Rogers Hornsby, a second baseman for the Cardinals, became the first National League player to hit more than 40 home runs (42) in a season. This remained a record for second basemen until 1973, when the Atlanta Braves' Davey Johnson hit 43. Hornsby, incidentally, would not go to the movies for fear they would hurt his eyes, and he restricted his reading to the *Racing Form*—which in fact was read to him by his handicapper. It should be added that Ted

Williams would have no truck with such a notion: he had a great passion for movies, his eyesight so keen on the field that it was said he could read the writing on a ball as it sped toward him.

1927 At Yankee Stadium on September 30, Babe Ruth hit a ball in the eighth inning that whistled just inside the foul pole and landed in the seats, according to the *New York Times,* with "a crash that was audible in all parts of the stadium." The home run, off Tom Zachary of the Washington Senators, was Ruth's 60th of the season. "Sixty, count 'em, sixty!" Ruth hollered afterward. "Let's see some other son of a bitch match that!"

1930 On June 27, Jack Quinn, a 46-year-old pitcher for the Philadelphia A's, became the oldest player to hit a home run.

1930 Hack Wilson of the Chicago Cubs set the National League home-run record with 56—a record that remained Wilson's until 1998, when both Mark McGwire and Sammy Sosa broke it.

1931 League officials decided to deaden the ball by wrapping its yarn more loosely, citing escalating home-run totals as one of the reasons. This was the first season in which balls that landed in fair territory and then bounced into the stands were ruled doubles and not home runs. The result was that the number of home runs in each league fell by nearly one-third from the previous season. Hack Wilson's total was only 13, a dubious record that stands as the biggest drop-off in homers (43) from one season to the next.

1932 "Charlie Root [of the Cubs] was pitching, and the first pitched ball was a called strike," Ruth will say later. "Well, I thought it was outside and didn't like it very much, and the boys over there [in the Cubs' dugout] were giving me an 'Oooiya! Oooiya!' [In fact, about as much verbal abuse as one can imagine.] Well, the second pitch was another called strike, and I didn't like that one either. So I let it go. I stepped out of the box, and by that time they were over there going crazy. Well, I looked out toward centerfield and I pointed and I said, 'I'm gonna hit the next pitch right past the flagpole.' Well, the good Lord must have been with me."

The "called-shot home run" has been debated for years. In Donald Honig's splendid *Baseball America,* the author devotes a couple of paragraphs of research to the subject:

> The eyewitness accounts break down pretty much according to party lines. Pitcher Charlie Root (who had to live with this for the rest of his life): "Ruth did not point at the fence before he swung. If he had made a gesture like that, he would have ended up on his ass." (Other players supported the contention that Ruth would never have taunted a pitcher as mean as Root was known to be.) Cubs second baseman Billy Herman: "When he held up his hand he was telling the Cub bench that he had only two strikes on him, that he still had another one coming. But he was pointing out toward Charlie Root when he did that, not toward the center-field bleachers." Chicago pitcher Burleigh Grimes: "After the second strike, Bush yells, 'Now, you big ape, what are you going to do now?' So Babe holds up his finger as if to say, 'I've got the big one left.' He's looking right at Guy Bush. Then he hits the next one out. But he never called it. Forget it." George Pipgras, Yankee pitcher: "Yes, sir, he called it. He pointed toward the bleachers and then he hit it right there. I saw him do it." Joe Sewell, Yankee third baseman: "I was there. I saw it. I don't care what anybody says. He called it." Interestingly enough, Yankee manager Joe McCarthy, who was disliked by Ruth and who returned the feeling, filed a minority report from his bench. "That's a good story, isn't it? A lot of people still believe today that he really did it. Did he? No.

Tell you the truth, I didn't see him point anywhere at all, but I might have turned my head for a moment."

It was an extraordinary, emotionally fevered moment. Not only were the Chicago bench and the Chicago pitcher yelling at him, so were over 50,000 Chicago fans. But the eye of the hurricane was prodigiously armed, with the only weapon he needed: a baseball bat. Whatever gesture he made, we can be sure it was not one of pacification; whatever words he threw back, we can be sure were utterances of defiance. The man had willfully put himself into a situation that demanded extravagant response. Failure meant thunderous catcalls and humiliation. So respond he did. With all his might, splendor, and glory. This was no mere home run. This was a clout among clouts, the longest ever struck at Wrigley Field up to that point. It was the dream shot of all dream shots, the personal circumstances surrounding it giving it a higher nobility even than that of Bobby Thomson's 1951 pennant-winning homer. Of all of Ruth's 729 homers (counting World Series play), this remains the most resounding, the consummate home run, a zenith shot that was as preposterous as the man, sending a baseball through the winds to the very summit of the game's tallest peak, where it remains shrouded in regal solitude.

Is the *Iliad* true? Was there an Achilles? Did Babe Ruth call his shot? The question is surely irrelevant.

1935 A tired and overweight Babe Ruth, 40, now a member of the Boston Braves, on May 25, hit a single and three home runs against the Pittsburgh Pirates at Forbes Field, the third home run over the double-deck stands and out of the ball park, a feat never accomplished before. It was the 714th, and final, home run of his career. Eight days later he retired.

1938 On September 28, a home run was hit whose flight very few of the 35,000 fans shivering in Wrigley Field were able to follow

because of the darkness—the so-called "Homer in the Gloaming."
It was hit by Gabby Hartnett, nicknamed "Old Tomato Face," who
had succeeded Charlie Grimm as the manager of the Cubs in mid-
season—thus a rare combination of player (he was a catcher), manager, and inspiration. He came to bat in the bottom of the ninth
against Pittsburgh, the score tied, two men out, the last chance before the umpires were bound to call the game because of darkness.
He hit the ball into the left-field bleachers—a shot that wasn't seen
as much as *heard.* Hartnett remembered: "A lot of people didn't
know the ball was in the bleachers. Well, I did. I knew it the minute
I hit it. When I got to second base I couldn't see third because of all
the people there. I don't think I walked a step to the plate—I was
carried in." It was a crucial win for the Cubs. It took the wind out
of the Pirates' sails; the Cubs clinched the pennant three days later.

1940 That year, Ted Williams of the Boston Red Sox stopped tipping
his cap to the stands after hitting a home run. He would not stand
on ceremony. He never wore ties. "Ties," he said, "get in your soup."

1946 In the All-Star game at Fenway Park, Ted Williams took a
long look at Rip Sewell's famed blooper pitch, its trajectory not unlike that of a pop fly, and when it finally reached home plate he supplied his own power and flicked it deep into the stands—the only
man who homered off that particular pitch. Williams seemed to
savor All-Star Games. In 1947, the American League All-Stars a run
behind, two out in the ninth, Williams hit a three-run home run off
the third deck of Detroit's right-field stands, where no home run had
ever been hit before.

1951 It was nearly four o'clock in the afternoon of October 3 when
Bobby Thomson of the New York Giants, a career .270 hitter,
stepped into the batter's box at the Polo Grounds to face the Brook-

lyn Dodgers' Ralph Branca. It was the ninth inning of the third and final game of the National League playoff series. Two men were on the bases, the Giants trailing 4–2. There was such interest in the pennant race that the prisoners on New York's Rikers Island were allowed to listen to the game on the radio. Thomson took an 0–1 fastball, high and outside, caught it flush, and drove it over the left-field wall, the so-called "Shot Heard Round the World." He said afterward: "If I was a good hitter, I would have taken that pitch."

Oddly enough, Thomson had hit a home run in the first game of the Series at Ebbets Field (the Giants won it 7–1) off none other than Ralph Branca.

In the *Wall Street Journal,* January 31, 2001, a staff writer, Joshua Harris Prager, wrote a feature story that suggested that Thomson, as well as other Giants, benefitted from signal-stealing via a telescope (situated 500 feet away in the Polo Grounds scoreboard) and a buzzer system set up in the dugout which allowed a coach to hand-signal to the batter what kind of pitch was coming. Prager interviewed Thomson whose manner suggested he knew about the sign-stealing. "Did you take the sign?" Prager asked. "My answer is no," Thomson said. He added, "I was always proud of that swing."

What surprised Prager (he interviewed twenty-one players and a coach) was how long they had kept mum about the sign-stealing. One reason would be that sign-stealing has been a part of baseball (in different degrees) since the turn of the century. A second reason might be Commissioner Ford Frick's bellicose and somewhat blustery statement made in an Associated Press story on March 22, 1962: "I am definitely opposed to such practices. If such a charge were substantiated, I would forfeit the game, but I certainly would not be guided by rumor."

Better to let sleeping dogs lie.

In sum, no one except perhaps the most die-hard Brooklyn fan, would ever question what Thomson did. Anyone who has watched batting practice can see how rarely even a fat pitch is hit out of the park.

1953 Early that season Casey Stengel, the Yankees' manager, grabbed a writer and pointed at Mickey Mantle in the batting cage. "See that kid?" He then motioned toward the far reaches of the field. "We're afraid for the lives of the people out there."

A few weeks later, on April 17, Stengel's words proved prescient when in the fifth inning at Griffith Stadium Mantle hit a home run off the Senator's Chuck Stobbs that many think is the longest home run ever hit. At 460 feet it hit the top of a National Bohemian Beer sign and bounced out of the park into the backyard of Perry L. Cool of 434 Oakdale Street. "I've never seen a ball hit farther," Stengel said afterward. "And I've seen a lot of home runs. I saw Ruth."

Arthur (Red) Patterson, the Yankees' publicity director, was so impressed by what he'd seen that he set off to measure the home run. He retraced his steps from Perry Cool's backyard and estimated the ball had traveled 565 feet. His method of calculation gave rise to the descriptive of an extra-long home run as a "a tape-measure job."

1954 On May 2, Stan Musial of the St. Louis Cardinals hit five home runs in a doubleheader against the Giants—a record tied in 1972 by Nate Colbert of the San Diego Padres. Though Musial never won a home-run title, he finished his 22-year career with 475 home runs.

Musial had a flair for the dramatic. In 1955 he hit a home run at the All-Star Game in Milwaukee that won the game in the twelfth inning, 6–5. Including that one, he hit a record *six* All-Star Game home runs, all from a curious crouched batting stance that reminded one observer of a guy peeping around a corner to see if the cops are coming.

1955 The Brooklyn Dodgers' Duke Snider hit a three-run home run over the screen into Bedford Avenue in the fourth game of the World Series. The Dodgers won the game 8–5 and went on to win its first (and last) World Series in the seventh game at Yankee Stadium.

1956 Dale Long of the Pittsburgh Pirates became the first major league player to hit home runs in eight straight games—a record eventually tied by Don Mattingly of the Yankees, in 1987, and Ken Griffey, Jr., of the Seattle Mariners, in 1993.

1960 On the cool, damp afternoon of September 28, Ted Williams of the Boston Red Sox came to bat for the last time. Facing Jack Fisher of the Baltimore Orioles, he hit an outside pitch over the right-field fence at Fenway Park. The next day a photo of Williams's follow-through swing appeared in several newspapers. In it his eyes are closed, as if to savor more intently what he has just done. Incidentally, the following year Jack Fisher gave up the home-run ball (60) to Roger Maris which set the stage for the breaking of Babe Ruth's record.

1960 The World Series between the New York Yankees and the Pittsburgh Pirates came down to the seventh game. In the last of the ninth, the score tied 9–9, Bill Mazeroski, who had hit into a double play in the seventh inning, came to the plate to face Ralph Terry. On Terry's second pitch, Mazeroski turned on a chest-high slider and drove it deep to left. Yogi Berra, playing there for the Yankees, took one step back, looked up, and then began trotting for the clubhouse. Coming down the third base line, Mazeroski was greeted by such an exuberant crowd of celebrants that it was doubted he ever touched home plate.

1961 On October 1, in front of a crowd of 23,154 in Yankee Stadium, Roger Maris broke Babe Ruth's home-run record with a drive into the right-field seats. The ball was caught by a 19-year-old kid from Coney Island, Sal Durante, who went to the locker room and tried to give the ball to Maris. Durante recalled later, "He must have known something I didn't, because he told me, 'Wait, you can make some money from it.' And he was right."

A Sacramento restaurateur named Sam Gordon gave Durante $5,000 for the ball, which five weeks later was returned to Maris, who in turn donated it to the Hall of Fame. Compare: Mark McGwire's 70th home-run ball was bought by a comic-book tycoon for three million dollars!

1969 Harmon Killebrew of the Minnesota Twins won his fifth American League home-run title in eight seasons. When he retired in 1975, he had hit 573 home runs, the second-most prolific home-run hitter in American League history after Ruth.

1972 Dave Kingman, known to his dismay as "King Kong," became the first player to hit a home run for four teams (the New York Mets, the San Diego Padres, the California Angels, and the New York Yankees) in the same season. When he retired in 1979, Kingman had hit 422 homers.

1974 During his pursuit of Babe Ruth's career home-run record, Henry Aaron had been bedeviled by threats, many of them with racial overtones. It had gone on during the latter part of the 1973 season when he was within a couple homers of tying the record. In the Houston Astrodome he hit 712 and then 713 on the second-to-last day. On April 4, he tied the record with his first swing of the new season: off a sailing fastball thrown by Jack Billingham, Aaron hit the ball on a line over the left center-field fence. On April 8, back home in Atlanta, he remarked to a teammate in the dugout, "I just hope I can get this thing over with tonight." In the fourth inning he did just that off an Al Downing fast ball. Between second and third as he rounded the bases, Aaron was joined by two Georgia Tech students who had jumped out of the stands. In the big celebrating crowd at home plate, his mother was waiting for him.

1976 Chris Chambliss of the Yankees hit the first pitch in the ninth off Mark Littell of the Kansas City Royals into the right-field stands of the stadium to win the pennant for New York. What is memorable about the moment is that the crowd exploded onto the field like a broken-apart beehive, such a swarm on the third-base line that Chambliss was never able to reach home plate. Questioned about this in the locker-room, Chambliss returned to the field with a policeman at either side and jumped with both feet on where home plate had been; moments before it had been uprooted by exuberant souvenir hunters.

1977 On September 3, Japan's Sadaharu Oh set the world record for home runs with his 756th and went on to finish his 22-year career with the Yomiuri (Tokyo) Giants with 868, an amazing 113 home runs ahead of Henry Aaron's recognized record.

1977 On October 18, Reggie Jackson of the New York Yankees hit three home runs, giving him a total of five in the World Series against the Los Angeles Dodgers. Astonishingly enough, the last four were hit with his first swing of the bat. On the 18th, the home runs were hit off Burt Hooton, Elias Sosa, and Charlie Hough. Hough complained of his knuckler: "It didn't move." "Not until I hit it," said Jackson.

For his spectacular performances at critical moments, most notably during a World Series, Jackson became known as "Mr. October."

1978 Until the one-game playoff against the Boston Red Sox on October 2, the Yankees' shortstop, Bucky Dent, had hit just four home runs. He was mired in one of the worst batting slumps of his career, hitting .140 over his last 20 games. He came up to bat against Boston's Mike Torrez in the top of the seventh inning with his team trailing 2–0. On a 1-and-1 count, he hit a ball to left that with the help of a strong tailwind barely cleared the high wall in left-field known as the Green Monster. The home run put the Yankees ahead 3–2, a lead they did not surrender as they went on to win 5–4 . . . yet another day of infamy for the Boston fans.

1982 In an Old-Timers Game on July 19th, Luke Appling, a Hall of Fame shortstop (for the Chicago White Sox) hit a home run off a gentle pitch thrown by Warren Spahn. Appling was seventy-five at the time.

1983 On July 24th, George Brett of the Kansas City Royals in a game against the New York Yankees hit a two-run home run off Goose Gossage that put his team ahead 5–4. Billy Martin, the Yankee skipper, came out of the Yankee dugout and complained that Brett had spread pine tar (used to get a better grip) too far up the barrel, which is against regulations and forfeits whatever is done with the bat. After measuring the bat against the known width of home plate, the umpires concurred. This brought Brett out of the Royal's dugout in a boil of rage, indeed to the point of being held back with great difficulty from a direct assault on the chief umpire. Woe to anyone who deigns to consign anything as important as a home run to oblivion! There was no further scoring, the Yankees had apparently won. Four days later the umpires' ruling was overturned, and the game was rescheduled to start with Brett's home run reinstated. The Royals held on to win 5–4. Baseball history refers to the episode as the Pine Tar Incident.

1986 Cliff Johnson, who played for seven teams in his 14-year career, retired after hitting 20 career pinch-hit home runs, more than any other player in history.

1987 On April 13, Marvell Wynne, Tony Gwynn, and John Kruk of the San Diego Padres led off the game by hitting back-to-back-to-back home runs off the San Francisco Giants' Roger Mason.

1990 On May 26, Carlos Martinez of the Cleveland Indians bounced a home run off Jose Canseco's head and over the right-field fence, helping the Indians beat the Texas Rangers 7–6. Canseco joked afterward: "Anybody got a Band-Aid?"

1993 Against the Cincinnati Reds on September 17, the St. Louis Cardinals outfielder Mark Whiten became the twelfth major leaguer to hit four home runs in one game. Other players to do this include Bob Horner (1986), Mike Schmidt (1976), Willie Mays (1961), Rocky Colavito (1959), Joe Adcock (1954), Gil Hodges (1950), Pat Seerey (1948), Chuck Klein (1936), Lou Gehrig (1932), Ed Delahanty (1896), and Bobby Lowe (1894).

1993 No one had ever hit a come-from-behind home run in the bottom of the ninth to win a World Series until October 23, at the SkyDome. Toronto Blue Jays' Joe Carter came up with two runners on, one out, and hit a 2-and-2 fastball over the left-field wall to give his team a series-clinching 8–6 victory. It prompted Carter to say afterward, "Yes, I do believe in miracles."

1999 The season saw one of the most dramatic spectacles in home-run history—the race to beat Roger Maris's single-season record of 61, a record that had stood for 38 years and was thought untouchable. Two men—Mark McGwire of the St. Louis Cardinals and Sammy Sosa of the Chicago Cubs—attempted to achieve that goal in a rivalry that captivated the nation and was widely credited with restoring baseball to the prominence it had enjoyed before the 1994 players' strike soured fans on the game. In New York City, the Dominican community marked their favorite son's home-run totals on their car windows with soap bars—for anyone not familiar with the home-run race, it must have seemed that the cars were being offered for sale at absurdly low prices. On April 8, at Busch Stadium in St. Louis, McGwire was the first to beat the Maris record, hitting a home run that barely cleared the wall just 15 feet from the left-field foul pole. It was McGwire's shortest home run of the season. The Maris family was seated in the stands. McGwire hoisted his son—a Cardinal batboy—on his shoulders as he crossed home plate, and Sosa came in from the outfield to offer his congratulations.

Over the three weeks left in the season, the lead shifted back and forth. In Houston's Astrodome, Sosa hit his 66th to pull ahead, but McGwire tied him 47 minutes later with a home run in St. Louis. McGwire hit two home runs in each of his last two games, hitting his 70th off Montreal's Carl Pavano. McGwire said of all this: "I don't play the game for records. I play the game because I love it. It just happened to be a milestone."

THAT MAN FROM MUDVILLE

Ernest Lawrence Thayer's "Casey at the Bat" is surely the best-known baseball, if not sports, poem ever written. It first appeared on June 3, 1888, in the *San Francisco Examiner* in a humor column, and thereafter achieved an astonishing popularity. Indeed, in answer to a publisher who wanted to pay for a reprinting, Thayer replied: "All I ask is never to be reminded of it again. Make it anything you wish."

Dozens of sequels, imitations, and parodies exist—even Casey's relatives get into the act: "Mrs. Casey," "Casey's Son," "Casey's Sisters at the Bat," each of whom strikes out. The last stanza of "Casey's Daughter at the Bat" (she is playing softball for the Mudvillettes) goes as follows:

> OH! somewhere in this favored land the moon is
>   shining bright
> And somewhere there are softball honeys winning
>   games tonight
> And somewhere there are softball fans
>   who scream and yell and shout
> But there is no joy in Mudville—Casey's daughter
>   has struck out.

A few writers, unable to bear the cruel twist of Casey striking out, reversed the outcome of the fateful ninth inning completely. The most familiar of these was Grantland Rice's "That Man from Mudville," also published under the title "Casey's Revenge." Rice, one of the best-known sportswriters of his era, often used snippets of self-penned verse in his columns, a noted example being "Game Called" on the date of Babe Ruth's death (*Game called by darkness—let the curtain fall / No more remembered thunder sweeps the field*).

CASEY'S REVENGE

There were saddened hearts in Mudville for a week or even more;
There were muttered oaths and curses—every fan in town was sore.
"Just think," said one, "how soft it looked with Casey at the bat,
And then to think he'd go and spring a bush-league trick like that!"

All his past fame was forgotten—he was now a hopeless "shine."
They called him "Strike-Out Casey," from the mayor down the line;
And as he came to bat each day his bosom heaved a sigh,
While a look of hopeless fury shone in mighty Casey's eye.

He pondered in the days gone by that he had been their king,
That when he strolled up to the plate they made the welkin ring;
But now his nerve had vanished, for when he heard them hoot
He "fanned" or "popped out" daily, like some minor-league recruit.

He soon began to sulk and loaf, his batting eye went lame;
No home runs on the scorecard now were chalked against his name;
The fans without exception gave the manager no peace,
For one and all kept clamoring for Casey's quick release.

The Mudville squad began to slump, the team was in the air;
Their playing went from bad to worse—nobody seemed to care.
"Back to the woods with Casey!" was the cry from Rooters' Row.
"Get someone who can hit the ball and let that big dub go!"

The lane is long, someone has said, that never turns again,
And Fate, though fickle, often gives another chance to men;

And Casey smiled; his rugged face no longer wore a frown—
The pitcher who had started all the trouble came to town.

All Mudville had assembled—ten thousand fans had come
To see the twirler who had put big Casey on the bum;
And when he stepped into the box, the multitude went wild;
He doffed his cap in proud disdain, but Casey only smiled.

"Play ball!" the umpire's voice rang out, and then the game began.
But in that throng of thousands there was not a single fan
Who thought that Mudville had a chance, and with the setting sun
Their hopes sank low—the rival team was leading "four to one."

The last half of the ninth came round, with no change in the score;
But when the first man up hit safe, the crowd began to roar;
The din increased, the echo of ten thousand shouts was heard
When the pitcher hit the second and gave "four balls" to the third.

Three men on base—nobody out—three runs to tie the game!
A triple meant the highest niche in Mudville's hall of fame;
But here the rally ended, and the gloom was deep as night,
When the fourth one "fouled to catcher" and the fifth "flew out to
    right."

A dismal groan in chorus came; a scowl was on each face
When Casey walked up, bat in hand, and slowly took his place;
His bloodshot eyes in fury gleamed, his teeth were clenched in
    hate;
He gave his cap a vicious hook and pounded on the plate.

But fame is fleeting as the wind, and glory fades away;
There were no wild and woolly cheers, no glad acclaim this day;
They hissed and groaned and hooted as they clamored: "Strike him
    out!"
But Casey gave no outward sign that he had heard this shout.

The pitcher smiled and cut one loose—across the plate it sped;
Another hiss, another groan. "Strike one!" the umpire said.
Zip! Like a shot the second curve broke just below the knee.
"Strike two!" the umpire roared aloud; but Casey made no plea.

No roasting for the umpire now—his was an easy lot;
But here the pitcher whirled again—was that a rifle shot?
A whack, a crack, and out through the space the leather pellet flew,
A blot against the distant sky, a speck against the blue.

Above the fence in center field in rapid whirling flight
The sphere sailed on—the blot grew dim and then was lost to sight.
Ten thousand hats were thrown in air, ten thousand threw a fit,
But no one ever found the ball that mighty Casey hit.

Oh, somewhere in this favored land dark clouds may hide the sun,
And somewhere bands no longer play and children have no fun!
And somewhere over blighted lives there hangs a heavy pall,
But Mudville hearts are happy now, *for Casey hit the ball.*

L'ENVOI

There is no sequel to this plot—except in Mudville's square
The bronze bust of a patriot—arms crossed—is planted there.
His cap is cocked above one eye—and from his rugged face
The sneer still curls above the crowd—across the marketplace.

And underneath, in solid bronze, these words are graved in flame—
"Here is a man who rose and fell—and rose again to fame—
He blew a big one in the pinch—but facing jeering throngs
He came through Hell to scramble back—and prove a champ
    belongs."

• •

FROM THE NATURAL

Bernard Malamud's *The Natural,* published in 1952, is one of the few notable American novels that uses a sports background—Don DeLillo's *Underworld* is a more recent example. The book, using many of baseball's myths (the called home run that inspired a sick boy to live), became a classic. It was made into a film starring Robert Redford, and many will remember him as Roy Hobbs in the scene in which armed with his bat, Wonderboy (made from the interior of a tree split by lightening), he hits a ball into a distant light standard and pitches the entire ballpark into darkness.

A S THE CAB PULLED UP before the hotel, a wild-eyed man in shirtsleeves, hairy-looking and frantic, rushed up to them.

"Any of you guys Roy Hobbs?"

"That's him," Pop said grimly, heading into the hotel with Red. He pointed back to where Roy was getting out of the cab.

"No autographs." Roy ducked past the man.

"Jesus God, Roy," he cried in a broken voice. He caught Roy's arm and held on to it. "Don't pass me by, for the love of God."

"What d'you want?" Roy stared, suspicious.

"Roy, you don't know me," the man sobbed. "My name's Mike Barney and I drive a truck for Cudahy's. I don't want a thing for myself, only a favor for my boy Pete. He was hurt in an accident, playin' in the street. They operated him for a broken skull a coupla days ago and he ain't doin' so good. The doctor says he ain't fightin' much."

Mike Barney's mouth twisted and he wept.

"What has that got to do with me?" Roy asked, white-faced.

The truck driver wiped his eyes on his sleeve. "Pete's a fan of yours, Roy. He got a scrapbook that thick fulla pictures of you. Yesterday they lemme go in and see him and I said to Pete you told me you'd sock a homer for him in the game tonight. After that he sorta smiled and looked better. They gonna let him listen a little tonight, and I know if you will hit one it will save him."

"Why did you say that for?" Roy said bitterly. "The way I am now I couldn't hit the side of a barn."

Holding to Roy's sleeve, Mike Barney fell to his knees. "Please, you gotta do it."

"Get up," Roy said. He pitied the guy and wanted to help him yet was afraid what would happen if he couldn't. He didn't want that responsibility.

Mike Barney stayed on his knees, sobbing. A crowd had collected and was watching them.

"I will do the best I can if I get the chance." Roy wrenched his sleeve free and hurried into the lobby.

"A father's blessing on you," the truck driver called after him in a cracked voice.

Dressing in the visitors' clubhouse for the game that night, Roy thought about the kid in the hospital. He had been thinking of him on and off and was anxious to do something for him. He could see himself walking up to the plate and clobbering a long one into the stands and then he imagined the boy, healed and whole, thanking him for saving his life. The picture was unusually vivid, and as he polished Wonderboy, his fingers itched to carry it into the batter's box and let go at a fat one.

But Pop had other plans. "You are still on the bench, Roy, unless you put that Wonderboy away and use a different stick."

Roy shook his head and Pop gave the line-up card to the ump without his name on it. When Mike Barney, sitting a few rows behind a box above third base, heard the announcement of the Knights' line-up without Roy in it, his face broke out in a sickish sweat.

The game began, Roy taking his non-playing position on the far corner of the bench and holding Wonderboy between his knees. It was a clear, warm night and the stands were just about full. The floods on the roof lit up the stadium brighter than day. Above the globe of light lay the dark night, and high in the sky the stars glittered. Though unhappy not to be playing, Roy, for no reason he could think of, felt better in his body than he had in a week. He had a hunch things could go well for him tonight, which was why he especially regretted not being in the game. Furthermore, Mike Barney was directly in his line of vision and sometimes stared at him. Roy's gaze went past him, farther down the stands, to where a young black-haired woman, wearing a red dress, was sitting at an aisle seat in short left. He could clearly see the white flower she wore pinned on her bosom and that she seemed to spend more time craning to get a look into the Knights' dugout—at him, he could swear—than in watching the game. She interested him, in that red dress, and he would have liked a close gander at her but he couldn't get out there without arousing attention.

Pop was pitching Fowler, who had kept going pretty well during the two dismal weeks of Roy's slump, only he was very crabby at everybody—especially Roy—for not getting him any runs, and causing him to lose two well-pitched games. As a result Pop had to keep after him in the late innings, because when Fowler felt disgusted he wouldn't bear down on the opposing batters.

Up through the fifth he had kept the Cubs bottled up but he eased off the next inning and they reached him for two runs with only one out. Pop gave him a fierce glaring at and Fowler then tightened and finished off the side with a pop fly and strikeout. In the Knights' half of the seventh, Cal Baker came through with a stinging triple, scoring Stubbs, and was himself driven in by Flores' single. That tied the score but it became untied when, in their part of the inning, the Cubs placed two doubles back to back, to produce another run.

As the game went on Roy grew tense. He considered telling Pop about the kid and asking for a chance to hit. But Pop was a stubborn cuss and Roy knew he'd continue to insist on him laying Wonderboy aside. This he was afraid to do. Much as he wanted to help the boy—and it really troubled him now—he felt he didn't stand a Chinaman's chance at a hit without his own club. And if he once abandoned Wonderboy there was no telling what would happen to him. Probably it would finish his career for keeps, because never since he had made the bat had he swung at a ball with any other.

In the eighth on a double and sacrifice, Pop worked a runner around to third. The squeeze failed so he looked around anxiously for a pinch hitter. Catching Roy's eye, he said, as Roy had thought he would, "Take a decent stick and go on up there."

Roy didn't move. He was sweating heavily and it cost him a great effort to stay put. He could see the truck driver suffering in his seat, wiping his face, cracking his knuckles, and sighing. Roy averted his glance.

There was a commotion in the lower left field stands. This lady in the red dress, whoever she was, had risen, and standing in a sea of gaping faces, seemed to be searching for someone. Then she looked toward the Knights' dugout and sort of half bowed her head. A murmur went up from the crowd. Some of them explained it that she had got mixed up about the seventh inning stretch and others an-

swered how could she when the scoreboard showed the seventh inning was over? As she stood there, so cleanly etched in light, as if trying to communicate something she couldn't express, some of the fans
were embarrassed. And the stranger sitting next to her felt a strong
sexual urge which he concealed behind an impatient cigarette. Roy
scarcely noticed her because he was lost in worry, seriously considering whether he ought to give up on Wonderboy.

Pop of course had no idea what was going on in Roy's head,
so he gave the nod to Ed Simmons, a substitute infielder. Ed picked
a bat out of the rack and as he approached the plate the standing
lady slowly sat down. Everyone seemed to forget her then. Ed flied out.
Pop looked scornfully at Roy and shot a stream of snuff into the dust.

Fowler had a little more trouble in the Cubs' half of the eighth
but a double play saved him, and the score was still 3–2. The ninth
opened. Pop appeared worn out. Roy had his eyes shut. It was
Fowler's turn to bat. The second guessers were certain Pop would
yank him for a pinch hitter but Fowler was a pretty fair hitter for a
pitcher, and if the Knights could tie the score, his pitching tonight
was too good to waste. He swung at the first ball, connecting for a
line drive single, to Pop's satisfaction. Allie Stubbs tried to lay one
away but his hard-hit fly ball to center was caught. To everybody's
surprise Fowler went down the white line on the next pitch and dove
safe into second under a cloud of dust. A long single could tie the
score, but Cal Baker, to his disgust, struck out and flung his bat away.
Pop again searched the bench for a pinch hitter. He fastened his gaze
on Roy but Roy was unapproachable. Pop turned bitterly away.

Mike Barney, a picture of despair, was doing exercises of grief.
He stretched forth his long hairy arms, his knobby hands clasped,
pleading. Roy felt as though they were reaching right into the dugout
to throttle him.

He couldn't stand it any longer. "I give up." Placing Wonderboy
on the bench he rose and stood abjectly in front of Pop.

Pop looked up at him sadly. "You win," he said. "Go on in."

Roy gulped. "With my own bat?"

Pop nodded and gazed away.

Roy got Wonderboy and walked out into the light. A roar of recognition drowned the announcement of his name but not the loud beating of his heart. Though he'd been at bat only three days ago, it felt like years—an ageless time. He almost wept at how long it had been.

Lon Toomey, the hulking Cub hurler, who had twice in the last two weeks handed Roy his lumps, smiled behind his glove. He shot a quick glance at Fowler on second, fingered the ball, reared and threw. Roy, at the plate, watched it streak by.

"Stuh-rike."

He toed in, his fears returning. What if the slump did not give way? How much longer could it go on without destroying him?

Toomey lifted his right leg high and threw. Roy swung from his heels at a bad ball and the umpire sneezed in the breeze.

"Strike two!"

Wonderboy resembled a sagging baloney. Pop cursed the bat and some of the Knights' rooters among the fans booed. Mike Barney's harrowed puss looked yellow.

Roy felt sick with remorse that he hadn't laid aside Wonderboy in the beginning and gone into the game with four licks at bat instead of only three miserable strikes, two of which he already used up. How could he explain to Barney that he had traded his kid's life away out of loyalty to a hunk of wood?

The lady in the stands hesitantly rose for the second time. A photographer who had stationed himself nearby snapped a clear shot of her. She was an attractive woman, around thirty, maybe more, and built solid but not too big. Her bosom was neat, and her dark hair, parted on the side, hung loose and soft. A reporter approached her and asked her name but she wouldn't give it to him, nor would she, blushing, say why she was standing now. The fans behind her hooted, "Down in front," but though her eyes showed she was troubled she remained standing.

Noticing Toomey watching her, Roy stole a quick look. He caught the red dress and a white rose, turned away, then came quickly back for another take, drawn by the feeling that her smile was for him. Now why would she do that for? She seemed to be wanting to say something, and then it flashed on him the reason she was standing was to show her confidence in him. He felt surprised that anybody would want to do that for him. At the same time he became aware that the night had spread out in all directions and was filled with an unbelievable fragrance.

A pitch streaked toward him. Toomey had pulled a fast one. With a sob Roy fell back and swung.

Part of the crowd broke for the exits. Mike Barney wept freely now, and the lady who had stood up for Roy absently pulled on her white gloves and left.

The ball shot through Toomey's astounded legs and began to climb. The second baseman, laying back on the grass on a hunch, stabbed high for it but it leaped over his straining fingers, sailed through the light and up into the dark, like a white star seeking an old constellation.

Toomey, shrunk to a pygmy, stared into the vast sky.

Roy circled the bases like a Mississippi steamboat, lights lit, flags fluttering, whistle banging, coming round the bend. The Knights poured out of their dugout to pound his back, and hundreds of their rooters hopped about in the field. He stood on the home base, lifting his cap to the lady's empty seat.

And though Fowler goose-egged the Cubs in the last of the ninth and got credit for the win, everybody knew it was Roy alone who had saved the boy's life.

ROBERT PETERSON

. . . .

JOSH

The selection that follows is from a book entitled *Only the Ball Was White* by Robert Peterson who in his hometown of Warren, Pennsylvania, saw many of the giants of black baseball perform against local semiprofessional teams. His book is a history of the legendary black players and all-black professional teams before Jackie Robinson entered major league baseball in 1946—Buck Leonard, Napoleon Cummings, Floyd (Jelly) Gardner, Cool Papa Bell. An epigram to *Only the Ball Was White* reads as follows:

> The other day Willie Mays hit his five hundred and twenty-second home run. He has gone past me, and he's pushing, and I say to him, "Go get 'em, Willie." Baseball gives every American boy a chance to excel. Not just to be as good as someone else, but to be better. This is the nature of man and the name of the game. I hope that some day Satchel Paige and Josh Gibson will be voted into the Hall of Fame as symbols of the great Negro players who are not here, only because they weren't given the chance. (Ted Williams upon his induction into the Hall of Fame, Cooperstown, New York, July 1966.)

In 1971, five years later, a special committee was established to vote players into the Hall of Fame who had starred in the Negro Leagues. Josh Gibson followed Satchel Paige into the Hall in 1972.

⚾

There is a catcher that any big-league club would like to buy for $200,000. His name is Gibson ... he can do everything. He hits

the ball a mile. And he catches so easy he might as well be in a
rocking chair. Throws like a rifle. Bill Dickey isn't as good a
catcher. Too bad this Gibson is a colored fellow.

—WALTER JOHNSON

THERE IS A STORY that one day during the 1930s the Pittsburgh Crawfords were playing at Forbes Field in Pittsburgh when their young catcher, Josh Gibson, hit the ball so high and far that no one saw it come down. After scanning the sky carefully for a few minutes, the umpire deliberated and ruled it a home run. The next day the Crawfords were playing in Philadelphia when suddenly a ball dropped out of the heavens and was caught by the startled center fielder on the opposing club. The umpire made the only possible ruling. Pointing to Gibson he shouted, "Yer out—yesterday in Pittsburgh!"

Gibson fans of those years might concede that there was an element of exaggeration in the story, but not much. Josh Gibson was not merely a home run hitter; he was *the* home run hitter. He was the black Babe Ruth, and like the Babe a legend in his own time whose prodigious power was celebrated in fact and fancy. But while it is relatively easy to separate fact from fancy in Ruth's legend, Gibson's suffers from the paucity of certified records about the quantity and quality of his home run production. Old-timers credit Gibson with eighty-nine home runs in one season and seventy-five in another; many of them, of course, were hit against semipro competition.

Whatever the truth of these claims, a strong case can be made for the proposition that Josh Gibson, a right-hand batter, had more power than the great Babe. The clincher in the argument is the generally accepted fact that Gibson hit the longest home run ever struck in Yankee Stadium, Ruth's home for twelve seasons.

Baseball's bible, *The Sporting News* [June 3, 1967], credits Gibson with a drive in a Negro league game that hit just two feet from the top of the stadium wall circling the bleachers in center field, about 580 feet from home plate. It was estimated that had the drive been two feet higher it would have sailed out of the park and traveled some 700 feet!

Some old Negro league players say that Gibson's longest shot in Yankee Stadium struck the rear wall of the bullpen in left field, about 500 feet from the plate. But Jack Marshall, of the Chicago American Giants, recalls an epic blast by Gibson that went *out* of the stadium—the only fair ball ever hit out of the Yankees' park.

In 1934, Josh Gibson hit a ball off of Slim Jones in Yankee Stadium in a four-team doubleheader that we had there—the Philadelphia Stars played the Crawfords in the second game; we had played the Black Yankees in the first game. They say a ball has never been hit out of Yankee Stadium. Well, that is a lie! Josh hit the ball over that triple deck next to the bullpen in left field. Over and out! I never will forget that, because we were getting ready to leave because we were going down to Hightstown, New Jersey, to play a night game and we were standing in the aisle when that boy hit this ball!

Both Ruth and Gibson played before the era of the tape-measure home run, when every long hit is carefully computed, almost to the inch. None of Ruth's towering smashes was ever officially measured, but the best guess of his longest is 550 feet. Only one of Gibson's home runs was ever measured. He was with the Homestead Grays in Monessen, Pennsylvania, one day in the late 1930s when he hit a homer of such impressive dimensions that the mayor ordered the game stopped and a tape measure applied. The result: 512 feet.

Unlike Babe Ruth, whose swing was awesome and whose body wound up like a pretzel when he missed the ball, Gibson's power was generated with little apparent effort. Judy Johnson, who was Gibson's first manager, said:

> It was just a treat to watch him hit the ball. There was no effort at all. You see these guys now get up there in the box and they dig and scratch around before they're ready. Gibson would just walk up there, and he would always turn his left sleeve.

And when Gibson raised his front foot, the infielders began edging backward onto the grass. If he met the pitch squarely and it came to them on one hop, they knew the ball would be in their glove before Gibson could drop his bat.

Josh Gibson was born December 21, 1911, in Buena Vista, Georgia, a village not far from Atlanta. His father scratched a bare living from a patch of ground outside the village. Josh, the first child of Mark and Nancy Gibson, was named Joshua after his grandfather.

At intervals of three years, two other children were born to the Gibsons: Jerry, who would follow Josh into professional baseball as a pitcher with the Cincinnati Tigers, and Annie. By 1923 the Gibson youngsters were growing up, and it became clear to Mark that if they were to have better opportunities than he had had he must join the swelling migration of black men to the North. And so, late that year, he went to Pittsburgh, where he had relatives, to find work. He quickly got a job as a laborer for Carnegie-Illinois Steel, which was later absorbed by U.S. Steel. In early 1924, Mark sent for his family. Josh was twelve years old when the Gibsons settled down in Pleasant Valley, a Negro enclave in Pittsburgh's North Side.

While equal opportunity was only a pleasant dream for a Negro boy in Pittsburgh, still, the change from the oppressive atmosphere of a southern small town was welcomed. "The greatest gift Dad gave me," Gibson said later, "was to get me out of the South."

Baseball was new to the migrant from Georgia, but he was soon the first one chosen for sandlot pickup games when he began demonstrating a talent for hitting the ball. He was always looking for a ballgame, to play or to watch, and he thought nothing of strapping on rollerskates and skating six miles downriver to Bellevue to see a game.

The young Josh did not care especially for football or basketball, the other neighborhood sports, but swimming caught his interest and as a teenager he brought home a number of medals from the city playground pools. At sixteen he was on his first uniformed baseball club—the Gimbels A.C., an all-Negro amateur team playing in Pittsburgh. He was already a catcher, as he would be throughout his career, except for an occasional game in the outfield.

His education was over. Josh had gone through fifth grade in the Negro school in Buena Vista and continued in elementary school in Pittsburgh. He dropped out after completing the ninth grade in Allegheny Pre-Vocational School, where he learned the rudiments of the electrician's trade. He immediately went to work as an apprentice in a plant that manufactured air brakes. But by this time it was clear that Gibson's vocation would be baseball. He was nearing his full size of 6 feet 1 inch and 215 pounds. He had a moon-round, trusting face, a friendly disposition, and the body of a dark Greek god. His broad shoulders sloped down to tremendous arms, thick with muscle, and his barrel chest tapered in the athlete's classic mold to a deceptively slim-looking waist. Like his arms, Gibson's legs were heavily muscled.

For a Pittsburgh Negro boy who loved baseball, his goal would have to be the Homestead Grays. He could envy the Pirates' heroes of his youth—the Waners, Lloyd and Paul, and Pie Traynor and Burleigh Grimes and Rabbit Maranville—but he could not hope to step into their shoes. The next best thing was the Homestead Grays, who had started twenty years before in the steel town a few miles upriver and were beginning to emerge as a national Negro baseball power. They had Smoky Joe Williams and Johnny Beckwith and

Sam Streeter and Vic Harris and Martin Dihigo—names that meant nothing to the typical Pirate fan but that loomed large in Negro baseball.

In 1929 and 1930, when the Grays were strengthening their position as one of the best Negro ballclubs in the country, Josh Gibson was catching for the Crawford Colored Giants of Pittsburgh. This was a semipro club that Josh had had a hand in organizing around a city recreation building in Pittsburgh's Hill District. The Crawfords (not to be confused with Gus Greenlee's powerhouse, which was formed in 1931) played other semipro clubs in and around Pittsburgh for a few dollars a game. No admission was charged for their games, and the collection rarely brought in more than fifty dollars, although crowds of 5,000, attracted by the growing awareness of Gibson's power at the plate, were not uncommon.

The Grays, naturally, soon heard of the big, raw slugger. Judy Johnson, who managed Homestead in 1930, said:

> I had never seen him play but we had heard so much about him. Every time you'd look in the paper you'd see where he hit a ball 400 feet, 500 feet. So the fans started wondering why the Homestead Grays didn't pick him up. But we had two catchers. Buck Ewing was the regular catcher, and Vic Harris, an outfielder, used to catch if we were playing a doubleheader.

In late July, the Kansas City Monarchs, Negro National League champions of 1929, came to Pittsburgh for a series with the Grays, bringing along their new portable lighting system. On July 25, the Grays and Monarchs were battling under these uncertain lights in Forbes Field. Johnson remembers:

> Joe Williams was pitching that night and we didn't know anything about lights. We'd never played under 'em before, and we couldn't use the regular catcher's signals, because if he put his hand down you couldn't see it. So we used the glove straight

up for a fastball and the glove down—that was supposed to be the curve.

Some way Joe Williams and the catcher got crossed up. The catcher was expecting the curve and Joe threw the fastball and caught him right there, and split the finger. Well, my other catcher was Vic Harris and he was playing the outfield and wouldn't catch. So Josh was sitting in the grandstand, and I asked the Grays' owner, Cum Posey, to get him to finish the game. So Cum asked Josh would he catch, and Josh said, "Yeah, oh yeah!" We had to hold the game up until he went into the clubhouse and got a uniform. And that's what started him out with the Homestead Grays.

Gibson got no hits that night, but he made no errors, either, and that was strange, for he was still a raw-boned eighteen-year-old and clumsy with the mitt. For the rest of that season, Johnson said, "Josh would catch batting practice and then catch the game, he was so anxious to learn. He wasn't much of a catcher then, but he came along fast."

Despite his shortcomings as a catcher, Gibson became an instant regular on the Grays, although he was often used in the outfield during his first year in top competition. His bat simply had to be in the lineup somewhere.

There remains a wide division of opinion among ballplayers who played with and against Gibson during his prime as to his skill as a catcher. Many maintain that he became a good receiver, but never a great one. They hold that he never learned to catch foul pop-ups, that his arm was adequate, but no more than that, and that as a receiver he was not in the same class with Bruce Petway, who threw out Ty Cobb twice trying to steal second in a series in Cuba in the winter of 1910, or Biz Mackey, whose career began in 1920 and spanned thirty years on top clubs, or Frank Duncan, Kansas City Monarchs catcher of the 1920s.

Walter Johnson's description of Gibson as a rocking-chair catcher with a rifle arm suggests otherwise. Joining Walter Johnson in his opinion that Josh was a superior catcher is Roy Campanella, who was beginning his career in professional baseball with the Baltimore Elite Giants in 1937, about the time Gibson reached his peak. Campanella said that Gibson was a graceful, effortless receiver with a strong, accurate arm. He was, said Campy, "not only the greatest catcher but the greatest ballplayer I ever saw."

The middle ground between these extreme opinions is held by Jimmie Crutchfield, an outfielder who was a teammate of Gibson on the Pittsburgh Crawfords from 1932 through 1936:

> I can remember when he couldn't catch this building if you threw it at him. He was only behind the plate because of his hitting. And I watched him develop into a very good defensive catcher. He was never given enough credit for his ability as a catcher. They couldn't deny that he was a great hitter, but they could deny that he was a great catcher. But I know!

In 1931, Josh Gibson was an established star on the Homestead Grays. He was credited with seventy-five home runs that year as the Grays barnstormed around Pennsylvania, West Virginia, Ohio, and into the southern reaches of New York State, feeding the growing legend about the young black catcher who could hit the ball a country mile. The next year he was lured to the Pittsburgh Crawfords by the free-spending Gus Greenlee to form with Satchel Paige perhaps the greatest battery in baseball history. Gibson stayed with Greenlee's Crawfords for five summers, his fame growing with each Brobdingnagian clout. In 1934 his record was sixty-nine home runs and in the other years his homer production, although not recorded, was from all accounts similarly Ruthian. Or perhaps Gibsonian.

As Greenlee's dream of a baseball dynasty soured, Gibson jumped back to the Grays near the end of the 1936 season. In 1937 he was listed on the Crawfords' spring roster, but by mid-March he was described as a holdout. John L. Clark, Greenlee's publicity man, wrote in the *Pittsburgh Courier* that Greenlee and Rufus (Sonnyman) Jackson, Grays' co-owner, were discussing a trade in which Gibson and Judy Johnson (who had been the Crawfords' third baseman since 1932) would go to the Grays for catcher Pepper Bassett and any infielder, plus $2,500. Here is a measure of Negro baseball's finances. The game's greatest slugger—who was also the paramount drawing card (always excepting Satchel Paige)—and Negro baseball's most accomplished third baseman were to be traded for two journeymen players and $2,500.

That the story was in part a ploy to bring Gibson to terms is evident from Clark's faint praise of the slugger. He said that Gibson was an asset to any club, "but not the kind of asset that more colorful and less capable players might be. With all this ability, he has not developed that 'it' which pulls the cash customers through the turnstiles—although he has been publicized as much as Satchel Paige." Gibson's lack of color, plus a rumor that he had an offer to manage an unnamed club at a higher salary than Greenlee would offer, made it likely that a trade would be made, Clark wrote. Gibson did not come to terms with Greenlee and a trade went through: Gibson and Johnson for Pepper Bassett and Henry Spearman. No money changed hands. Johnson did not report to the Grays.

And so Josh Gibson returned to the Homestead Grays, his first team. Spring training had hardly begun when he heard the siren call of the dollar to be made with Satchel Paige in the Dominican Republic. He heeded the call. The *Pittsburgh Courier* reported, most improbably, that Gibson had gone to Trujillo-land with the consent of the Grays. In any event, he stayed only until July, returning in time to help the Grays win their first Negro National League championship.

For the next two years, Gibson's big bat was the piledriving punch on the strongest club in Negro baseball. Boasting Buck Leonard, Sam Bankhead, Vic Harris, and other sluggers in addition to Josh, the Grays dominated the league and toyed with their foes on the barnstorming trail. It was such a powerful and well-balanced team that it could survive the loss of Gibson and continue its mastery over the NNL in the 1940 and 1941 seasons after Gibson had jumped to the Mexican League. He earned $6,000 a season with Veracruz, according to the *Courier*, $2,000 more than he was paid by the Grays. If Cum Posey and Sonnyman Jackson had looked on with favor when he had gone to the Dominican Republic in 1937, they were not pleased by his contract-jumping in later years. They won a court judgment against Gibson for $10,000 and laid claim to his Pittsburgh home. But when he signed with the Grays for 1942, all was forgiven and they dropped the suit. Josh Gibson was at the height of his fame and near the peak of his incredible power, envied but popular with other Negro professional ballplayers, and the toast of Pittsburgh's black community. There was nowhere to go but down, and the slide would soon begin.

He had come into big-time Negro baseball twelve years before as a rookie of uncommon rawness, a young man so shy and retiring that when he visited in another player's home he spent the evening looking at his shoes. Now he was self-assured, the main attraction at any party, and he had developed a fondness for the bottle. Gibson's drinking never reached the point where he failed to show up for ballgames—or to hit with power—but in his final five seasons he was occasionally suspended for a few days for "failing to observe training rules," in Cum Posey's delicate phrase.

Another, more ominous, portent of the dark days ahead appeared when he began suffering from recurring headaches. On January 1, 1943, he blacked out, lapsing into a coma that lasted all day and hospitalized him for about ten days. The diagnosis was a brain tumor. Doctors at Pittsburgh's St. Francis Hospital wanted to operate, but he would not permit it, according to his sister, Mrs. Annie Mahaffey. "He figured that if they operated, he'd be like a vegetable."

Gibson's knees, too, were giving him trouble, apparently the result of cartilage damage, and he was slowing to a snail's pace compared with his former speed. In his heyday, Gibson, despite his size, had been one of the fastest runners on the Grays. Yet, even while his troubles were pyramiding, Gibson was still the symbol of power. In 1944 he led the Negro National League in homers with six while batting .338 in 39 league games. The next year he was again home-run champion with eight and boasted a league-leading .393 average in 44 games. As a matter of course, he was chosen as the East's catcher in the East-West all-star games in 1944 and 1946. He missed the 1945 all-star game because it was played during one of his periodic suspensions for violating training rules.

Josh Gibson had played baseball the year-round every year from 1933 through 1945, spending the winter seasons in Puerto Rico, Cuba, Mexico, and Venezuela. His greatest thrill, he said, had been winning the batting title and the most-valuable-player award in the Puerto Rican League in 1941. (He was without doubt the most valuable player in the Negro National League for several seasons, but no MVP award was ever given in the NNL.)

Now, in the winter of 1946, his headaches and blackouts were increasing in frequency and severity, and for the first time since 1933 he stayed home in Pittsburgh. Outwardly, he remained a cheerful, easy-going giant, gregarious and friendly, and only his increasing attachment to liquor betrayed his concern about his illness. "He never got drunk so that he was staggering or anything like that," Mrs. Mahaffey recalled, "but still it worried you, because he wasn't really a drinking man."

On the evening of January 20, 1947, Josh came home and told

his mother that he felt sick. He said that he believed he was going to have a stroke. Mrs. Gibson said, "Shush, Josh, you're not going to have no stroke," but she sent him to bed. The family gathered around his bedside and waited for a doctor while Josh laughed and talked. Then he sent his brother Jerry to the homes of friends to collect his scattered trophies and his radio and bring them home. "So Jerry came back about ten-thirty," Mrs. Mahaffey said, "and we were all laughing and talking, and then he had a stroke. He just got through laughing and then he raised up in bed and went to talk, but you couldn't understand what he was saying. Then he lay back down and died right off."

There are those who believe his death was caused by his disappointment at being denied the opportunity to play in the big leagues. Ted Page, an outfielder who was Gibson's teammate on the Crawfords, said, "Josh knew he was major-league quality. We would go to a major-league game if we had a day off. He was never the kind of a guy to say, 'I'm the great Josh Gibson,' but if he saw a player make a mistake he would say what should have been done, or he might say, 'I would have been expecting that.'"

Page said that Gibson never complained about the hard lot of the Negro professional.

He wouldn't have traded his life for anything. One weekend, I remember, we played a twilight game at Forbes Field in Pittsburgh. Afterward we jumped in two cars and drove the 600 miles to St. Louis for a 2 P.M. game the next day. And the next day we drove 350 miles to Kansas City for a doubleheader. It was 110 in the shade, but he loved it. That night Josh and I were sitting on the back porch of the hotel and we saw a kid ballgame and we went and joined it. That's the kind of guy he was.

By the standards of Negro baseball, Gibson was well-paid for such labors. During the boom of the early 1940s, he was, next to

Satchel Paige, the highest-salaried performer in the game, earning about $6,000 from the Homestead Grays for a five-month season and adding perhaps $3,000 in winter baseball. (A journeyman black player made about $1,250 for the summer and considerably less during the winter, if he played at all.) While Gibson's salary was higher than that of the average major-leaguer during this period, it was nowhere near that of white stars of his stature like Joe DiMaggio, Hank Greenberg, and Ted Williams.

Like them, he hit for a high average as well as for distance. Only for the last three years of his career are official records available, but they show him among the batting leaders in the Negro National League and suggest that in his prime he would have boasted a batting average not far below .400 against strong pitching.

As John L. Clark noted during Gibson's salary wrangle with the Crawfords in 1937, he was "colorless" in the same sense that Joe DiMaggio was. It was the colorlessness of perfection, the ability to do the difficult effortlessly. He loved the game and he played to win, but his performance excited only admiration and awe while Satchel Paige, with equally memorable though different skills, added to them a talent for showmanship. The result was that while hundreds went to the ballgame to see Gibson, thousands went to watch Paige.

Gibson died the year after Jackie Robinson had broken organized baseball's color line at Montreal and only months before Robinson would become the first Negro in the major leagues since Fleet and Weldy Walker in 1884. Gibson himself had had two tantalizing nibbles that suggested he might become the first to cross the line. In 1939, Wendell Smith of the *Courier* reported that Bill Benswanger, president of the Pittsburgh Pirates, had promised a trial for Josh and Buck Leonard, the Grays' slugging first baseman. Smith said Cum Posey had agreed to sell his two stars but Benswanger changed his mind. Benswanger's version was different. He said Cum Posey asked him not to sign Gibson because then other Negro stars would be taken and the Negro National League would be wrecked. In any case, no tryout was held.

A few years later, when the Homestead Grays were playing in Griffith Stadium regularly, Gibson and Leonard were called up to the Washington Senators' offices by Clark Griffith, the owner. "He talked to us about Negro baseball and about the trouble there would be if he took us into the big leagues," Leonard said. "But he never did make us an offer."

Griffith must have been sorely tempted to sign the two black men. His Senators were usually mired deep in the American League's second division, and when they were on the road he could look out of his office and watch Gibson and Leonard busting the fences in his park. In one game in 1943, Gibson hit three home runs there, one of them landing two feet from the top of the left-center-field bleachers, 485 feet from the plate. For the season, he belted eleven home runs to left field, the deep field in Griffith Stadium, playing there only once or twice a week, reportedly more than were hit to left in all American League action in that ballpark.

That Josh Gibson would have been one of baseball's superstars if the color line had been lowered earlier is beyond dispute. It is likely that he would have posed the most serious threat ever to Babe Ruth's lifetime record of 714 home runs in the major leagues.

Gibson did achieve a considerable measure of fame, parochial as it was, as the greatest hitter in Negro baseball. After Satchel Paige, his was easily the most famous name among black players. He is remembered with admiration, affection, and even wonder by old teammates and opponents alike, no small legacy for any man. Since Josh Gibson was not a man to pine for what might have been, perhaps the most fitting epitaph that could be devised was pronounced by Ted Page: "He was a big, overgrown kid who was glad for the chance he had. He loved his life."

• •

HIS MAJESTY THE KING

Paul Gallico was the highest paid sportswriter in the so-called Golden Age of Sport of the 1930s (Babe Ruth, Jack Dempsey, Bobby Jones, Bill Tilden, Red Grange). A large, burly, bespectacled man with a stooped but powerful build, he was skillful enough with an épée in his hand to win fencing championships. Writing a thousand-word column, seven days a week, for the *New York Daily News,* Gallico, a skilled pilot, often went from one sports event to another in an amphibian named "Daisy-the-Duck." In 1936 he gave up sportswriting for fiction: *The Snow Goose,* the famous parable about World War II; the *Mrs. 'Arris* stories; and *The Poseidon Adventure* are perhaps the most familiar. He also wrote a recollection of his *Daily News* days entitled *Farewell to Sport.* Dedicated to a number of his fellow sportswriters, it was among the most popular of his books.

⊘

O NE OF THE GREAT characters of my time was George Herman (Babe) Ruth, the baseball-player. I do not mean to write like an old man reminiscing, but of course Babe Ruth is through as a ball-player. His legs went back on him (it is the legs that go first with practically all athletes), and my adjectives were beginning to look a trifle shopworn. A great many of them I managed to wear thin in over twelve years of writing about Ruth. For the Babe was and still is a wonderful person and a great human being. I do not write this as a pop-eyed cub or even as an exponent of the "Gee whiz, ain't he grand?" school of sportswriting, but in sober retrospection over the career of a man I genuinely love and admire.

The last time I saw Babe Ruth was at Jones Beach State Park on Long Island, where I was putting on a water circus for my paper. Ruth, finished as an active ball-player, had been brutally discarded by the game and its operators, for whom he did so much. It made me angry to see this glamorous figure suddenly completely neglected and out of the picture. I invited him to come down to the beach as guest star of the day's shows.

It was a warm, bright sunshiny seashore afternoon in August, a Saturday, and there were some seventy-five thousand people jammed around the flat, sandy area of Zach's Bay, many of them standing waist-deep in the water to see the fun. Midway during the program Ruth was led out from the show control station, down the aisle bordering the bay, and out across the catwalk that led to our big water stage. No announcement had been made or was to be made until he reached the stage and the act then going on was concluded.

But as we walked, a murmur began in the vast crowd as they recognized the big, burly man with the ugly face, blob nose, curly black hair, cigar stuck out of the side of his mouth. There were individual cries of "Hi, Babe! Oh you Babe! Hey, Babe, look up here!" The name passed from lip to lip. The crowd caught fire like a blaze running over a dry meadow, and the murmur swelled and rose, gained and grew and took on volume, until by the time he reached the stage it was one thundering, booming roar drowning out the pounding of the surf on the beach a few hundred yards away. It shook the stands and the glassy surface of the water. It shook Ruth a little too, the man who had heard so many of these crowd roars. He stood facing into this gale of sound, grinning, his little eyes shining. The ringmaster had a stroke of genius. He dispensed with his microphone and simply swept his arm in Ruth's direction. The greeting redoubled.

And this was not a baseball crowd. Many of the people there had never seen a major-league baseball game. They were simply Mr. and Mrs. Average Citizen out for a day's fun at the beach. But they all knew Ruth and somehow loved him.

A few minutes later Babe began to hit fungo flies out into the bay. "Hitting fungo flies" is the baseball term for the act of throwing the ball up and out in front of you a little way and then hitting it up into the air with a specially constructed bat. It is used to knock flies out to the outfielders to give them practice. Ruth, incidentally, holds the world's record for distance in fungo-hitting. A most curious sight followed.

The first three baseballs had hardly splashed into the bay, the fourth was still in its arching flight, when the shore line—a half-mile or so of it—suddenly became frothed with white. The line of foam extended around the U of the bay and grew in width, white splash-ings in which dark heads bobbed, the beginning of one of the strangest and most exciting races I have ever witnessed. More than a thousand youngsters, girls as well as boys, with one sudden, simul-taneous impulse, had taken to the water and were threshing out to-wards those tiny white baseballs bobbing on the blue surface of Zach's Bay. Many of them were competitors who had been waiting for their swimming races to be called and who should have been rest-ing and husbanding their strength. They didn't care. There was but one immediate goal for that army of splashing, water-churning youngsters. It seems that there was magic on those baseballs.

There has always been a magic about that gross, ugly, coarse, Gargantuan figure of a man and everything he did. It is all the more remarkable because George Herman Ruth is not sculptured after the model of the hero. He is one of the ugliest men I have ever known. He was kneaded, rough-thumbed out of earth, a golem, a figurine that might have been made by a savage.

He is six feet in height, or close to it, with an unshapely body that features a tremendous, barrel-shaped torso that tapers down into too small legs and an amazingly fragile and delicate pair of ankles. But his head is even more remarkable. It is enormous, too large even for his big, bulky frame. His eyes are brown, small, and deep sunk, but clear and bright. His nose is flat and pushed in. Nobody did it for him; it grew that way. It gives him a quaintly appealing porcine look, emphasized by the little, glittering eyes. His mouth is large and thick-lipped and featured by fine white teeth. His hair is a dark brown, almost black, and crisp and curling.

His voice rumbles from the deep caverns of his massive chest, a great, deep, masculine voice, and his speech is coarse, salty, and completely man's talk, peppered with strong ribald oaths. It is the talk I used to hear in the Navy, with "son of a bitch" used so frequently, genially, and pleasantly that it loses all of its antisocial qualities and becomes merely another word that does not particularly disturb the ears any more than "guy" or "I'm blessed"—a peculiarity one often notices about strong speech. Habitual use of what is technically termed an oath eventually robs it of its sting. When Babe Ruth used to say casually: "I'm a bastard if that feller ain't hitten' 'em to left field now," he was merely using an accepted colloquialism of his early youth and stratum to indicate surprise, and therefore the word meant no more than if he had said: "I'm a wood nymph." Less.

Like all people who spring from what we like to call low origins, Ruth never had any inhibitions. The polite evasions of civilized speech and their interdictions, until recent years, were never for him, and sometimes he said shocking things. That is, they would have been shocking coming from an archbishop or a Princeton graduate or a virgin, but to me they never were because he was always so completely natural and never said them with the purpose of startling or shocking, but merely for the more utilitarian purpose of expressing himself and his meaning. His language for many years remained the robust, expressive, if thoroughly gutter speech of the asphalt and gutter world.

He was, after all, when first noticed, a tough kid in a Baltimore Catholic semi-correction school. His true antecedents—that is, his father and mother—apparently will always remain misty and unexplored. After all, Ruth was an orphan. What he remembers about his parents is hardly pleasant, and he will not talk of it. Suffice it to say that they, too, were made of gray clay, and that Ruth's youth was hard and bitter as was Dempsey's, but the rancid bitterness and hardness of cobblestones and back-yard city slums, a drabness differing from those sections in the small country towns known as "across the railroad tracks" only by its components.

That, of course, is one of the never dimming miracles of this inexplicable country, that half-brutes like Dempsey or Ruth can and do emerge from the filth and ashes to shine more brightly than any phoenix as the beloved heroes of the nation, rich beyond maddest fantasies, and, above all, looked up to and worshipped by children. And I marvel, too, how, as they age, these men who were toughies and hard nuts in their early years begin to take on a patina of civilization and gentleness. True, the layer never waxed very thick over Ruth's uncouth exterior, but he acquired it nevertheless. He can talk refined and gentle as long as you please now. It nearly kills him, but he can.

I am not equipped to tamper with the question of Ruth's mental age, because he was always a boyish, direct fellow who spent most of his time playing a game, but he is possessed of plenty of shrewdness and intelligence. Of his psychic age, however, I am prepared to suggest that it never grew beyond that of a nine-year-old.

I get a little tired when I read of prizefighters, ball-players, football heroes, and the like who are just "big, playful boys who never grew up." Ruth grew up, very slowly, it is true, but his spirit, or whatever it is that inhabits and animates his gross body, never did and never will. He merely has learned to discipline his appetites and desires. He never got over having them.

His reasoning and behavior were always engagingly childlike and wholly understandable. When he was poor and an orphan boy he had nothing and must have wanted everything. There was a time when he was undernourished and sometimes starving. No man who has ever gone hungry ever quite forgets it. Now, consider that in the years between 1914 and 1934 Babe Ruth in salary and prize money alone earned the sum of $1,000,000. With the perquisites that fall to every successful athlete in the United States, the endorsings, the syndicated articles, the sporting-goods material and candy bar bearing his name, the moving pictures, the radio, and the royalties, he must have made that sum over again. In 1914 his salary with the Baltimore team was $600 a year, in five years with Boston it was $5,000, and in ten years with New York it was $52,000 and eventually rose to $70,000.

Is any man who has starved and lived meanly, geared to accept and handle sudden wealth? And yet the most harmful thing that Ruth in all his life ever did with his money was one time nearly to kill himself through overeating. Whether or not it grew out of his early unsatisfied hungers, he was a glutton. One hot afternoon in some dreadful little Southern whistle stop on the training swing up through the cotton states on the way north, he was hungry and thirsty. Therefore he bought as many greasy, railroad-station hot dogs and bottles of arsenic green and jaundice-yellow soda pop as he could eat and drink. Eyewitnesses say he ate twelve frankfurters washed down with eight bottles of pop.

The result was the stomach-ache heard and felt around the world. Ruth never did anything in a small way. The biggest-pain-ever griped his middle. His training trip was interrupted. In New York he was carted from the train on a stretcher and taken to the hospital, where he very nearly died. Few if any American citizens have ever had such a death watch or caused so much public concern while lying on a sick-bed.

There was an inside story current at the time that actually, the dogs and the soda pop were successfully digested and that Ruth was suffering from something a little more sinister. Actually, which story was true I do not know. Both were easily applicable to Ruth. But in this instance the cause was far less important than the effect. A baseball-player lay close to death, and an entire nation held its breath, worried and fretted, and bought every edition of the newspapers to read the bulletins as though the life of a personal friend or a member of the family were at stake.

There was published at the time one of the most touching news pictures of the day. It was a shot of a couple of grimy street Arabs standing on the sidewalk beneath the hospital, looking up at the curtained window behind which lay the Babe. In their hands they clasped little bunches of flowers for their hero.

When you have worked on a great newspaper for many years you come to regard such touching pictures with more than a faint tinge of suspicion. You can almost hear the photographers saying: "Hey! Wouldn't it make a swell shot to get a couple of dirty-faced kids looking up at the Babe's window? Let's grab a couple and pose 'em. Hey, Jack, run down to the corner—there's a florist there—and get a couple of cheap bunches of flowers. We'll get 'em to hold 'em and look up at his window, sad. Boy, that'll be a knockout." Photographers are that way—good ones.

But the point is that, whether or not the pictures were on the level, there was behind them a sound basis of fact. Ruth was loved and admired by children the country over. He had a magic about him; he was a character out of a fairy story, that drew youngsters to his side as well as grown-ups. Success and wealth had been showered upon him as it is in the stories and there he was in the flesh, to be looked at, touched, spoken to.

He was perhaps the most accessible of all our heroes. From April 14 through the first week in October he was in some ball park every day, a familiar and easily distinguished figure with his funny little mincing run, but there was nothing mincing about the cut he took at the ball, or the speed and amazing accuracy of his throw to home plate from deep right field. And if you could get down onto the field before a game, and youngsters with a little nerve usually could, he would pat you on top of the head and say: "Hullo, son. Shake hands"; or autograph a program or a baseball. Sometimes he did not do this with utter good grace, but always until the later years, when autograph-hunters had become a nerve-racking public menace, he did it. And sometimes when there was time out or a delay on the diamond he would back up to the right-field screen behind which were the bleachers and chat with the youngsters there.

One of the penalties of too close association with heroes and daily sports-reporting is the suspicion and cynicism already indicated. You learn eventually that, while there are no villains, there are no heroes either. And until you make the final discovery that there are only human beings, who are therefore all the more fascinating, you are liable to miss something.

One of the most beautiful of the Ruth stories is this one: There was a handsome kid aged around twelve or thirteen, son of a pleasant, middle-class suburban family, who had undergone an operation. The operation had been successful, but the boy failed to improve. He had slipped too far downhill. Something tremendous was needed to bring him back. The boy's idol was Babe Ruth. A baseball autographed by the Babe might prove the right stimulus to quicken that nearly extinct flame. A newspaperman went to Ruth and told him the story and asked him to autograph a baseball for the boy.

The next morning the nurse came into the room and said: "Johnny! Johnny! You must open your eyes and sit up for a moment. Someone is here to see you."

The door opened and it was God Himself who walked into the room, straight from His glittering throne, God dressed in a camel's hair polo coat and a flat, camel's hair cap, God with a flat nose and little piggy eyes, a big grin, and a fat black cigar sticking out of the side of it.

God gave His alias as Babe Ruth and sat at the foot of the bed and talked baseball as man to man for a little while with the earth child and then promised him a personal and private miracle all for himself. He said: "Ya know what I'm going to do this afternoon? I'm gonna hit a home run just for you. You watch. It's gonna be your home run. Now you hurry up and get well so you can come out and see me play."

When he left, the boy knew that God had been there, because He left a shiny white American League baseball with the familiar "Babe Ruth" traced on the horsehide in ink as evidence of His presence. And what is more, he performed the miracle. He hit that home run that afternoon. How did he know that he would be able to do it? Ruth always seemed to know. The boy could not die after that; not after he had thus been held close to the august breast of divinity and been a party to a genuine grade-A special Number One miracle.

Did Babe Ruth think up and execute that wonderful, simple visit to a sick child? Or was it cooked up by his wise, hard-boiled syndicate manager or some smart newspaperman scenting a heart story that would thrill the country? I don't know. I never really wanted to know, but I remember that at the time I had my suspicions. There were too many photographers and reporters present.

But does it really matter? He went. He sat and talked to the boy as long as the doctors would permit him to stay. And he did hit that home run in the afternoon, the boy's private, personal home run, promised and dedicated to him, the sweetest and most thrilling gift a child could want. The pictures and the story covered the country. People looked, read, gulped, and felt an emotion and said in effect: "You gotta love a guy like that, don't you?" And so they loved him.

I learned to love him because he was all man. In his early days before the great reformation he drank, he smoked, he cursed, he wenched, he indulged himself, he brawled and sulked, and got the swelled head and got over it. He was discovering, living and enjoying this wonderful thing called life with all of his senses, enjoying it more than anyone I have ever known. God, life was swell! All the food he could eat, beer and whisky, girls with red or black or yellow hair and soft lips, baseball every day, nice warm places to sleep, silk underwear, fine warm clothing, plenty of pals, money in the pants pocket, more where that came from, name and pictures in the papers, a big shiny automobile to ride around in—wow!

And yet it never made him mean. He never forgot his early days. For that matter, he didn't want to forget them, because thinking of them sharpened his enjoyment of the new ones so much more. And he always had a tremendous earnestness and sincerity and, above all, something that only a great and really simple man could have: a sense of responsibility to the millions of people, young and old, who loved him and thought that he was a hero and a fine man.

This is perhaps the greatest truth about the Babe—that no matter how phony or drippingly sentimental the situation in which he found himself might be, whether it was the outcome of natural instincts on his part to be kind or whether it was as carefully stage-managed as the first visit of a cub columnist to the home of a particularly vicious prizefighter, Ruth was always the honest and sincere element in the situation. He, if no one else, believed in it and played it up to the hilt, not ever for his own personal gain or glory or to build up an elaborate false character to be sold to his public, but because he believed that that was the kind of person he was. His generosity and his affections were just as Gargantuan as his appetites.

Consider for instance the brilliantly phony plea to Babe Ruth made by his friend Senator Jimmy Walker at a baseball-writers' banquet at the close of a season during which Ruth had been a particularly bad boy, had broken training, had quarreled with Miller Huggins, his manager, had been fined and suspended and sent home, had, in short, acted the part of a spoiled, willful, naughty brat.

The Senator rose to speak in a banquet hall filled with tough, hard-boiled, worldly-wise baseball-writers whose daily job it is to peddle treacle about the baseball heroes and soft-pedal the sour stuff, baseball managers, perhaps as tough and hard a group of men as there is in sports, celebrities of every kind; and he made a personal plea to Babe Ruth to reform himself and behave because he owed it to the dirty-faced kids in the streets who worshipped him; the Babe, he said, had a great responsibility to the youth of the country and he must not shirk it.

It was maudlin; it was in some ways cheap and tear-jerking. But, as I have suggested, it was likewise brilliant, and the brittely hard, cynical Senator of the State of New York knew what he was doing. Because Ruth robbed it of all cheapness, of all sensationalism, or everything that was vulgarly maudlin, by getting to his feet and, with tears streaming down his big, ugly face, promising the dirty-faced kids of the nation to behave—for their sake. And then he kept his promise. He was never in trouble again. From that time on he began to learn a little about moderation and restraint. Nor did it make him any the less a picturesque character, because he never went sissy or holy on the boys. He retained all of his appetites and gusto for living. He merely toned them down. He learned what every celebrity in the United States eventually must learn—to perform his peccadillos in strict privacy if possible. Formerly Ruth had perpetrated his right out in public.

Ruth's baseball record is a remarkable one and deserves inclusion even in such an informal estimate of him as this. He has an all-time total of 708 home runs and 723 homers, adding those he hit in World Series. He holds the record for the most home runs hit in one season: namely, 60, scored in 1927 in a season of 151 league games. He likewise holds the world's record for the total number of bases on balls during a playing career, 2,036, an indication of what the opposing pitchers thought of him. For twelve years he led his American League in home runs hit, and for eleven years hit forty or more out of the park each season. There are dozens of other minor records that one could dig out of the files and the record-books, all connected with his prodigious hitting, such as runs batted in, runs scored, extra base hits, and so on; but they still remain dusty figures and reveal nothing of the manner of his making these numbers—numbers which in two or three generations will be all that will remain of George Herman Ruth, except legend.

For he played ball on the same enormous scale on which he lived his life, intensely, fervently, and with tremendous sincerity and passion. It was impossible to watch him at bat without experiencing an emotion. I have seen hundreds of ball-players at the plate, and none of them managed to convey the message of impending doom to a pitcher that Babe Ruth did with the cock of his head, the position of his legs, and the little, gentle waving of the bat, feathered in his two big paws.

And, curiously, no home run that Ruth ever hit managed to hint at the energy, power, effort, and sincerity of purpose that went into a swing as much as one strike-out. Just as when he connected the result was the most perfect thing of its kind, a ball whacked so high, wide, and handsome that no stadium in the entire country could contain it, so was his strike-out the absolute acme of frustration. He would swing himself twice around until his legs were braided. Often he would twist himself clear off his feet. If he had ever connected with that one...

Every move that Ruth made brought some kind of answering sound from the crowd in the stands. Each swung strike left a trail of laughter, but backed by a chorus of respectful and awed "Oooooooohs" as the audience realized the power that had gone to waste and the narrow escape the pitcher had had. Ruth's throws to home plate from the outfield, or to a base, so accurate that the receiver never had to move a step from his position to receive them, always brought ripples of incredulous laughter, the "I'm seeing it, but I don't believe it" kind.

And of course his home runs brought forth pandemonium, a curious double rejoicing in which the spectator celebrated not only Babe's feat and its effect upon the outcome of the game, but also his excellent luck in being present and with his own eyes beholding the great happening. There must be an enormous amount of fetishism in our hero-worship of successful athletes, and seeing Ruth hit a home run always seemed to have definitely a stimulating effect upon people, almost as though by having been there when it happened, some of his magic stuck to them. Behind the autograph craze which sends the crowd clamoring around Ruth and other celebrities for signatures there is pure fetishism, with the touch of the signature of the great one desired for a talisman.

Because Ruth will always be one of the great success stories, the fairy tale come true—From Rags to Riches, or the Orphan Who Made Good. It is one of the favorite fables of our democracy, and when it comes to life as it sometimes does in startling places, we are inclined to regard the lucky character as more royal than royalty.

We apply the titles of Kings and Queens to our successful athletes, as expressions of a belief in their fortunate birth, anointed and under a lucky star. Thus Ruth was always and always will be the King of Swat, a distinct and royal personage to whom the ordinary rules of life do not seem to apply. For among the other blessings with which he was apparently showered when he entered this world— blessings which, it is true, were not apparent at the time—was the gift of being able to deliver where there was something important at stake, when it meant the most, when the greatest number of eyes were upon him. We admire this trait greatly, and all our fictional heroes are endowed with it. They always come through at the right time, just as Ruth hit his home run for the sick boy the day he promised to do so.

And so when I think back over the great deeds of sport that I have witnessed and think particularly of the ones that have warmed my heart and made it glow beyond all cynicism, I remember with most pleasure the last World Series in which Ruth played, back in 1932, and which involved the New York Yankees and the Chicago Cubs. The game took place in Chicago, and Root was pitching for the Western team. The Cubs were giving Ruth an unmerciful riding down on the field, and the sallies were deliberately vicious and foul, having chiefly to do with his origin, upon which, as I have indicated, there may be considerable speculation. He had already hit one home run, and when he came to bat in the latter part of the game, the entire Cub bench came out to the edge of the dugout and began to shout filth and abuse at him.

Root put over the first pitch and Ruth swung at it and missed. There was a great roar of delight from the partisan crowd, which hated everything that came from New York, and the players redoubled their insults. Ruth held up one finger so that everyone could see it. He was indicating that that was just one strike. The crowd hooted him. Root pitched again and Ruth missed for the second time, and the park rocked with laughter. The Cub players grew louder and more raucous. The Babe held up two fingers. The crowd razzed him, and there was nothing good-natured about it, because his magnificent effrontery was goading them badly.

Two balls, wide pitches, intervened. And at this point, Ruth made the most marvelous and impudent gesture I have ever seen. With his forefinger extended he pointed to the flagpole in center field, the farthest point removed from the plate. There was no mistaking his meaning. He was advising crowd, pitcher, and jeering Cubs that that was the exact spot where Root's next pitch would leave the park.

The incensed crowd gave forth a long-drawn-out and lusty "Booooooo!" Ruth made them choke on it by slugging the ball out of the premises at exactly that point, the center-field flagpole, for his second home run of the day and probably the only home run in the entire history of baseball that was ever called in advance, as to both time and place.

Ruth could do those things, take those chances and get away with them, because he was The Babe and because his imagination told him that it was a fine, heroic, and Ruthian thing to do. And he had the ability to deliver. I suppose in fifty or sixty years the legend will be that Ruth could call his shots any time.

But once is sufficient for me, and I saw him do that.

· ·

KALEIDOSCOPE: PERSONALITY OF THE BABE

The chapter that follows is from Robert W. Creamer's *Babe: A Legend Come to Life*. Creamer writes: "The baseball purists in that era (1894–1919) were forever frowning on home runs and deploring their increasing prevalence as a sign the game was degenerating. Henry Chadwick, the English-born sportswriter, who invented the box score (and this is the man responsible for baseball's preoccupation with statistics), looked upon baseball as a slightly forward child he had reared and educated. He wrote a strong attack on the insidious home run as early as 1890."

Babe Ruth, of course, changed all this, and here Creamer provides a vivid portrait of the man responsible.

⚾

ONE DAY IN 1930, before the first of a routine series of games in St. Louis between the Yankees and the Browns, Ruth was behind the batting cage talking with Bill Killefer, the Browns' manager, Tony Lazzeri, and a reporter.

"Your face is getting fatter and fatter," Killefer said.

"Yeah?" said Ruth. He spat some tobacco juice. "Well, I don't hit with my face."

"Is the wife on the trip with you?"

"Sure."

"Having a hard time dodging the old phone calls?" Killefer said, grinning.

"Oh, go to hell."

"Who do you like in the Derby?" the reporter asked.

"I'm not playing the ponies."

"What books are you reading?"

"Books?" Ruth looked at him. "Reading isn't good for a ballplayer. Not good for his eyes. If my eyes went bad even a little bit I couldn't hit home runs. So I gave up reading."

"You must do some reading. Who are your favorite authors?" The reporter pronounced it in the midwestern way, alien to Ruth's semisouthern ear.

"My favorite Arthurs? Nehf and Fletcher."

"Not Arthurs," the reporter said patiently. "Authors, writers."

"Oh, writers. My favorite writer is Christy Walsh."

"Seriously, what President of the United States do you admire most?"

"Well, I liked Harding a lot, and I liked Wilson a lot. Coolidge was all right. Hoover is okay with me, but Al Smith was my favorite for the job."

"What is the psychology of home runs?"

"Say, are you kidding me?"

"No, of course not. I just want an explanation of why you get so many home runs."

Ruth spat again. "Just swinging," he said.

"Have you ever had an idol, someone you thought more of than anyone else?"

"Sure he has," Lazzeri said. "Babe Ruth."

"Go to hell," Ruth said, and to the reporter, "Excuse me, it's my turn to hit."

When he finished he ducked under the stands for a few minutes and came back with a hot dog. He sat on the Browns' bench next to Killefer and the reporter.

"What was the biggest thrill you ever got out of a ballgame?" the reporter asked.

"Biggest thrill?" Ruth said. He bit off half the hot dog and gulped it down. "That's easy. It happened right here in St. Louis when I got three home runs in one World Series game and made that running catch off Frankie Frisch. Picked the ball right out of the stands. And I got a thrill out of little Sherdel trying to sneak that strike over on me when I wasn't looking and then hitting one out."

"How much did you earn last year? I mean, from everything—baseball, exhibitions, testimonials, everything."

"A hundred and ten thousand dollars."

"Are you saving any money?"

"Lots of it," Ruth replied. He finished the hot dog. "I started a trust fund three years ago and I've got $120,000 in it right now. I got an older one with $50,000 in it. Right now I'm good for $500 a month for as long as I live."

"What are you going to do when your baseball days are over?"

"Take life easy," Ruth said. "Excuse me, I've got to hit again."

Later the Yankee batboy and mascot, Eddie Bennett, a hunchback, came down to the runway into the Browns' dugout. He was carrying a cup of some sort of whitish liquid.

"What have you got there?" Killefer asked.

"Some bicarbonate of soda for the Babe."

"How many hot dogs did he have?" Killefer asked.

"Three."

"How often does he do that?" asked the reporter.

"Every day," Bennett said, shaking his head. "Every day."

Ruth drank bicarbonate of soda every day in the dugout. He called it his milk. He began the habit one day after he gobbled down a couple of hot dogs too quickly and felt bloated just before game time. The trainer recommended bicarbonate. It made him feel good and he decided that was the ideal diet before a game: a couple of hot dogs and a glass of bicarb. He chewed tobacco and gum, smoked cigars and occasionally cigarettes or a pipe, took snuff in such vast amounts that some of the dust became impacted in his nasal passages. A doctor ordered him to quit taking it after that.

Before the game that day in St. Louis a photographer asked Ruth to pose for pictures and he willingly complied. He always went along. A photographer asked him one day to have his picture taken with "another champion, the greatest egglayer in Nebraska." He was handed a chicken and an egg. He posed amiably with the chicken cuddled in one hand, the egg in the other, a huge grin on his face and his eyes all crinkled up from laughing. He was relaxed with reporters, and would go out of his way to be cooperative with them, although he was often subjected to bizarre questions. "What do you think of the Chinese situation?" he was asked. "The hell with it," he replied. But when Will Grimsley of the Associated Press was a young reporter, Ruth patiently answered all his questions one day even though his teammates were yelling at him to hurry up.

On the road he always had a suite, sometimes in a different hotel from the one the team was staying at. He liked to lounge around in red slippers and a red robe, smoking a cigar. Dozens of people streamed in and out of the suite day and night. He always carried a wind-up portable phonograph with him on road trips. He loved to sing. Occasionally he would strum a ukulele. He was always shaved by a barber. ("That's what they're for, aren't they?") In St. Louis he liked to eat at a German restaurant that made barbecued spare ribs. Often, on the day the Yankees were leaving town, he'd go from the ballpark to the restaurant and order a mess of ribs and home brew and take it to the train. He would set up shop in a washroom and sell the ribs to the players for fifty cents a portion. He insisted on being paid too, but he also provided beer, and the players could have all the beer they wanted for their fifty cents.

He was apolitical, although he called himself a Democrat until Franklin D. Roosevelt ran for a third term, and apparently he never cast a vote in a national election until 1944. Yet he created a mild political furor in September 1928, when Herbert Hoover was running for President. Hoover appeared at the ballpark and a publicity man ran down to the Yankee clubhouse to get Ruth to come and pose with the Republican candidate.

"No, sir," said Ruth, "nothing doing on politics." He had been burned a few days earlier by a story saying he was supporting Hoover. He denied it, saying he was for Al Smith, and now he declined to appear with Smith's rival. But, graciously, he said, "Tell him I'll be glad to talk to him if he wants to meet me under the stands." No doubt here as to which was king.

Reporters with Hoover heard about all this, and it became a headline story: "RUTH REFUSES TO POSE WITH HOOVER." Christy Walsh almost died. Republican newspapers were threatening to drop Ruth's syndicated column. Walsh got in touch with Babe and hurriedly prepared a statement, ostensibly by Ruth, saying he regretted that because of a misunderstanding he had been unable to pose with the Republican candidate. He would be happy to, he declared, and a photo was duly taken of Ruth and Hoover together.

Despite the earlier publicity, Hoover's camp was happy to have the photograph, because Ruth's personality was pervasive. The crudity, the vulgarity, the indifference, the physical humor that bordered on brutality, the preoccupation with his own needs that ignored Hoover and hurt Helen—none of it mattered when Ruth smiled or laughed or moved or did almost anything. "He was one of those exciting people who make life fun, and who give more to life than they take from it," said Arthur Robinson, a New York sportswriter who was another of the Babe's ghosts. "God, we liked that big son of a bitch," said Hoyt. "He was a constant source of joy." When Roger Maris was chasing Ruth's home run record in 1961, Jimmy Dykes said, "Maris is a fine ballplayer, but I can't imagine him driving down Broadway in a low-slung convertible, wearing a coonskin coat." Dugan said, "What a fantastic ballplayer he was, the things he could do. But he wasn't human. He dropped out of a tree."

He was so alive, so attractive, like an animal or a child: ingenuous, unselfconscious, appealing. Frank Graham said, "He was a very simple man, in some ways a primitive man. He had little education, and little need for what he had." Tom Meany said he had the supreme self-confidence of the naïve. On a stifling hot day at the Washington ballpark he said to President Harding, "Hot as hell, ain't it, Prez?" He met Marshal Foch when that renowned French hero of World War I was making a tour of the United States early in the 1920s and said politely, "I suppose you were in the war?"

Introduced before a game to a man he had never seen before, Ruth said, "You sound like you have a cold." The man admitted he did. Ruth reached into the hip pocket of his uniform and pulled out a big onion. "Here, gnaw on this," he said. "Raw onions are cold-killers." During a blistering heat wave Ruth brought a cabbage into the dugout and put it in the team's old-fashioned water cooler, and each inning before he went on the field he took a fresh cabbage leaf and put it under his cap to keep himself cool.

Famous for not remembering names (when Waite Hoyt was leaving the Yankees in 1930 after eleven seasons as Babe's teammate in Boston and New York, Ruth shook hands and said solemnly, "Goodbye, Walter"), he had nicknames for other players, not necessarily complimentary nicknames. His teammates were Chicken Neck, Flop Ears, Duck Eye, Horse Nose, Rubber Belly. People he did not know or remember he called Doc or Kid, which he usually pronounced Keed, in the flashy slang pronunciation of the time. He called older men Pop, older women Mom. Younger women he needed no special name for. He usually called Claire [his second wife], Clara. He himself was called Jidge by the Yankees, a corruption of George that was apparently first used by Dugan.

His appetite was enormous, although accounts of it were often exaggerated. A report of one dinner says he had an entire capon, potatoes, spinach, corn, peas, beans, bread, butter, pie, ice cream, and three or four cups of coffee. He was known to have eaten a huge omelet made of eighteen eggs and three big slices of ham, plus half a dozen slices of buttered toast and several cups of coffee. Ty Cobb, no stickler for accuracy in his memoirs of baseball life, said, "I've seen him at midnight, propped up in bed, order six club sandwiches, a platter of pigs' knuckles, and a pitcher of beer. He'd down all that while smoking a big black cigar. Next day, if he hit a homer, he'd trot around the bases complaining about gas pains and a bellyache." He belched magnificently and, I was told, could fart at will.

He was, as noted, a sexual athlete. In a St. Louis whorehouse he announced he was going to go to bed with every girl in the house during the night, and did, and after finishing his rounds sat down and had a huge breakfast. In the early 1930s the Yankees signed a superior pitcher named Charlie Devens out of Harvard, who abandoned a promising major league career a year or two later to join his family's banking business in Boston. Devens joined the team in St. Louis, reporting in at the hotel. He was given the key to his room and went up and unpacked. His roommate, some secondary figure on the team, was not around. Just as he finished unpacking, the phone rang and a voice asked, "Devens?"

"Yes."

"Bring your room key with you and come down to the lobby."

Obediently Devens took his key and went downstairs. When the elevator doors opened at the lobby floor, there was Babe Ruth, a girl on each arm.

"You Devens?" Ruth asked.

Devens nodded. Ruth put out his hand. Devens looked at him dumbly.

"The key," Ruth snapped. Devens gave him the key and Babe and his friends swept into the elevator. Later Devens learned that when Mrs. Ruth was with Babe on road trips he occasionally preempted teammates' rooms for extracurricular activities.

There were inevitable stories that Ruth was exceptionally well equipped sexually, and a male nurse who took care of him in his terminal illness was impressed by the size of Ruth's genitals. But apparently any abnormality in size then was a product of illness. One teammate, asked if Ruth had an exceptionally big penis, frowned a little as he searched his memory and shook his head. "No," he said. "It was normal size, judging from locker room observation. Nothing extraordinary. Del Pratt's was. And Home Run Baker's. My God, you wouldn't believe Home Run Baker's. It looked like it belonged to a horse. But Babe's wasn't noticeably big. What was extraordinary was his ability to keep doing it all the time. He was continually with women, morning and night. I don't know how he kept going." He was very noisy in bed, visceral grunts and gasps and whoops accompanying his erotic exertions. "He was the noisiest fucker in North America," a whimsical friend recalled.

There is a story, probably apocryphal, about a time he and Meusel were barnstorming together. They shared a hotel suite. Meusel was half asleep when Ruth came in with a girl, went into his room, and made love to her in his usual noisy fashion. Afterwards he came out to the living room of the suite, lit a cigar, and sat in a chair by the window, smoking it contemplatively. When he finished the cigar he went back into the bedroom and made love again. And then came out and smoked another cigar. In the morning Meusel asked, "How many times did you lay that girl last night?" Ruth glanced at the ashtray, and so did Meusel. There were seven butts in the tray. "Count the cigars," said Ruth.

On the other side of the coin there is another story, about a barnstorming trip with Gehrig. Ruth came back to the suite boisterously drunk with two girls and went into the bedroom with both of them. During the night one of the girls came out to Gehrig and said, "You better come and see if you can straighten out your friend." Lou went into the bedroom and found Ruth sitting naked on the side of the bed, sobs racking his shoulders, tears running down his face. In bits, from Ruth and the girls, Gehrig discovered what was wrong. However successful he had been earlier in the night with his friends, Ruth was crying because he was unable now to service both girls.

Everything about him reflected sexuality—the restless, roving energy; the aggressive skills; fastball pitching; home run hitting; the speed with which he drove cars; the loud, rich voice; the insatiable appetite; the constant need to placate his mouth with food, drink, a cigar, chewing gum, anything. When he played poker, he liked to raise even when his cards did not justify a raise, and when he lucked into a pot he chortled happily. He was a fairly skillful bridge player, but he wanted to play every hand himself and often outbid his partner as well as their opponents. In retirement his favorite sports were golf and bowling; he liked to hit a golf ball a long way, and in bowling to keep track of the total number of pins he knocked down rather than his average score. He loved to win in whatever he did. He received absolute physical joy from cards, baseball, golf, bowling, punching the bag, sex.

He liked to fish and would go with Gehrig before their friendship became strained, but he was a better hunter than a fisherman. His physical stamina, superb eyesight, and quick reflexes helped his hunting, and he also had a quality seldom in evidence anywhere else: extraordinary patience. Once in Georgia he stalked a wild turkey for seven hours before getting close enough to shoot. Then he picked it off the top of a tree with one shot.

Physically he was a paradox. He was big, strong, muscular, exceptionally well coordinated, yet he was often injured and he suffered from a surprising number of colds and infections. This would indicate a low resistance to disease, yet he had an amazing ability to recover quickly. He dramatized injuries; no player in big league history was carried off the field on his shield as often as the massive Bambino. But he could ignore both illness and injury and play superlatively well despite them.

In his later years Ruth was often babied by the Yankees. He and Jimmy Reese, a rookie second baseman who weighed seventy-five pounds less than the Babe, crashed into each other running for a fly ball. They staggered apart and fell to the ground, both apparently hurt. The trainer and others ran from the bench, past Reese's prostrate form, and gathered around Babe. When Lefty Gomez was a rookie, he was pitching batting practice in spring training. Hoyt came past the mound just as Ruth was stepping in to hit. "Nothing but fastballs right down the pipe," Hoyt told Gomez. "Don't get cute, kid. And for God's sake, don't hit him or you're gone."

In the summer of 1931, going after a fly ball, Babe smashed into a chicken-wire screen that was serving as a temporary outfield fence during renovations. A strand of loose wire ripped into his finger, cutting it badly and tearing the nail off. The trainer ran out, took one look, and said Ruth would have to come out of the game. Holding the damaged hand with the other, his face screwed up in pain, Ruth limped all the way in from right field, even though his legs had not been hurt. In the trainer's room he was told the damaged nail would have to be cut away. "Not without gas," he declared. "Nobody's going to cut me unless I have gas." He made a great fuss before the nail was removed and the finger bandaged, and everybody laughed about the limp and the gas. But the next day he played, torn finger and all, and stole a base. His second wife reacted to the well-publicized stories about Mickey Mantle having to have his legs bandaged each day during his career because of his osteomyelitis by saying, "No one ever mentions that my husband played with bandaged legs practically every day of his career." Old teammates verified this. When Ruth slid into base he slid with abandon, and because he would not wear sliding pads under his uniform his thighs and hips were scraped raw by the rough pebbly soil of the old infields. His legs were richly decorated with raw "strawberry" wounds which persisted all season. He would have them doused with alcohol and wrapped in bandages and go on playing.

"He was very brave at the plate," Casey Stengel said. "You rarely saw him fall away from a pitch. He stayed right in there. No one drove him out."

His weight fluctuated throughout his career. When he signed with the Orioles he weighed about 185 and with the Red Sox he went up to 198 and then to 212 in a couple of seasons. He got down below 200 again, but not for long, and after 1919 his weight was seldom below 220. It soared to 240 in Cuba late in 1920 and stayed around 230 in 1921 and 1922. In the spring of 1923, after his first reformation, he was down briefly to 215, but a year later he was up to 230 again. In January 1925 he weighed 256 and was probably more than 260 at the time of his collapse in Asheville. Determined work at McGovern's gymnasium the following winter got him down to 212; thereafter his weight as a player varied from about 225 to 240, depending on the time of the year. But he continued to work with McGovern every winter, and he was in much better shape at that weight than he used to be. When he first went to McGovern during the winter of 1925–26 his chest measured 43 inches normal and 45 inches expanded; both his waist (49¾ inches) and his hips (47 inches) were larger than his chest. But in the winter of 1931–32, approaching his thirty-eighth birthday and weighing 235½, his waist was 38 and his hips 40, and his chest was 41 normal and 48 expanded.

Because of Ruth's bulk, Ruppert decided to dress the Yankees in their now-traditional pinstripe uniform and dark blue stockings. The natty, clothes-conscious Ruppert felt the new uniform would make Ruth look trimmer. The Yankees also introduced uniform numbers to the major leagues in 1929. Ruth's number was number 3 because he batted third, Gehrig's 4 because he batted fourth, and so on.

When Ruth left the ballpark or the hotel, usually to meet a girl, he would say, "I'm going to see a party." He seldom if ever went to popular night clubs or famous restaurants. He much preferred out-of-the-way places where he knew the owner and could relax in relative peace and quiet. One of his favorites was a spot in northern New Jersey called Donahue's. The owner fixed up a private room for him where he could eat and drink and talk with his guests without being bothered by strangers. He seldom had many people with him, usually four or five at the most.

His voice was rich and warm, his accent very slightly southern. "Less go out to the *bowl* game," he would say, pronouncing "ball" that way and stressing it heavily. His speech was splattered with vulgarities. "Piss pass the butter," he would say childishly if he was dining with a teammate. Or, asked how he was feeling, he'd reply, "Pussy good, pussy good." In the early 1920s he saw a teammate on the street with a pretty girl. Next day he asked, "Who was that cunt you were with?" The teammate said, "For God's sake, Babe, that was my wife."

"Oh," Ruth said. "I'm sorry. I *knew* she wasn't no whore."

He was sitting around a table with several players and their wives in Hot Springs in 1923. "Excuse me," he said, getting up. "I've got to take a piss."

Herb Pennock, very much a gentleman and also very much a friend of Ruth's, followed Babe out to the men's room. "Babe," he said, "you shouldn't say that in front of the ladies."

"Say what?"

"Say piss like that. You just don't say that in front of women. You should say, 'Excuse me, I have to go to the bathroom,' or something like that."

"I'm sorry, Herb."

"Okay."

They went back to the table and sat down, and Ruth said to the women, "I'm sorry I said piss."

After Ruth came back from a trip to the Far East in the 1930s, a friend who had just been married came to visit, bringing along his new wife. Babe told them stories about the trip, including a long anecdote about a game in Manila.

"Then these Hawaiians tried to tell us—" he began.

"Not Hawaiians, Babe," said Mrs. Ruth, "Filipinos."

"Yeah, Filipinos." He went on and after another couple of sentences said, "Then this little Hawaiian—"

"Filipino," said Mrs. Ruth.

"Filipino. This little guy came over..." He went on to the end of the story, laughed uproariously, and said, "Those Hawaiians thought they were pulling a fast one on us."

"Filipinos."

"Oh, Christ, call them Eskimos. Who gives a goddamn?"

He told another story about sitting next to Lefty Gomez's wife at dinner one evening on the trip. "They brought out this great caviar, and they started it around the table from one side of me. Lefty's wife was sitting on the other side. It goes all the way around the table, and there's only a little left when it gets to her, and she takes it all. 'Oh, I love this stuff,' she said. So I asked the waiter to bring some more, and they bring it and it goes around the table again, and damn if she didn't take the last bit again. She was sitting there eating it on bits of toast. My God, she ate so much of that stuff she looked like a seagull eating shit."

The friend was wondering uneasily how his lovely new wife was taking this, and he got Ruth to talking instead about his trophies. Babe gave them a quick guided tour. He pointed to one silver cup and said, "Look at this one. You know what I got it for?"

"No, what?"

"I won first place in a farting contest. Honest. Read the writing on it. Boy, I had to down a lot of beer and limburger to win that one."

The friend left the apartment a bit shaken. In the elevator he looked nervously at his wife. But she seemed exhilarated.

"What a fascinating man," she said.

"Ruth's language *was* pretty bad," Frick said, "but, you know, it's a remarkable thing. My wife is a very genteel lady, *very* genteel, yet she always enjoyed seeing Ruth, and we were with him a great deal in those years. In all the time we knew him, I cannot recall one instance when he ever said anything crude or obscene in front of her." Meany said he was with Ruth at a party on Long Island when Babe decided to tell a joke, something he rarely did. Before he began, he insisted that all the women leave the room. And the anecdote turned out to be fairly innocuous.

Many stories about Ruth were turned into legend by the encrustations of time. Here are three of them, with a factual basis for each. The story of Johnny Sylvester is one of the most famous in Ruth lore. The simplest version says that Johnny, a young boy, lay dying in a hospital. Ruth came to visit him and promised him he would hit a home run for him that afternoon. And he did, which so filled Johnny with the will to live that he miraculously recovered. The facts are parallel, if not so melodramatic. In 1926 eleven-year-old Johnny Sylvester was badly hurt in a fall from a horse and was hospitalized. To cheer him up, a friend of Johnny's father brought him baseballs autographed by players on the Yankees and the Cardinals just before the World Series that year, as well as a promise from Ruth that he would hit a home run for him. Ruth hit four homers in the Series, and after it was over paid a visit to Johnny in the hospital, which thrilled the boy. The visit was given the tears-and-lump-in-the-throat treatment in the press, and the legend was born. After that, few writers reviewing Ruth's career failed to mention a dying boy and the home run that saved his life.

The following spring Ruth was sitting with a couple of baseball writers when a man came up to him and said, "Mr. Ruth, I'm Johnny Sylvester's uncle. I just want to thank you again for what you did for him."

"That's all right," Ruth said, "glad to do it. How is Johnny?"

"He's fine. He's home, and everything looks okay."

"That's good," said Ruth. "Give him my regards."

The man left. Ruth watched him walk away and said, "Now who the hell is Johnny Sylvester?"

There is a legend that Ruth once hit a ball so hard that it went between the pitcher's legs and over the center fielder's head for a home run. In 1927 the Yankees played the Senators when Hod Lisenbee was pitching for Washington and Tris Speaker was playing center field. Lisenbee was in his first year in the majors and Speaker in his next to last. There was a runner on second taking a big lead, although he was keeping his eyes on both the shortstop and the second baseman. Speaker began a favorite maneuver of his: sneaking in from center field toward second base in the hopes of getting a quick throw from the pitcher and picking the runner off second. Lisenbee ignored Speaker's move and threw to the plate. Ruth hit a low line drive directly back at the pitcher, who leaped and lifted his right leg frantically to avoid being hit by it. The ball ticked the underside of his thigh as it went past. It hit the ground a few feet past second, took a huge bounce, and went over Speaker's head. One of the other outfielders retrieved it, but Ruth got an extra-base hit out of it—not a home run.

And there is a legend, seldom printed but often talked about in baseball circles, that says Leo Durocher stole Babe Ruth's watch, which is not true. What is true is that Ruth did not like Durocher. When he saw Leo, a rookie, wearing a tuxedo in the lobby of a spring-training hotel, Ruth asked with considerable distaste, "Who's the little gink in the monkey suit?" He resented Leo's cockiness, and the two never got along, although Leo tried to—at first.

Durocher was in a hotel elevator late one night with a couple of other players when Ruth got on. "Oh, am I drunk," said the Babe. "Somebody's got to undress me and put me to bed. You guys have to help me."

The other players backed away rapidly, but Leo said, "I'll help you, pal."

"Thank you, pal," Ruth said. Leo helped him off the elevator and down the hall to Babe's room. The next morning Ruth decided that he was missing something—money in one version of the story, his watch in another. Although he was drunk on the town the night before and had been in the Lord knows what places, he blamed Durocher. As Leo said, in a half-angry, half-mocking tone, "Jesus Christ, if I was going to steal anything from him I'd steal his goddamned Packard."

Ruth continued to harass Durocher. One night on the train as he was getting undressed by his berth, he called to Durocher.

"Hey, Leo, you want to see something?" He held up a glittering bit of jewelry. "See that, Leo? Isn't that beautiful? That cost me seventy-five hundred bucks, Leo. I'm going to give it to Claire when we get to New York. Tonight I'm putting it under my pillow. And, Leo, I want it to be there when I wake up in the morning."

After that, Durocher disliked Ruth as much as Babe disliked him, although in a year or so their paths parted. After the 1929 season Durocher was sold out of the American League to Cincinnati. Explaining the sale, which was made when he was manager, Shawkey said, "You'll never see a better fielding shortstop than Leo, but he couldn't hit. And he was a little too much of an individual."

Ruth did not like Ty Cobb much either, primarily because of Cobb's bench jockeying, which was cruel and humorless. When the story about Ruth never changing his underwear got around the league during his early years with the Red Sox, Cobb would say the same thing whenever he saw Ruth: "You fellows smell something around here? Oh, hello, Babe." Ruth's usual reply to Cobb's gibes was a stream of obscenity. Cobb and some of the other Tigers were riding Ruth about the 1922 Series, and Cobb said, "We hear that little Johnny Rawlings ran you out of the Giant clubhouse. Is that true?" Ruth said, "It ain't a goddamned bit true, and you sons of bitches can go fuck yourselves." Cobb said that when Ruth extended himself he had a vocabulary that stood alone, even in the purple atmosphere of dugout and clubhouse. Ruth and Cobb had a fight of sorts on the field in 1924 when a free-for-all broke out between the Yankees and Tigers, but they were separated before anything much happened. Ruth was not much of a brawler. His quick temper got him into a lot of mixups, but, according to Meany, he never won a fight. He never really lost one either. He had a lot of No Decisions. He seldom stayed angry very long.

Ruth's tendency to get into trouble, particularly during his first decade in the majors, gave rise to a fairly widespread opinion that he was subnormal mentally (Ban Johnson said he had the mind of a fifteen-year-old) or else was so primitive that he could not accept a moral code. "He was an animal," Dugan said. "He ate a hat once. He did. A straw hat. Took a bite out of it and ate it."

But Ernie Shore said, "You have to remember, he had grown up in that Catholic reformatory. When they let him out it was like turning a wild animal out of a cage. He wanted to *go* every place and *see* everything and *do* everything."

"Ruth recognized the difference between right and wrong," Frick said. "What he did not recognize, or could not accept, was the right of society to tell him what he should do, or not do."

He had a perceptive understanding of things in certain areas and, in his own way, a refreshing sense of taste. When he met Red

Grange after the Illinois football hero turned professional in the mid-1920s, Ruth said to him, "Kid, don't ever forget two things I'm going to tell you. One, don't believe everything that's written about you. Two, don't pick up too many checks." Someone introduced him to Max Schmeling when he and the then heavyweight champion of the world happened to be riding on the same train. After Schmeling returned to his own compartment, a friend said to Ruth, "You should have asked him for his autograph." Ruth said, "Who the hell wants to collect that crap?" Frick said, "He drank a great deal and he was a ladies' man, but he never led a young ballplayer astray and he never took advantage of an innocent girl."

He understood clearly what he was doing when he batted, despite his habit of saying, "I just keep swinging," when people asked him the secret of hitting home runs. Once, seriously discussing his batting, he said, "I swing as hard as I can, and I try to swing right through the ball. In boxing, your fist usually stops when you hit a man, but it's possible to hit so hard that your fist doesn't stop. I try to follow through the same way. The harder you grip the bat, the more you can swing it through the ball, and the farther the ball will go. I swing big, with everything I've got. I hit big or I miss big. I like to live as big as I can." He held his bat at the very end, with his right hand curled over the knob. He had a big callus in the palm of his right hand as a result, along with the usual calluses that all batters have on their fingers and thumbs.

"He liked anything connected with playing baseball," Frick said, "but he liked home runs best. Whenever he hit one, he laughed. Sometimes before a game he'd say, 'I feel hitterish today. I'm due to hit one.' And if he did hit one, he'd talk about it long after the game."

He could be thoughtlessly cruel at times. Bud Mulvey, whose family used to own a substantial part of the Brooklyn Dodgers and still retains an interest in the Los Angeles Dodgers, remembered a baseball writers' dinner he was taken to as a boy. Ruth, retired by then, was there, and before the dinner he began to fool with Jackie Farrell, a tiny man literally half Ruth's weight, who later worked in the Yankee publicity department. Mulvey watched in distaste as Ruth playfully twisted Farrell's arm. "Jackie was really in pain," Mulvey said, "and Ruth was roaring with laughter. I never could like him after that."

Bob Condon, whose father knew Charlie McManus, the Yankee Stadium supervisor, was sometimes a backstage guest at the Stadium when he was a boy, which was relatively late in the Babe's career. Once, while a game was going on outside on the field, Condon was playing by himself in an open area under the stands behind the Yankee dugout. Ruth left the game for some reason, possibly a minor injury, and came angrily up the runway from the dugout. As he did, the ball Condon was playing with took a freak bounce directly into Ruth's path. The boy dove for it and fell flat in front of the Babe, who irritably shoved him out of the way with his foot. Kick may be too strong a word for the action, but substantially that is what Ruth did. "Stay out of the Babe's way," someone warned the tearful boy.

Alice Doubleday Rhodes recalled a time when Ruth played an exhibition in her small town when she was about ten. For some reason she accepted a dare to get Ruth's autograph, and well before the game she sneaked onto the field and walked to the Yankee bench. She had to ask, "Which one is Babe Ruth?" and this, to her confusion, made everyone laugh. He was pointed out and when she walked over to him he said, pleasantly enough, "You want to see me, sister?" She handed him her school notebook and a pen, a brand new pen that had just been given to her for her birthday. "Here," she said. He signed his name, in "a beautiful, even hand" and gave her back her schoolbook and pen. "There you are, sister," he said. "Now don't go home and sell it." But she had promised to get autographs for her schoolmates too. She handed book and pen back to him and said,

"Write some more. Write on all the lines." The other players broke up laughing. Ruth shrugged and slowly wrote his name on line after line until the page was filled. "That okay now?" he said, not smiling. He handed her the book and, looking out at the field, absentmindedly put the pen in his own pocket. Her marvelous birthday pen. She did not know what to do. Ruth looked at her coldly. "Something else on your mind, little girl?" he asked. She shook her head and said, "No, sir," and left. Chagrined and not a little afraid, it took her some time to get up the courage to tell her father what had happened, and she was totally unable to understand his hilarity when she did tell him. "Babe Ruth swiped your pen?" he howled.

Yet his affection for children was genuine, and it remained with him all his life. In 1943 he played a round of golf in the rain at the Commonwealth Country Club near Boston. As he was teeing up on the first hole he noticed two boys staring through a chain-link fence.

"Hey," he called to them. "You want to follow me around? It won't be any drier but it'll be more fun. You want to?"

The kids nodded. "Show them how to get into this joint," Ruth said to Russ Hale, the club pro. He waited until the boys reached the tee before he hit his drive, and he walked down the fairway with one arm around each, talking. He played nine holes in the rain, most of the time laughing and joking with the other men in his foursome but always returning to the kids to make sure they were enjoying themselves.

A decade earlier Jack Redding, who was to become librarian of the National Baseball Library at Cooperstown, caddied for him at Wheatley Hills on Long Island. "He'd give us a two-dollar tip if he won, a dollar and a half if he lost," Redding said. Was that a good tip? "Hell, yes," Redding said. "The usual tip was a quarter, or at best a half dollar. And on the thirteenth hole, where the refreshment stand was, that's where you tested your man. Some golfers would buy you a soft drink, some wouldn't buy you anything. Ruth always said, 'Get whatever you want.'"

He was a frequent and interested visitor to hospitals, orphanages, children's wards, and the like. He could create a holiday spirit in a ward merely by being himself. Many of his visits were well publicized—Walsh saw to that—but they were not done for publicity. Ruth always, or almost always, made himself available to the press, but the publicity was coincidental. After someone made fun of all the newspaper copy he received from such visits, he avoided mention of them, and for every one that got public notice several more did not.

Stories about the time and trouble he took to call on the sick and distressed are innumerable. Even when he was ill himself, he continued the practice. A year or so before he died, racked with pain from the cancer that was to kill him, he went with Paul Carey to visit a man who had gone blind. After they left, Ruth said of the blind man, "Some guys get all the bad breaks, don't they?"

He liked seeing children the best. He enjoyed them. He was comfortable with them. "He's just a big kid" was a common description of him, and perhaps the only time he was truly at ease was when he was with children. With them there were no rules, no authority, no need to apologize, to explain, to explode, to drink, to fuck, to prove himself over and over. Without thinking about it, he knew who they were and they knew who he was. They got along. Like a child, he did not like to wait or plan for the right moment. He did not like to wait for anything. "It might rain tomorrow," he would say.

He did things impulsively, the way a child does. Children are emotionally neutral to things that deeply affect adults. Without malice, they casually hurt the feelings of a close friend. Without love, they do an act of exceptional thoughtfulness for a casual acquaintance. In his novel *Stop-Time* Frank Conroy wrote, "Like all children, I was unsentimental." Hoyt said of Ruth, "Babe was not a sentimentalist and generally made no outward demonstration of affection either by word or action."

This may explain a curious thing that Paul Carey, his great friend, said when he was asked about Ruth's feelings toward Claire. "I don't think the Babe really loved Claire," Carey said. "I don't think he really loved anybody."

THE BABE

Ty Cobb had an interesting idea about Ruth's home-run hitting, speaking of it when Ruth was still a pitcher: "He could experiment at the plate. He didn't have to get a piece of the ball. He didn't have to protect the plate the way a regular batter was expected to. No one cares much if a pitcher strikes out or looks bad at bat, so Ruth could take that big swing. If he missed it didn't matter. And when he didn't miss, the ball went a long way. As time went on he learned more and more about how to control that big swing and put the wood on the ball. By the time he was a fulltime outfielder he was ready."

Robert Frost always wanted to write a poem about a ball hit so far by Babe Ruth that it circled the earth like a satellite—an idea long before the scientists ever thought it possible to send up an artificial moon. As the following story attests, Frost is not the only one to come up with this startling image.

⚾

THE BABE HAD RETIRED in 1935 and was dying of cancer, but even a dying man has bills to pay, and so he took to the road for Sorbasol, and Lake Wobegon was the twenty-fourth stop on the trip, a day game on November 12. The All-Star train of two sleepers and a private car for the Babe backed up the sixteen-mile spur into Lake Wobegon, arriving at 10:00 A.M. with a blast of whistle and a burst of steam, but hundreds already were on hand to watch it arrive.

The Babe was a legend then, much like God is today. He didn't give interviews, in other words. He rode around on his train and appeared only when necessary. It was said that he drank Canadian rye whiskey, ate hot dogs, won thousands at poker, and kept beautiful women in his private car, *Excelsior*, but that was only talk.

The sleepers were ordinary deluxe Pullmans; the *Excelsior* was royal green with gold-and-silver trim and crimson velvet curtains tied shut—not that anyone tried to look in; these were proud country people, not a bunch of gawkers. Men stood by the train, their backs to it, talking purposefully about various things, looking out across the lake, and when other men straggled across the field in twos and threes, stared at the train, and asked, "Is he really in there?" the first-comers said, "Who? Oh! You mean the Babe? Oh, yes, I reckon he's here all right—this is his train, you know. I doubt that his train would go running around without the Babe in it, now, would it?" and resumed their job of standing by the train, gazing out across the lake. A proud moment for them.

At noon the Babe came out in white linen knickers. He looked lost. A tiny black man held his left arm. Babe tried to smile at the people and the look on his face made them glance away. He stumbled on a loose plank on the platform and men reached to steady him and noticed he was hot to the touch. He signed an autograph. It was illegible. A young woman was carried to him who'd been mysteriously ill for months, and he laid his big hand on her forehead and she said she felt something. (Next day she was a little better. Not recovered but improved.)

However, the Babe looked shaky, like a man who ate a bushel of peaches whole and now was worried about the pits. He's drunk, some said, and a man did dump a basket of empty beer bottles off the train, and boys dove in to get one for a souvenir—but others who came close to his breath said no, he wasn't drunk, only dying. So it was that an immense crowd turned out at the Wally (Old Hard

Hands) Bunsen Memorial Ballpark: twenty cents per seat, two bits to stand along the foul line, and a dollar to be behind a rope by the dugout, where the Babe would shake hands with each person in that section.

He and the All-Stars changed into their red Sorbasol uniforms in the dugout, there being no place else, and people looked away as they did it (nowadays people would look, but then they didn't), and the Babe and his teammates tossed the ball around, then sat down, and out came the Schroeders. They ran around and warmed up and you could see by their nonchalance how nervous they were. E.J. batted grounders to them and hit one grounder zinging into the visitors' dugout, missing the Babe by six inches. He was too sick to move. The All-Stars ran out and griped to the ump but the Babe sat like he didn't know where he was. The ump was scared. The Babe hobbled out to home plate for the ceremonial handshakes and photographs, and E.J. put his arm around him as the crowd stood cheering and grinned and whispered, "We're going to kill ya, ya big mutt. First pitch goes in your ear. This is your last game. Bye, Babe." And the game got under way.

It was a good game, it's been said, though nobody remembers much about it specifically, such as the score, for example. The All-Stars were nobodies, only the Babe mattered to the crowd, and the big question was Would he play? He looked too shaky to take the field, so some said, "Suspend the rules! Why not let him just go up and bat! He can bat for the pitcher! Why not? It wouldn't hurt anything!" And nowadays they might do it, but back then you didn't pick up the bat unless you picked up your glove and played a position, and others said that maybe it wouldn't hurt anything but once you start changing the rules of the game for convenience, then what happens to our principles? Or do we change those, too?

So the game went along, a good game except that the Babe sat sprawled in the dugout, the little black man dipping cloths in a bucket of ice and laying them on the great man's head—a cool fall day but he was hot—and between innings he climbed out and waved to the fans and they stood and cheered and wondered would he come to bat. E.J. said to Bernie, "He'll bat all right, and when he comes, remember the first pitch: hard and high and inside."

"He looks too weak to get the bat off his shoulder, Dad. He looks like a breeze would blow him over. I can't throw at Babe Ruth."

"He's not sick, he's pretending so he don't have to play like the rest of us. Look at him: big fat rich New York son of a bitch, I bet he's getting five hundred dollars just to sit there and have a pickaninny put ice on him. Boy, I'd put some ice on him you-know-where, boy, he'd get up quick then, he'd be ready to play then. He comes up, I want you to give him something to think about so he knows we're not all a bunch of dumb hicks out here happy just to have him show up. I want him to know that some of us *mean it.* You do what I say. I'm serious."

It was a good game and people enjoyed it, the day cool and bright, delicious, smelling of apples and leather and woodsmoke and horses, blazed with majestic colors as if in a country where kings and queens ride through the cornfields into the triumphant reds and oranges of the woods, and men in November playing the last game of summer, waiting for the Babe, everyone waiting for the Babe as runs scored, hours passed, the sky turned red and hazy. It was about time to quit and go home, and then he marched out, bat in hand, and three thousand people threw back their heads and yelled as loud as they could. They yelled for one solid minute and then it was still.

The Babe stood looking toward the woods until everything was silent, then stepped to the plate and waved the bat, and Bernie looked at him. It was so quiet you could hear coughing in the crowd. Way to the rear a man said, "Merle, you get your hands off her and shut up now," and hundreds turned and shushed *him.* Then Bernie wound up. He bent way down and reached way back and kicked up high and the world turned and the ball flew and the umpire said, "BALL ONE!" and the catcher turned and said, "Be quiet, this doesn't concern you," and the umpire blushed. He knew immediately that he was in the wrong. Babe Ruth was not going to walk, he would sooner strike out and would do it himself, with no help from an umpire. So the umpire turned and walked away.

The Babe turned and spat and picked up a little dirt and rubbed his hands with it (people thought, Look, that's our dirt and he's putting it on his hands, as if the Babe might bring his own) and then stood in and waved the bat and Bernie bent way down and reached way back and kicked high and the world turned and the ball flew and the Babe swung and missed; he said *huhhhnnnn* and staggered And the next pitch. He swung and cried in pain and the big slow curve slapped into the catcher's mitt.

It was so still, they heard the Babe clear his throat, like a board sliding across dirt. They heard Bernie breathing hard througn his nose.

The people were quiet, wanting to see, hear, and smell everything and remember it forever: the wet fall dirt, the pale-white bat, the pink cotton candy and the gentlemen's hats, the smell of wool and the glimmer of a star in the twilight, the touch of your dad's big hand and your little hand in it. Even E.J. was quiet, chewing, watching his son. The sun had set beyond right field, darkness was settling, you had to look close to see—Bernie took three steps toward home and pointed at the high outside corner of the plate, calling his pitch, and the Babe threw back his head and laughed four laughs. (People were glad to hear he was feeling better, but it was scary to hear a man laugh at home plate; everyone knew it was bad luck.) He touched the corner with his bat. Bernie climbed back on the mound, he paused, he bent down low and reached way back and kicked real high and the world turned and the ball flew and the Babe swung and it cracked and the ball became a tiny white star in the sky. It hung there as the Babe went around the bases in his famous Babe Ruth stride, the big graceful man trotting on slim little feet, his head down until the roar of the crowd rose like an ocean wave on the prairie and he looked up as he turned at third, he smiled, lifted his cap, strode soundlessly across home plate looking like the greatest ballplayer in the history of the world. The star was still in the sky, straight out due northwest of the centerfield fence, where he hit it. The ball was never found, though they searched for it for years.

DREAM OF A BASEBALL STAR

I dreamed Ted Williams
leaning at night
against the Eiffel Tower, weeping.

He was in uniform
and his bat lay at his feet
—knotted and twiggy.

"Randall Jarrell says you're a poet!" I cried.
"So do I! I say you're a poet!"

He picked up his bat with blown hands;
stood there astraddle as he would in the batter's box,
and laughed! flinging his schoolboy wrath
toward some invisible pitcher's mound
—waiting the pitch all the way from heaven.

It came; hundreds came! all afire!
He swung and swung and swung and connected not one
sinker curve hook or right-down-the-middle.
A hundred strikes!

The umpire dressed in strange attire
thundered his judgment: YOU'RE OUT!
And the phantom crowd's horrific boo
dispersed the gargoyles from Notre Dame.

And I screamed in my dream:
God! throw thy merciful pitch!
Herald the crack of bats!
Hooray the sharp liner to left!
Yea the double, the triple!
Hosannah the home run!

· ·

HUB FANS BID KID ADIEU

I once asked John Updike about this much-anthologized piece. He wrote me back as follows: "I wasn't sure I wanted to go to Williams's last game, but another engagement fell through and I went, and the events were so stirring that I was moved to write my only extended sports piece. I wrote it in five days with very little research material on hand. But, though I was not a great student of baseball, I was a keen student of Williams, and twenty years of doting Williams-watching came back to me. I loved Ted, in the way that adolescents can love an unattainable celebrity-object, and the love comes through, as Boston's love for the Splendid Splinter came through that day."

⊘

FENWAY PARK, in Boston, is a lyric little bandbox of a ball park. Everything is painted green and seems in curiously sharp focus, like the inside of an old-fashioned peeping-type Easter egg. It was built in 1912 and rebuilt in 1934, and offers, as do most Boston artifacts, a compromise between Man's Euclidean determinations and Nature's beguiling irregularities. Its right field is one of the deepest in the American League, while its left field is the shortest; the high left-field wall, three hundred and fifteen feet from home plate along the foul line, virtually thrusts its surface at right-handed hitters. On the afternoon of Wednesday, September 28, as I took a seat behind third base, a uniformed groundskeeper was treading the top of this wall, picking batting-practice home runs out of the screen, like a mushroom gatherer seen in Wordsworthian perspective on the verge of a cliff. The day was overcast, chill, and uninspirational. The Boston team was the worst in twenty-seven seasons. A jangling medley of incompetent youth and aging competence, the Red Sox were finishing in seventh place only because the Kansas City Athletics had locked them out of the cellar. They were scheduled to play the Baltimore Orioles, a much nimbler blend of May and December, who had been dumped from pennant contention a week before by the insatiable Yankees. I, and 10,453 others, had shown up primarily because this was the Red Sox's last home game of the season, and therefore the last time in all eternity that their regular left fielder, known to the headlines as TED, KID, SPLINTER, THUMPER, TW, and, most cloyingly, MISTER WONDERFUL, would play in Boston. "WHAT WILL WE DO WITHOUT TED? HUB FANS ASK" ran the headline on a newspaper being read by a bulb-nosed cigar smoker a few rows away. Williams's retirement had been announced, doubted (he had been threatening retirement for years), confirmed by Tom Yawkey, the Red Sox owner, and at last widely accepted as the sad but probable truth. He was forty-two and had redeemed his abysmal season of 1959 with a—considering his advanced age—fine one. He had been giving away his gloves and bats and had grudgingly consented to a sentimental ceremony today. This was not necessarily his last game; the Red Sox were scheduled to travel to New York and wind up the season with three games there.

I arrived early. The Orioles were hitting fungos on the field. The day before, they had spitefully smothered the Red Sox, 17–4, and neither their faces nor their drab gray visiting-team uniforms seemed very gracious. I wondered who had invited them to the party. Between our heads and the lowering clouds a frenzied organ was thundering through, with an appositeness perhaps accidental, "You *maaaade* me love you, I didn't wanna do it, I didn't wanna do it..."

The affair between Boston and Ted Williams has been no mere summer romance; it has been a marriage, composed of spats, mutual disappointments, and, toward the end, a mellowing hoard of shared memories. It falls into three stages, which may be termed Youth, Maturity, and Age; or Thesis, Antithesis, and Synthesis; or Jason, Achilles, and Nestor.

First, there was the by now legendary epoch when the young bridegroom came out of the West, announced "All I want out of life is that when I walk down the street folks will say 'There goes the greatest hitter who ever lived.'" The dowagers of local journalism attempted to give elementary deportment lessons to this child who spake as a god, and to their horror were themselves rebuked. Thus began the long exchange of backbiting, hat-flipping, booing, and spitting that has distinguished Williams's public relations. The spitting incidents of 1957 and 1958 and the similar dockside courtesies that Williams has now and then extended to the grandstand should be judged against this background: The left-field stands at Fenway for twenty years have held a large number of customers who have bought their way in primarily for the privilege of showering abuse on Williams. Greatness necessarily attracts debunkers but in Williams's case the hostility has been systematic and unappeasable. His basic offense against the fans has been to wish that they weren't there. Seeking a perfectionist's vacuum, he has quixotically desired to sever the game from the ground of paid spectatorship and publicity that supports it. Hence his refusal to tip his cap to the crowd or turn the other cheek to newsmen. It has been a costly theory—it has probably cost him, among other evidences of goodwill, two Most Valuable Player awards, which are voted by reporters—but he has held to it from his rookie year on. While his critics, oral and literary, remained beyond the reach of his discipline, the opposing pitchers were accessible, and he spanked them to the tune of .406 in 1941. He slumped to .356 in 1942 and went off to war.

In 1946, Williams returned from three years as a marine pilot to the second of his baseball avatars, that of Achilles, the hero of incomparable prowess and beauty who nevertheless was to be found sulking in his tent while the Trojans (mostly Yankees) fought through to the ships. Yawkey, a timber and mining maharajah, had surrounded his central jewel with many gems of slightly lesser water, such as Bobby Doerr, Dom DiMaggio, Rudy York, Birdie Tebbetts, and Johnny Pesky. Throughout the late forties, the Red Sox were the best paper team in baseball, yet they had little three-dimensional to show for it, and if this was a tragedy, Williams was Hamlet. A succinct review of the indictment—and a fair sample of appreciative sports-page prose—appeared the very day of Williams's valedictory, in a column by Huck Finnegan in the *Boston American* (no sentimentalist, Huck):

> Williams's career, in contrast [to Babe Ruth's], has been a series of failures except for his averages. He flopped in the only World Series he ever played in (1946) when he batted only .200. He flopped in the playoff game with Cleveland in 1948. He flopped in the final game of the 1949 season with the pennant hinging on the outcome (Yanks 5, Sox 3). He flopped in 1950 when he returned to the lineup after a two-month absence and ruined the morale of a club that seemed pennant-bound under Steve O'Neill. It has always been Williams's records first, the team second, and the Sox non-winning record is proof enough of that.

There are answers to all this, of course. The fatal weakness of the great Sox slugging teams was not-quite-good-enough pitching rather than Williams's failure to hit a home run every time he came to bat. Again, Williams's depressing effect on his teammates has never been proved. Despite ample coaching to the contrary, most insisted that they *liked* him. He has been generous with advice to any player who asked for it. In an increasingly combative baseball atmosphere, he continued to duck beanballs docilely. With umpires he was gracious to a fault. This courtesy itself annoyed his critics, whom there was no pleasing. And against the ten crucial games (the seven World Series games with the St. Louis Cardinals, the 1948 play-off with the Cleveland Indians, and the two-game series with the Yankees at the end of the 1949 season, winning either one of which would have given the Red Sox the pennant) that make up the Achilles' heel of Williams's record, a mass of statistics can be set showing that day in and day out he was no slouch in the clutch. The correspondence columns of the Boston papers now and then suffer a sharp flurry of arithmetic on this score; indeed, for Williams to have distributed all his hits so they did nobody else any good would constitute a feat of placement unparalleled in the annals of selfishness.

Whatever residue of truth remains of the Finnegan charge those of us who love Williams must transmute as best we can, in our own personal crucibles. My personal memories of Williams begin when I was a boy in Pennsylvania, with two last-place teams in Philadelphia to keep me company. For me, "W'ms, if" was a figment of the box scores who always seemed to be going 3-for-5. He radiated, from afar, the hard blue glow of high purpose. I remember listening over the radio to the All-Star Game of 1946, in which Williams hit two singles and two home runs, the second one off a Rip Sewell "blooper" pitch; it was like hitting a balloon out of the park. I remember watching one of his home runs from the bleachers of Shibe Park; it went over the first baseman's head and rose meticulously along a straight line and was still rising when it cleared the fence. The trajectory seemed qualitatively different from anything anyone else might hit. For me, Williams is the classic ballplayer of the game on a hot August weekday, before a small crowd, when the only thing at stake is the tissue-thin difference between a thing done well and a thing done ill. Baseball is a game of the long season, of relentless and gradual averaging-out. Irrelevance—since the reference point of most individual games is remote and statistical—always threatens its interest, which can be maintained not by the occasional heroics that sportswriters feed upon but by players who always *care;* who care, that is to say, about themselves and their art. Insofar as the clutch hitter is not a sportswriter's myth, he is a vulgarity, like a writer who writes only for money. It may be that, compared to managers' dreams such as Joe DiMaggio and the always helpful Stan Musial, Williams is an icy star. But of all team sports, baseball, with its graceful inter-mittences of action, its immense and tranquil field sparsely settled with poised men in white, its dispassionate mathematics, seems to me, best suited to accommodate, and be ornamented by, a loner. It is an essentially lonely game. No other player visible to my genera-tion has concentrated within himself so much of the sport's poignance, has so assiduously refined his natural skills, has so con-stantly brought to the plate that intensity of competence that crowds the throat with joy.

By the time I went to college, near Boston, the lesser stars Yawkey had assembled around Williams had faded, and his crafts-manship, his rigorous pride, had become itself a kind of heroism. This brittle and temperamental player developed an unexpected quality of persistence. He was always coming back—back from Korea, back from a broken collarbone, a shattered elbow, a bruised heel, back from drastic bouts of flu and ptomaine poisoning. Hardly a season went by without some enfeebling mishap, yet he always came back, and always looked like himself. The delicate mechanism of timing and power seemed locked, shockproof, in some case out-side his body. In addition to injuries, there were a heavily publicized divorce, and the usual storms with the press, and the Williams Shift—the maneuver, custom-built by Lou Boudreau, of the Cleve-land Indians, whereby three infielders were concentrated on the right side of the infield, where a left-handed pull hitter like Williams generally hits the ball. Williams could easily have learned to punch singles through the vacancy on his left and fattened his average hugely. This was what Ty Cobb, the Einstein of average, told him to do. But the game had changed since Cobb; Williams believed that his value to the club and to the game was as a slugger, so he went on pulling the ball, trying to blast it through three men, and paid the price of perhaps fifteen points of lifetime average. Like Ruth before him, he bought the occasional home run at the cost of many directed singles—a calculated sacrifice certainly not, in the case of a hitter as average-minded as Williams, entirely selfish.

After a prime so harassed and hobbled, Williams was granted by the relenting fates a golden twilight. He became at the end of his career perhaps the best *old* hitter of the century. The dividing line came between the 1956 and the 1957 seasons. In September of the first year, he and Mickey Mantle were contending for the batting championship. Both were hitting around .350, and there was no one else near them. The season ended with a three-game series between the Yankees and the Sox, and living in New York then, I went up to the Stadium. Williams was slightly shy of the four hundred at-bats needed to qualify; the fear was expressed that the Yankee pitchers would walk him to protect Mantle. Instead, they pitched to him—a wise decision. He looked terrible at the plate, tired and discouraged and unconvincing. He never looked very good to me in the Stadium. (Last week, in *Life,* Williams, a sportswriter himself now, wrote gloomily of the Stadium, "There's the bigness of it. There are those high stands and all those people smoking—and, of course, the shadows....It takes at least one series to get accustomed to the Stadium and even then you're not sure.") The final outcome in 1956 was Mantle .353, Williams .345.

The next year, I moved from New York to New England, and it

made all the difference. For in September of 1957, in the same situation, the story was reversed. Mantle finally hit .365; it was the best season of his career. But Williams, though sick and old, had run away from him. A bout of flu had laid him low in September. He emerged from his cave in the Hotel Somerset haggard but irresistible; he hit four successive pinch-hit home runs. "I feel terrible," he confessed, "but every time I take a swing at the ball it goes out of the park." He ended the season with thirty-eight home runs and an average of .388, the highest in either league since his own .406, and, coming from a decrepit man of thirty-nine, an even more supernal figure. With eight or so of the "leg hits" that a younger man would have beaten out, it would have been .400. And the next year, Williams, who in 1949 and 1953 had lost batting championships by decimal whiskers to George Kell and Mickey Vernon, sneaked in behind his teammate Pete Runnels and filched his sixth title, a bargain at .328.

In 1959, it seemed all over. The dinosaur thrashed around in the .200 swamp for the first half of the season, and was even benched ("rested," Manager Mike Higgins tactfully said). Old foes like the late Bill Cunningham began to offer batting tips. Cunningham thought Williams was jiggling his elbows; in truth, Williams's neck was so stiff he could hardly turn his head to look at the pitcher. When he swung, it looked like a Calder mobile with one thread cut; it reminded you that since 1953 Williams's shoulders had been wired together. A solicitous pall settled over the sports pages. In the two decades since Williams had come to Boston, his status had imperceptibly shifted from that of a naughty prodigy to that of a municipal monument. As his shadow in the record books lengthened, the Red Sox teams around him declined, and the entire American League seemed to be losing life and color to the National. The inconsistency of the new superstars—Mantle, Colavito, and Kaline—served to make Williams appear all the more singular. And off the field, his private philanthropy—in particular his zealous chairman-ship of the Jimmy Fund, a charity for children with cancer—gave him a civic presence somewhat like that of Richard Cardinal Cush-ing. In religion, Williams appears to be a humanist, and a selective one at that, but he and the cardinal, when their good works inter-sect and they appear in the public eye together, make a handsome and heartening pair.

Humiliated by his 1959 season, Williams determined, once more, to come back. I, as a specimen Williams partisan, was both glad and fearful. All baseball fans believe in miracles; the question is, how *many* do you believe in? He looked like a ghost in spring train-ing. Manager Jurges warned us ahead of time that if Williams didn't come through he would be benched, just like anybody else. As it turned out, it was Jurges who was benched. Williams entered the 1960 season needing eight home runs to have a lifetime total of 500; after one time at bat in Washington, he needed seven. For a stretch, he was hitting a home run every second game that he played. He passed Lou Gehrig's lifetime total, then the number 500, then Mel Ott's total, and finished with 521, thirteen behind Jimmy Foxx, who alone stands between Williams and Babe Ruth's unapproachable 714. The summer was a statistician's picnic. His two-thousandth walk came and went, his eighteen-hundredth run batted in, his six-teenth All-Star Game. At one point, he hit a home run off a pitcher, Don Lee, off whose father, Thornton Lee, he had hit a home run a generation before. The only comparable season for a forty-two-year-old man was Ty Cobb's in 1928. Cobb batted .323 and hit one homer. Williams batted .316 but hit twenty-nine homers.

In sum, though generally conceded to be the greatest hitter of his era, he did not establish himself as "the greatest hitter who ever lived." Cobb, for average, and Ruth, for power, remain supreme. Cobb, Rogers Hornsby, Joe Jackson, and Lefty O'Doul, among play-ers since 1900, have higher lifetime averages than Williams's .344.

Unlike Foxx, Gehrig, Hack Wilson, Hank Greenberg, and Ralph Kiner, Williams never came close to matching Babe Ruth's season home-run total of sixty. In the list of major league batting records, not one is held by Williams. He is second in walks drawn, third in home runs, fifth in lifetime averages, sixth in runs batted in, eighth in runs scored and in total bases, fourteenth in doubles, and thirtieth in hits. But if we allow him merely average seasons for the four-plus seasons he lost to two wars, and add another season for the months he lost to injuries, we get a man who in all the power totals would be second, and not a very distant second, to Ruth. And if we further allow that these years would have been not merely average but prime years, if we allow for all the months when Williams was playing in sub-par condition, if we permit his early and later years in baseball to be some sort of index of what the middle years could have been, if we give him a right-field fence that is not, like Fenway's, one of the most distant in the league, and if—the least excusable "if"— we imagine him condescending to outsmart the Williams Shift, we can defensibly assemble, like a colossus induced from the sizable fragments that do remain, a statistical figure not incommensurate with his grandiose ambition. From the statistics that are on the books, a good case can be made that in the *combination* of power and average Williams is first; nobody else ranks so high in both categories. Finally, there is the witness of the eyes; men whose memories go back to Shoeless Joe Jackson—another unlucky natural—rank him and Williams together as the best-looking hitters they have seen. It was for our last look that ten thousand of us had come.

Two girls, one of them with pert buckteeth and eyes as black as vest buttons, the other with white skin and flesh-colored hair, like an underdeveloped photograph of a redhead, came and sat on my right. On my other side was one of those frowning, chestless young-old men who can frequently be seen, often wearing sailor hats, attending ball games alone. He did not once open his program but instead tapped it, rolled up, on his knee as he gave the game his disconsolate attention. A young lady, with freckles and a depressed, dainty nose that by an optical illusion seemed to thrust her lips forward for a kiss, sauntered down into the box seats and with striking aplomb took a seat right behind the roof of the Oriole dugout. She wore a blue coat with a Northeastern University emblem sewed to it. The girls beside me took it into their heads that this was Williams's daughter. She looked too old to me, and why would she be sitting behind the visitors' dugout. On the other hand, from the way she sat there, staring at the sky and French-inhaling, she clearly was *some-body*. Other fans came and eclipsed her from view. The crowd looked less like a weekday ball park crowd than like the folks you might find in Yellowstone National Park, or emerging from automobiles at the top of scenic Mount Mansfield. There were a lot of competitively well-dressed couples of tourist age, and not a few babes in arms. A row of five seats in front of me was abruptly filled with a woman and four children, the youngest of them two years old, if that. Someday, presumably, he could tell his grandchildren that he saw Williams play. Along with these tots and second-honeymooners, there were Harvard freshmen, giving off that peculiar nervous glow created when a quantity of insouciance is saturated with insecurity; thick-necked army officers with brass on their shoulders and lead in their voices; pepperings of priests; perfumed bouquets of Roxbury Fabian fans; shiny salesmen from Albany and Fall River; and those gray, hoarse men—taxidrivers, slaughterers, and bartenders—who will continue to click through the turnstiles long after everyone else has deserted to television and tramporamas. Behind me, two young male voices blossomed, cracking a joke about God's five proofs that Thomas Aquinas exists—typical Boston College levity.

The batting cage was trundled away. The Orioles fluttered to the sidelines. Diagonally across the field, by the Red Sox dugout, a cluster of men in overcoats were festering like maggots. I could see a splinter of white uniform, and Williams's head, held at a self-deprecating and evasive tilt. Williams's conversational stance is that of a six-foot-three-inch man under a six-foot ceiling. He moved away to the patter of flash bulbs, and began playing catch with a young Negro outfielder named Willie Tasby. His arm, never very powerful, had grown lax with the years, and his throwing motion was a kind of muscular drawl. To catch the ball, he flicked his glove hand onto his left shoulder (he batted left but threw right, as every schoolboy ought to know) and let the ball plop into it comically. This catch session with Tasby was the only time all afternoon I saw him grin.

A tight little flock of human sparrows who, from the lambent and pampered pink of their faces, could only have been Boston politicians moved toward the plate. The loudspeakers mammothly coughed as someone huffed on the microphone. The ceremonies began. Curt Gowdy, the Red Sox radio and television announcer, who sounds like everybody's brother-in-law, delivered a brief sermon, taking the two words "pride" and "champion" as his text. It began, "Twenty-one years ago, a skinny kid from San Diego, California..." and ended, "I don't think we'll ever see another like him." Robert Tibolt, chairman of the board of the Greater Boston Chamber of Commerce, presented Williams with a big Paul Revere silver bowl. Harry Carlson, a member of the sports committee of the Boston Chamber, gave him a plaque, whose inscription he did not read in its entirety, out of deference to Williams's distaste for this sort of fuss. Mayor Collins presented the Jimmy Fund with a thousand-dollar check.

Then the occasion himself stooped to the microphone, and his voice sounded, after the others, very Californian; it seemed to be coming, excellently amplified, from a great distance, adolescently young and as smooth as a butternut. His thanks for the gifts had not died from our ears before he glided, as if helplessly, into "In spite of all the terrible things that have been said about me by the maestros of the keyboard up there..." He glanced up at the press rows sus-pended above home plate. (All the Boston reporters, incidentally, re-ported the phrase as "knights of the keyboard," but I heard it as "maestros" and prefer it that way.) The crowd tittered, appalled. A frightful vision flashed upon me, of the press gallery pelting Williams with erasers, of Williams clambering up the foul screen to slug jour-nalists, of a riot, of Mayor Collins being crushed. "...And they *were* terrible things," Williams insisted, with level melancholy, into the mike. "I'd like to forget them, but I can't." He paused, swallowing his memories, and went on. "I want to say that my years in Boston have been the greatest thing in my life." The crowd, like an immense sail going limp in a change of wind, sighed with relief. Taking all the parts himself, Williams then acted out a vivacious little morality drama in which an imaginary tempter came to him at the beginning of his career and said, "Ted, you can play anywhere you like." Leap-ing nimbly into the role of his younger self (who in biographical ac-tuality had yearned to be a Yankee), Williams gallantly chose Boston over all the other cities, and told us that Tom Yawkey was the great-est owner in baseball and we were the greatest fans. We applauded ourselves heartily. The umpire came out and dusted the plate. The voice of doom announced over the loudspeakers that after Williams's retirement his uniform number, 9, would be permanently retired—the first time the Red Sox had so honored a player. We cheered. The national anthem was played. We cheered. The game began.

Williams was third in the batting order, so he came up in the bot-tom of the first inning, and Steve Barber, a young pitcher who was not yet born when Williams began playing for the Red Sox, offered him four pitches, at all of which he disdained to swing, since none of them were within the strike zone. This demonstrated simultane-ously that Williams's eyes were razor-sharp and that Barber's control wasn't. Shortly, the bases were full, with Williams on second. "Oh, I hope he gets held up at third! That would be wonderful," the girl beside me moaned, and, sure enough, the man at bat walked and Williams was delivered into our foreground. He struck the pose of Donatello's David, the third-base bag being Goliath's head. Fiddling with his cap, swapping small talk with the Oriole third baseman (who seemed delighted to have him drop in), swinging his arms with a sort of prancing nervousness, he looked fine—flexible, hard, and not unbecomingly substantial through the middle. The long neck, the small head, the knickers whose cuffs were worn down near his ankles—all these points, often observed by caricaturists, were visible in the flesh.

One of the collegiate voices behind me said, "He looks old, doesn't he, old; big deep wrinkles in his face..."

"Yeah," the other voice said, "but he looks like an old hawk, doesn't he?"

With each pitch, Williams danced down the baseline, waving his arms and stirring dust, ponderous but menacing, like an attacking goose. It occurred to about a dozen humorists at once to shout "Steal home! Go, go!" Williams's speed afoot was never legendary. Lou Clinton, a young Sox outfielder, hit a fairly deep fly to center field. Williams tagged up and ran home. As he slid across the plate, the ball, thrown with unusual heft by Jackie Brandt, the Oriole center fielder, hit him on the back.

"Boy, he was really loafing, wasn't he?" one of the boys behind me said.

"It's cold," the other explained. "He doesn't play well when it's cold. He likes heat. He's a hedonist."

The run that Williams scored was the second and last of the inning. Gus Triandos, of the Orioles, quickly evened the score by plunking a home run over the handy left-field wall. Williams, who had had this wall at his back for twenty years, played the ball flawlessly. He didn't budge. He just stood there, in the center of the little patch of grass that his patient footsteps had worn brown, and, limp with lack of interest, watched the ball pass overhead. It was not a very interesting game. Mike Higgins, the Red Sox manager, with nothing to lose, had restricted his major league players to the left-field line— along with Williams, Frank Malzone, a first-rate third baseman, played the game—and had peopled the rest of the terrain with un-predictable youngsters fresh, or not so fresh, off the farms. Other than Williams's recurrent appearances at the plate, the *maladresse* of the Sox infield was the sole focus of suspense; the second baseman turned every grounder into a juggling act, while the shortstop did a breathtaking impersonation of an open window. With this sort of as-sistance, the Orioles wheedled their way into a 4–2 lead. They had early replaced Barber with another young pitcher, Jack Fisher. For-tunately (as it turned out), Fisher is no cutie; he is willing to burn the ball through the strike zone, and inning after inning this tactic punctured Higgins's string of test balloons.

Whenever Williams appeared at the Plate—pounding the dirt from his cleats, gouging a pit in the batter's box with his left foot, wringing resin out of the bat handle with his vehement grip, switch-ing the stick at the pitcher with an electric ferocity—it was like hav-ing a familiar Leonardo appear in a shuffle of *Saturday Evening Post* covers. This man, you realized—and here, perhaps, was the differ-ence, greater than the difference in gifts—really intended to hit the ball. In the third inning, he hoisted a high fly to deep center. In the fifth, we thought he had it; he smacked the ball hard and high into the heart of his power zone, but the deep right field in Fenway and the heavy air and a casual east wind defeated him. The ball died. Al Pilarcik leaned his back against the big "380" painted on the right-field wall and caught it. On another day, in another park, it would have been gone. (After the game, Williams said, "I didn't think I could hit one any harder than that. The conditions weren't good.")

The afternoon grew so glowering that in the sixth inning the arc lights were turned on—always a wan sight in the daytime, like the burning headlights of a funeral procession. Aided by the gloom, Fisher was slicing through the Sox rookies, and Williams did not come to bat in the seventh. He was second up in the eighth. This was almost certainly his last time to come to the plate in Fenway Park, and instead of merely cheering, as we had at his three previous appearances, we stood, all of us—stood and applauded. Have you ever heard applause in a ball park? Just applause—no calling, no whistling, just an ocean of handclaps, minute after minute, burst after burst, crowding and running together in continuous succession like the pushes of surf at the edge of the sand. It was a somber and considered tumult. There was not a boo in it. It seemed to renew itself out of a shifting set of memories as the kid, the marine, the veteran of feuds and failures and injuries, the friend of children, and the enduring old pro evolved down the bright tunnel of twenty-one summers toward this moment. At last, the umpire signaled for Fisher to pitch; with the other players, he had been frozen in position. Only Williams had moved during the ovation, switching his bat impatiently, ignoring everything except his cherished task. Fisher wound up, and the applause sank into a hush.

Understand that we were a crowd of rational people. We knew that a home run cannot be produced at will; the right pitch must be perfectly met and luck must ride with the ball. Three innings before, we had seen a brave effort fail. The air was soggy; the season was exhausted. Nevertheless, there will always lurk, around a corner in a pocket of our knowledge of the odds, an indefensible hope, and this was one of the times, which you now and then find in sports, when a density of expectation hangs in the air and plucks an event out of the future.

Fisher, after his unsettling wait, was wide with the first pitch. He put the second one over, and Williams swung mightily and missed. The crowd grunted, seeing that classic swing, so long and smooth and quick, exposed, naked in its failure. Fisher threw the third time, Williams swung again, and there it was. The ball climbed on a diagonal line into the vast volume of air over center field. From my angle, behind third base, the ball seemed less an object in flight than the tip of a towering, motionless construct, like the Eiffel Tower or the Tappan Zee Bridge. It was in the books while it was still in the sky. Brandt ran back to the deepest corner of the outfield grass; the ball descended beyond his reach and struck in the crotch where the bullpen met the wall, bounced chunkily, and, as far as I could see, vanished.

Like a feather caught in a vortex, Williams ran around the square of bases at the center of our beseeching screaming. He ran as he always ran out home runs—hurriedly, unsmiling, head down, as if our praise were a storm of rain to get out of. He didn't tip his cap. Though we thumped, wept, and chanted "We want Ted" for minutes after he hid in the dugout, he did not come back. Our noise for some seconds passed beyond excitement into a kind of immense open anguish, a wailing, a cry to be saved. But immortality is nontransferable. The papers said that the other players, and even the umpires on the field, begged him to come out and acknowledge us in some way, but he never had and did not now. Gods do not answer letters.

Every true story has an anticlimax. The men on the field refused to disappear, as would have seemed decent, in the smoke of Williams's miracle. Fisher continued to pitch, and escaped further harm. At the end of the inning, Higgins sent Williams out to his left-field position, then instantly replaced him with Carrol Hardy, so we had a long last look at Williams as he ran out there and then back, his uniform jogging, his eyes steadfast on the ground. It was nice, and we were grateful, but it left a funny taste.

One of the scholasticists behind me said, "Let's go. We've seen everything. I don't want to spoil it." This seemed a sound aesthetic decision. Williams's last word had been so exquisitely chosen, such a perfect fusion of expectation, intention, and execution, that already it felt a little unreal in my head, and I wanted to get out before the castle collapsed. But the game, though played by clumsy midgets under the feeble glow of the arc lights, began to tug at my attention, and I loitered in the runway until it was over. Williams's homer had, quite incidentally, made the score 4–3. In the bottom of the ninth inning, with one out, Marlin Coughtry, the second-base juggler, singled. Vic Wertz, pinch-hitting, doubled off the left-field wall, Coughtry advancing to third. Pumpsie Green walked, to load the bases. Willie Tasby hit a double-play ball to the third baseman, but in making the pivot throw Billy Klaus, an ex–Red Sox infielder, reverted to form and threw the ball past the first baseman and into the Red Sox dugout. The Sox won, 5–4. On the car radio as I drove home I heard that Williams had decided not to accompany the team to New York. So he knew how to do even that, the hardest thing. Quit.

MIRACLE OF COOGAN'S BLUFF

I was always struck by the fact that Red Smith never identified himself (at least to my knowledge) in his columns with the personal pronoun "I," although obviously he was the witness of whatever event he was describing. He invariably disguised his presence with various pseudonyms—"a friend" or "a passerby" or "a guy" as in "a guy wondered if Stan Musial..." Almost perversely self-deprecatory, he described himself as a "seedy amateur with watery eyes behind glittering glasses, a retiring chin, a hole in his frowzy haircut." Whatever he thought of himself and what he did for a living (he always held the view that "sports isn't Armageddon") he was considered "The Master" by his peers.

⟨⦿⟩

NOW IT IS DONE. Now the story ends. And there is no way to tell it. The art of fiction is dead. Reality has strangled invention. Only the utterly impossible, the inexpressibly fantastic, can ever be plausible again.

Down on the green and white and earth-brown geometry of the playing field, a drunk tries to break through the ranks of ushers marshaled along the foul lines to keep profane feet off the diamond. The ushers thrust him back and he lunges at them, struggling in the clutch of two or three men. He breaks free, and four or five tackle him. He shakes them off, bursts through the line, runs head-on into a special park cop, who brings him down with a flying tackle.

Here comes a whole platoon of ushers. They lift the man and haul him, twisting and kicking, back across the first-base line. Again he shakes loose and crashes the line. He is through. He is away, weaving out toward center field, where cheering thousands are jammed beneath the windows of the Giants' clubhouse.

At heart, our man is a Giant, too. He never gave up.

From center field comes burst upon burst of cheering, pennants are waving, uplifted fists are brandished, hats are flying. Again and again the dark clubhouse windows blaze with the light of photographers' flash bulbs. Here comes that same drunk out of the mob, back across the green turf to the infield. Coattails flying, he runs the bases, slides into third. Nobody bothers him now.

And the story remains to be told, the story of how the Giants won the 1951 pennant in the National League. The tale of their barreling run through August and September and into October. . . . Of the final day of the season, when they won the championship and started home with it from Boston, to hear on the train how the dead, defeated Dodgers had risen from the ashes in the Philadelphia twilight. . . . Of the three-game playoff in which they won, and lost, and were losing again with one out in the ninth inning yesterday when— Oh, why bother?

Maybe this is the way to tell it: Bobby Thomson, a young Scot from Staten Island, delivered a timely hit yesterday in the ninth inning of an enjoyable game of baseball before 34,320 witnesses in the Polo Grounds. . . . Or perhaps this is better:

"Well!" said Whitey Lockman, standing on second base in the second inning of yesterday's playoff game between the Giants and Dodgers.

"Ah, there," said Bobby Thomson, pulling into the same station after hitting a ball to left field. "How've you been?"

"Fancy," Lockman said, "meeting you here!"

"Ooops!" Thomson said. "Sorry."

And the Giants' first chance for a big inning against Don Newcombe disappeared as they tagged Thomson out. Up in the press
section, the voice of Willie Goodrich came over the amplifiers announcing a macabre statistic: "Thomson has now hit safely in fifteen
consecutive games." Just then the floodlights were turned on, en-
abling the Giants to see and count their runners on each base.

It wasn't funny, though, because it seemed for so long that the
Giants weren't going to get another chance like the one Thomson
squandered by trying to take second base with a playmate already
there. They couldn't hit Newcombe, and the Dodgers couldn't do
anything wrong. Sal Maglie's most splendrous pitching would avail
nothing unless New York could match the run Brooklyn had scored
in the first inning.

The story was winding up, and it wasn't the happy ending that
such a tale demands. Poetic justice was a phrase without meaning.

Now it was the seventh inning and Thomson was up, with runners on first and third base, none out. Pitching a shutout in Philadelphia last Saturday night, pitching again in Philadelphia on
Sunday, holding the Giants scoreless this far, Newcombe had now
gone twenty-one innings without allowing a run.

He threw four strikes to Thomson. Two were fouled off out of
play. Then he threw a fifth. Thomson's fly scored Monte Irvin. The
score was tied. It was a new ball game.

Wait a moment, though. Here's Pee Wee Reese hitting safely in
the eighth. Here's Duke Snider singling Reese to third. Here's Maglie
wild-pitching a run home. Here's Andy Pafko slashing a hit through
Thomson for another score. Here's Billy Cox batting still another
home. Where does his hit go? Where else? Through Thomson at
third.

So it was the Dodgers' ball game, 4 to 1, and the Dodgers' pennant. So all right. Better get started and beat the crowd home. That
stuff in the ninth inning? That didn't mean anything.

A single by Al Dark. A single by Don Mueller. Irvin's pop-up, Lockman's one-run double. Now the corniest possible sort of Hollywood schmaltz—stretcher-bearers plodding away with an injured Mueller between them, symbolic of the Giants themselves.

There went Newcombe and here came Ralph Branca. Who's at bat? Thomson again? He beat Branca with a home run the other day. Would Charley Dressen order him walked, putting the winning run on base, to pitch to the dead-end kids at the bottom of the batting order? No, Branca's first pitch was a called strike.

The second pitch—well, when Thomson reached first base he turned and looked toward the left-field stands. Then he started jumping straight up in the air, again and again. Then he trotted around the bases, taking his time.

Ralph Branca turned and started for the clubhouse. The number on his uniform looked huge. Thirteen.

• •

PAFKO AT THE WALL

At the instant of Bobby Thomson's home run, Don DeLillo was sitting in a dentist's chair with his mouth full of appliances. All around him joyous cries went up—the staff and those in the waiting area were apparently New York Giants' fans. DeLillo remained "aloof" (as he puts it), in part because of his mouth's condition but more particularly because he was a Yankee fan. At the time, the Yankees were already in the World Series, having won the American League pennant and were simply awaiting the outcome of the Giant–Dodger game.

Forty years later, on the day of the anniversary of the "shot heard 'round the world" (October 1), DeLillo was reading an account of the game, realized its importance, and decided to go back and research it. Using the game as a kind of canvas for his fiction, he said in an interview with the *Paris Review*: "I started writing something new and didn't know what it would be—a novel, a short story, a long story. It was simply a piece of writing, and it gave me more pleasure than any other writing I've done. It turned into a novella, 'Pafko at the Wall' [inspired by a famous photo of Andy Pafko, the Dodgers right-fielder, leaning against the wall at the 315-foot mark and looking up into the stands where the home run ball has just landed], and it appeared in *Harper's* about a year after I started it. At some point I decided I wasn't finished with the piece. I was sending signals into space and getting echoes back, like a dolphin or a bat."

Subsequently, "Pafko at the Wall" with a new title, "The Triumph of Death"—from a Brueghel painting (a reproduction in a copy of *Life* magazine falls on J. Edgar Hoover's head at the end of the game)—became the prologue of DeLillo's extraordinary picaresque novel *Underworld*. The celebrities who appear in the fiction—Hoover, Jackie Gleason, Frank Sinatra, Toots Shor—were, in fact, at the game, though how each is affected by what happens is, of course, through the author's pure and wondrous invention.

Slight cuts have been made in what follows—inevitably where characters and plot lines are introduced that would require explanation.

⊘

H E SPEAKS IN YOUR VOICE, American, and there's a shine in his eye that's halfway hopeful.

It's a school day, sure, but he's nowhere near the classroom. He wants to be here instead, standing in the shadow of this old rust-hulk of a structure, and it's hard to blame him—this metropolis of steel and concrete and flaky paint and cropped grass and enormous Chesterfield packs aslant on the scoreboards, a couple of cigarettes jutting from each.

Longing on a large scale is what makes history. This is just a kid with a local yearning but he is part of an assembling crowd, anonymous thousands off the buses and trains, people in narrow columns tramping over the swing bridge above the river, and even if they are not a migration or a revolution, some vast shaking of the soul, they bring with them the body heat of a great city and their own small reveries and desperations, the unseen something that haunts the day—men in fedoras and sailors on shore leave, the stray tumble of their thoughts, going to a game.

The sky is low and gray, the roily gray of sliding surf.

He stands at the curbstone with the others. He is the youngest, at fourteen, and you know he's flat broke by the edgy leaning look he hangs on his body. He has never done this before and he doesn't know any of the others and only two or three of them seem to know each other but they can't do this thing singly or in pairs so they have found one another by means of slidy looks that detect the fellow foolhard and here they stand, black kids and white kids up from the subways or off the local Harlem streets, lean shadows, bandidos, fifteen in all, and according to topical legend maybe four will get through for every one that's caught.

They are waiting nervously for the ticket holders to clear the turnstiles, the last loose cluster of fans, the stragglers and loiterers. They watch the late-arriving taxis from downtown and the brilliantined men stepping dapper to the windows, policy bankers and supper club swells and Broadway hotshots, high aura'd, picking lint off their mohair sleeves. They stand at the curb and watch without seeming to look, wearing the sourish air of corner hangabouts. All the hubbub has died down, the pregame babble and swirl, vendors working the jammed sidewalks waving scorecards and pennants and calling out in ancient singsong, scraggy men hustling buttons and caps, all dispersed now, gone to their roomlets in the beaten streets.

They are at the curbstone, waiting. Their eyes are going grim, sending out less light. Somebody takes his hands out of his pockets. They are waiting and then they go, one of them goes, a mick who shouts *Geronimo.*

There are four turnstiles just beyond the pair of ticket booths. The youngest boy is also the scrawniest, Cotter Martin by name, scrawny tall in a polo shirt and dungarees and trying not to feel doom-struck—he's located near the tail of the rush, running and shouting with the others. You shout because it makes you brave or you want to announce your recklessness. They have made their faces into scream masks, tight-eyed, with stretchable mouths, and they are running hard, trying to funnel themselves through the lanes between the booths, and they bump hips and elbows and keep the shout going. The faces of the ticket sellers hang behind the windows like onions on strings.

Cotter sees the first jumpers go over the bars. Two of them jostle in the air and come down twisted and asprawl. A ticket taker puts a headlock on one of them and his cap comes loose and skims down his back and he reaches for it with a blind swipe and at the same time—everything's at the same time—he eyes the other hurdlers to keep from getting stepped on. They are running and hurdling. It's a witless form of flight with bodies packed in close and the gate-crashing becoming real. They are jumping too soon or too late and hitting the posts and radial bars, doing cartoon climbs up each other's back, and what kind of stupes must they look like to people at the hot dog stand on the other side of the turnstiles, what kind of awful screwups—a line of mostly men beginning to glance this way, jaws working at the sweaty meat and grease bubbles flurrying on their tongues, the gent at the far end going dead-still except for a hand that produces automatic movement, swabbing on mustard with a brush.

The shout of the motley boys comes banging off the deep concrete.

Cotter thinks he sees a path to the turnstile on the right. He drains himself of everything he does not need to make the jump. Some are still jumping, some are thinking about it, some need a hair-cut, some have girlfriends in woolly sweaters and the rest have landed in the ruck and are trying to get up and scatter. A couple of stadium cops are rumbling down the ramp. Cotter sheds these elements as they appear, sheds a thousand waves of information hitting on his skin. His gaze is trained on the iron bars projected from the post. He picks up speed and seems to lose his gangliness, the slouchy funk of hormones and unbelonging and all the stammering things that seal his adolescence. He is just a running boy, a half-seen figure from the streets, but the way running reveals some clue to being, the way a runner bares himself to consciousness, this is how the dark-skinned kid seems to open to the world, how the bloodrush of a dozen strides brings him into eloquence.

Then he leaves his feet and is in the air, feeling sleek and unmussed and sort of businesslike, flying in from Kansas City with a briefcase full of bank drafts. His head is tucked, his left leg is clearing the bars. And in one prolonged and aloof and discontinuous instant he sees precisely where he'll land and which way he'll run and even though he knows they will be after him the second he touches ground, even though he'll be in danger for the next several hours— watching left and right–there is less fear in him now.

He comes down lightly and goes easy-gaiting past the ticket taker groping for his fallen cap and he knows absolutely—knows it all the way, deep as knowing goes, he feels the knowledge start to hammer in his runner's heart—that he is uncatchable.

Here comes a cop in municipal bulk with a gun and cuffs and a flashlight and a billy club all jigging on his belt and a summons pad wadded in his pocket. Cotter gives him a juke step that sends him nearly to his knees and the hot dog eaters bend from the waist to watch the kid veer away in soft acceleration, showing the cop a little finger-wag bye-bye.

He surprises himself this way every so often, doing some gaudy thing that whistles up out of unsuspected whim.

He runs up a shadowed ramp and into a crossweave of girders and pillars and spilling light. He hears the crescendoing last chords of the national anthem and sees the great open horseshoe of the grandstand and that unfolding vision of the grass that always seems to mean he has stepped outside his life—the rubbed shine that sweeps and bends from the raked dirt of the infield out to the high green fences. It is the excitement of a revealed thing. He runs at quarter speed craning to see the rows of seats, looking for an inconspicuous wedge behind a pillar. He cuts into an aisle in section 35 and walks down into the heat and smell of the massed fans, he walks into the smoke that hangs from the underside of the second deck, he hears the talk, he enters the deep buzz, he hears the warm-up pitches crack into the catcher's mitt, a series of reports that carry a comet's tail of secondary sound.

Then you lose him in the crowd.

In the radio booth they're talking about the crowd. Looks like thirty-five thousand and how do you figure it. When you think about the textured histories of the teams and the faith and passion of the fans and the way these forces are entwined citywide, and when you think about the game itself, live-or-die, the third game in a three-game play-off, and you say the names Giants and Dodgers, and you calculate the way the players hate each other openly, and you recall the kind of year this has turned out to be, the pennant race that has brought the city to a strangulated rapture, an end-shudder requiring a German loan-word to put across the mingling of pleasure and dread and suspense, and when you think about the blood loyalty, this is what they're saying in the booth—the love-of-team that runs across the boroughs and through the snuggled suburbs and out into the apple counties and the raw north, then how do you explain twenty thousand empty seats?

The engineer says, "All day it looks like rain. It affects the mood. People say the hell with it." ...

Russ Hodges, who broadcasts the games for WMCA, he is the voice of the Giants—Russ has an overworked larynx and the makings of a major cold and he shouldn't be lighting up a cigarette but here he goes, saying, "That's all well and good but I'm not sure there really is a logical explanation. When you deal with crowds, nothing's predictable."

Russ is going jowly now but there are elements of the uncomplicated boy in his eyes and smile and in the hair that looks bowl-cut and the shapeless suit that might belong to almost anyone. Can you do games, can you do play-by-play almost every day through a deep summer and not be located in some version of the past?

He looks out at the field with its cramped corners and the over-compensating spaces of the deep alleys and dead center. The big square Longines clock that juts up from the clubhouse. Strokes of color all around, a frescoing of hats and faces and the green grandstand and tawny base paths. Russ feels lucky to be here. Day of days and he's doing the game and it's happening at the Polo Grounds—a name he loves, a precious echo of things and times before the century went to war. He thinks everybody who's here ought to feel lucky because something big's in the works, something's building. Okay, maybe just his temperature. But he finds himself thinking of the time his father took him to see Dempsey fight Willard in Toledo and what a thing that was, what a measure of the awesome, the Fourth of July and a hundred and ten degrees and a crowd of shirtsleeved men in straw hats, many wearing handkerchiefs spread beneath their hats and down to their shoulders, making them look like play-Arabs, and the greatness of the beating big Jess took in that white hot ring, the way the sweat and blood came misting off his face every time Dempsey hit him.

When you see a thing like that, a thing that becomes a newsreel, you begin to feel you are a carrier of some solemn scrap of history.

In the second inning Thomson hits a slider on a line over third.

Lockman swings into an arc as he races toward second, looking out at left field.

Pafko moves to the wall to play the carom.

People stand in both decks in left, leaning out from the rows up front, and some of them are tossing paper over the edge, torn-up scorecards and bits of matchbook covers, there are crushed paper cups, little waxy napkins they got with their hot dogs, there are germ-bearing tissues many days old that were matted at the bottoms of deep pockets, all coming down around Pafko.

Thomson is loping along, he is striding nicely around first, leaning into his run.

Pafko throws smartly to Cox.

Thomson moves head-down toward second, coasting in, and then sees Lockman standing on the bag looking at him semi-spellbound, the trace of a query hanging on his lips.

Days of iron skies and all the mike time of the past week, the sore throat, the coughing, Russ is feverish and bedraggled—train trips and nerves and no sleep and he describes the play in his familiar homey ramble, the grits-and-tater voice that's a little scratchy today.

Cox peers out from under his cap and snaps the ball sidearm to Robinson.

Look at Mays meanwhile strolling to the plate dragging the barrel of his bat on the ground.

Robinson takes the throw and makes a spin move toward Thomson, who is standing shyly maybe five feet from second.

People like to see the paper fall at Pafko's feet, maybe drift across his shoulder or cling to his cap. The wall is nearly seventeen feet high so he is well out of range of the longest leaning touch and they have to be content to bathe him in their paper.

Look at Durocher on the dugout steps, manager of the Giants, hard-rock Leo, the gashouse scrapper, a face straight from the Gallic Wars, and he says into his fist, "Holy fuggin shit almighty."

Near the Giants' dugout four men are watching from Leo's own choice box when Robinson slaps the tag on Thomson. They are three-quarters show biz, Frank Sinatra, Jackie Gleason and Toots Shor, drinking buddies from way back, and they're accompanied by a well-dressed man with a bulldog mug, one J. Edgar Hoover. What's the nation's number one G-man doing with these crumbums? Well, Edgar is sitting in the aisle seat and he seems to be doing just fine, smiling at the rude banter that rolls nonstop from crooner to joke-smith to saloonkeeper and back. He would rather be at the racetrack but is cheerful enough in this kind of company whatever the venue.

He likes to be around movie idols and celebrity athletes, around gossip-meisters such as Walter Winchell, who is also at the game today, sitting with the Dodger brass. Fame and secrecy are the high and low ends of the same fascination, the static crackle of some libidinous thing in the world, and Edgar responds to people who have access to this energy. He wants to be their dearly devoted friend provided their hidden lives are in his private files, all the rumors collected and indexed, the shadow facts made real.

Gleason says, "I told you chumps, it's all Dodgers today. I feel it in my Brooklyn bones."

"What bones?" says Frank. "They're rotted out by booze."

Thomson's whole body sags, it loses vigor and resistance, and Robinson calls time and walks the ball to the mound in the pigeon-toed gait that makes his path seem crooked.

"The Giants'll have to hire that midget if they want to win, what's-his-name, because their only hope is some freak of nature," Gleason says. "An earthquake or a midget. And since this ain't California, you better pray for an elf in flannels."

Frank says, "Fun-nee."

The subject makes Edgar nervous. He is sensitive about his height even though he is safely in the middle range. He has added weight in recent years and when he sees himself in the mirror getting dressed, thick-bodied and Buddha-headed, it is a short round man that looks back at him. And this is something the yammerheads in the press have reported to be true, as if a man can wish his phantom torment into public print. And today it's a fact that taller-than-average agents are not likely to be assigned to headquarters. And it's a further fact that the midget his pal Gleason is talking about, the three-foot seven-inch *sportif* who came to bat one time for the St. Louis Browns some six weeks ago in a stunt that was also an act, Edgar believes, of political subversion—this fellow is called Eddie Gaedel and if Gleason recalls the name he will flash-pair Eddie with

Edgar and then the short-man jokes will begin to fly like the storied shit that hits the fan. Gleason got his start doing insult comedy and never really stopped—does it for free, does it for fun and leaves shattered lives behind.

Toots Shor says, "Don't be a shlump all your life, Gleason. It's only one-zip. The Giants didn't come from thirteen and a half games back just to blow it on the last day. This is the miracle year. Nobody has a vocabulary for what happened this year."

The slab face and meatcutter's hands. You look at Toots and see a speakeasy vet, dense of body, with slicked-back hair and a set of chinky eyes that summon up a warning in a hurry. This is an ex-bouncer who throws innocent people out of his club when he is drinking.

He says, "Mays is the man."

And Frank says, "This is Willie's day. He's due to bust loose. Leo told me on the phone."

Gleason does a passable clipped Britisher saying, "You're not actually telling me that this fellow stepping up to the wicket is going to do something extraordinary."

Edgar, who hates the English, falls forward laughing even as Jackie takes a breathless bite of his hot dog and begins to cough and choke, sending quidbits of meat and bread in many directions, pellets and smithereens, spitball flybys.

But it is the unseeable life-forms that dismay Edgar most and he faces away from Gleason and holds his breath. He wants to hurry to a lavatory, a zinc-lined room with a bar of untouched oval soap, a torrent of hot water and a swansdown towel that has never been used by anyone else. But of course there is nothing of the kind nearby. Just more germs, an all-pervading medium of pathogens, microbes, floating colonies of spirochetes that fuse and separate and elongate and spiral and engulf, whole trainloads of matter that people cough forth, rudimentary and deadly.

The crowd, the constant noise, the breath and hum, a basso rumble building now and then, the genderness of what they share in their experience of the game, how a man will scratch his wrist or shape a line of swearwords. And the lapping of applause that dies down quickly and is never enough. They are waiting to be carried on the sound of rally chant and rhythmic handclap, the set forms and repetitions. This is the power they keep in reserve for the right time. It is the thing that will make something happen, change the structure of the game and get them leaping to their feet, flying up together in a free thunder that shakes the place crazy.

Sinatra saying, "Jack, I thought I told you to stay in the car until you're all done eating."

Mays takes a mellow cut but gets under the ball, sending a routine fly into the low October day. The sound of the ash bat making contact with the ball reaches Cotter Martin in the left-field stands, where he sits in a bony-shouldered hunch. He is watching Willie instead of the ball, seeing him sort of shrug-run around first and then scoop his glove off the turf and jog out to his position.

The arc lights come on, catching Cotter by surprise, causing a shift in the way he feels, in the freshness of his escapade, the airy flash of doing it and not getting caught. The day is different now, grave and threatened, rain-hurried, and he watches Mays standing in center field looking banty in all that space, completely kid-size, and he wonders how the guy can make those throws he makes, whirl and sling, with power. He likes looking at the field under lights even if he has to worry about rain and even if it's only afternoon and the full effect is not the same as in a night game when the field and the players seem completely separate from the night around them. He has been to one night game in his life, coming down from the bluff with his oldest brother and walking into a bowl of painted light. He thought there was an unknown energy flaring down out of the light towers, some intenser working of the earth, and it isolated the players and the grass and the chalk-rolled lines from anything he'd ever seen or imagined. They had the glow of first-time things.

The way the runner skid-brakes when he makes the turn at first.

The empty seats were Cotter's first surprise, well before the lights. On his prowl through the stands he kept seeing blank seats, too many to be explained by people buying a beer or taking a leak, and he found a spot between a couple of guys in suits and it's all he can do to accept his good luck, the ease of an actual seat, without worrying why there's so many.

The man to his left says, "How about some peanuts hey?"

Peanut vendor's coming through again, a coin-catching wiz about eighteen, black and rangy. People know him from games past and innings gone and they quicken up and dig for change. They're calling out for peanuts, *hey, here, bag,* and tossing coins with thumb flicks and discus arcs and the vendor's hands seem to inhale the flying metal. He is magnet-skinned, circus-catching dimes on the wing and then sailing peanut bags into people's chests. It's a thrill-a-minute show but Cotter feels an obscure danger here. The guy is making him visible, shaming him in his prowler's den. Isn't it strange how their common color jumps the space between them? Nobody saw Cotter until the vendor appeared, black rays phasing from his hands. One popular Negro and crowd pleaser. One shifty kid trying not to be noticed.

The man says, "What do you say?"

Cotter raises a hand no.

"Care for a bag? Come on."

Cotter leans away, the hand going to his midsection to mean he's already eaten or peanuts give him cramps or his mother told him not to fill up on trashy food that will ruin his dinner.

The man says, "Who's your team then?"

"Giants."

"What a year hey?"

"This weather, I don't know, it's bad to be trailing."

The man looks at the sky. He's about forty, close-shaved and Brylcreemed but with a casual quality, a free-and-easy manner that Cotter links to small-town life in the movies.

"Only down a run. They'll come back. The kind of year it's been, it can't end with a little weather. How about a soda?"

Men passing in and out of the toilets, men zipping their flies as they turn from the trough and other men approaching the long receptacle, thinking where they want to stand and next to whom and not next to whom, and the old ballpark's reek and mold are consolidated here, generational tides of beer and shit and cigarettes and peanut shells and disinfectants and pisses in the untold millions, and they are thinking in the ordinary way that helps a person glide through a life, thinking thoughts unconnected to events, the dusty hum of who you are, men shouldering through the traffic in the men's room as the game goes on, the coming and going, the lifting out of dicks and the meditative pissing.

Man to his left shifts in the seat and speaks to Cotter from off his shoulder, using a crafty whisper. "What about school? Having a private holiday?" Letting a grin slide across his face.

Cotter says, "Same as you," and gets a gunshot laugh.

"I'd a broken out of prison to see this game. Matter of fact they're broadcasting to prisoners. They put radios in cell blocks in the city jails."

"I was here early," Cotter says. "I could have gone to school in the morning and then cut out. But I wanted to see everything."

"A real fan. Music to my ears."

"See the people showing up. The players going in the players' entrance."

"My name's Bill Waterson by the way. And I'd a gladly gone AWOL from the office but I didn't actually have to. Got my own little business. Construction firm."

Cotter tries to think of something to say.

"We're the people that build the houses that are fun to live in."

Peanut vendor's on his way up the aisle and headed over to the next section when he spots Cotter and drops a knowing smile. The kid thinks here comes trouble. This gatemouth is out to expose him in some withering way. Their glances briefly meet as the vendor moves up the stairs. In full stride and double-quick he dips his hand for a bag of peanuts and zings it nonchalant to Cotter, who makes the grab in a one-hand blur that matches the hazy outline of the toss. And it is one sweetheart of a moment, making Cotter crack the smile of the week and sending a wave of goodwill through the area.

Cotter unrolls the pleated top of the brown bag and extends it to Bill. They sit there shelling the peanuts and rubbing off the tissuey brown skin with a rolling motion of thumb and index finger and eating the oily salty flesh and dropping the husks on the ground without ever taking their eyes off the game.

Bill says, "Next time you hear someone say they're in seventh heaven, think of this."

"All we need is some runs."

He pushes the bag at Bill once more.

"They'll score. It's coming. Don't worry. We'll make you happy you skipped school."

Look at Robinson at the edge of the outfield grass watching the hitter step in and thinking idly, Another one of Leo's country-boy krauts.

"Now there's a law of manly conduct," Bill says. "And it states that since you're sharing your peanuts with me, I'm duty-bound to buy us both some soda pop."

"That sounds fair enough."

"Good. It's settled then." Turning in his seat and flinging up an arm. "A couple of sportsmen taking their ease."

Stanky the pug sitting in the dugout.

Mays trying to get a jingle out of his head, his bluesy face slightly puffed, some catchy tune he's been hearing on the radio lately.

The batboy comes down the steps a little daydreamy, sliding Dark's black bat into the rack.

The game turns inward in the middle innings. They fall into waiting, into some unshaped anxiety that stiffens the shoulder muscles and sends them to the watercooler to drink and spit.

Across the field Branca is up in the Dodger bullpen, a large man with pointy elfin ears, tight-armed and throwing easily, just getting loose.

Mays thinking helplessly, Push-pull click-click, change blades that quick....

Gleason has two sudsy cups planted at his feet and there's a hot dog he has forgotten about that's bulging out at each end of his squeezed fist. He is talking to six people at once and they are laughing and asking questions, season box holders, old-line fans with their spindly wives. They see he is half swacked and they admire the clarity of his wit, the fine edge of insult and derision. They want to be offended and Jackie's happy to do it, bypassing his own boozy state to do a detailed imitation of a drunk. He goes heavy-lidded and growly, making sport of one man's ragmop toupee, ridiculing a second for the elbow patches on his tweed jacket. The women enjoy it enormously and they want more. They watch Gleason, they look at Sinatra for his reaction to Gleason, they watch the game, they listen to Jackie do running lines from his TV show, they watch the mustard slide down his thumb and feel too shy to tell him....

Gleason isn't even supposed to be here. There's a rehearsal going on right now at a midtown studio and that's where he's supposed to be, preparing a skit called "The Honeymooners," to be shown for the first time in exactly two days. This is material that's close to Jackie's heart, involving a bus driver named Ralph Kramden who lives with his wife Alice in a shabby Brooklyn flat. Gleason sees nothing strange about missing a rehearsal to entertain fans in the stands. But it's making Sinatra uneasy, all these people lapping at their seat backs. He is used to ritual distances. He wants to encounter people in circumstances laid out beforehand. Frank doesn't have his dago secret service with him today. And even with Jackie on one flank and Toots on the other—a couple of porkos who function as natural barriers—people keep pressing in, showing a sense of mission. He sees them decided one by one that they must speak to him. The rigid grins floating near. And the way they use him as a reference for everything that happens. Somebody makes a nice play, they look at Frank to see how he reacts. The beer vendor trips on a step, they look at Frank to see if he has noticed.

He leans over and says, "Jack, it's a great boot being here but you think you can put a towel over your face so these people can go back to watching the game?"

People want Gleason to do familiar lines of dialogue from the show. They're calling out the lines they want him to do.

Then Frank says, "Where the hell is Hoover by the way? We need him to keep these women off our beautiful bodies."

The catcher works up out of his squat, dirt impacted in the creases that run across the back of his ruddled neck. He lifts his mask so he can spit. He is padded and bumpered, lips rough and scored and sun-flaked. This is the freest thing he does, spitting in public. His saliva bunches and wobbles when it hits the dirt, going sandy brown.

Russ Hodges is over on the TV side for the middle innings, talking less, guided by the action on the monitor. Between innings the statistician offers him part of a chicken sandwich he has brought along for lunch.

He says to Russ, "What's the wistful look today?"

"I didn't know I had a look. Any look. I don't feel capable of a look. Maybe hollow-eyed."

"Pensive," says the statman.

And it's true and he knows it, Russ is wistful and drifting and this is so damn odd, the mood he's been in all day, a tilting back, an old creaky easing back, as of a gray-haired man in a rocker.

"This is chicken with what?"

"I'm guessing mayonnaise."

"It's funny, you know," Russ says, "but I think it was Charlotte put the look in my face."

"The lady or the city?"

"Definitely the city. I spent years in a studio doing re-creations of big league games. The telegraph bug clacking in the background and blabbermouth Hodges inventing ninety-nine percent of the action. And I'll tell you something scout's honor. I know this sounds far-fetched but I used to sit there and dream of doing real baseball from a booth in the Polo Grounds in New York."

"Real baseball."

"The thing that happens in the sun."

Somebody hands you a piece of paper filled with letters and numbers and you have to make a ball game out of it. You create the weather, flesh out the players, you make them sweat and grouse and hitch up their pants, and it is remarkable, thinks Russ, how much earthly disturbance, how much summer and dust the mind can manage to order up from a single Latin letter lying flat.

"That's not a bush curve Maglie's throwing," he says into the mike.

When he was doing ghost games he liked to take the action into the stands, inventing a kid chasing a foul ball, a carrot-topped boy with a cowlick (shameless, ain't I) who retrieves the ball and holds it aloft, this five-ounce sphere of cork, rubber, yarn, horsehide and spiral stitching, a souvenir baseball, a priceless thing somehow, a thing that seems to recapitulate the whole history of the game every time it is thrown or hit or touched.

He puts the last bite of sandwich in his mouth and licks his thumb and remembers where he is, far from the windowless room with the telegraph operator and the Morse-coded messages. . . .

Down in the field boxes they want Gleason to say, "You're a dan-dan-dandy crowd."

Russ makes his way back to the radio side after the Giants go down in their half of the sixth still trailing by a run. He's glad he doesn't have a thermometer because he might be tempted to use it and that would be demoralizing. It's a mild day, glory be, and the rain's holding off.

Producer says, "Going to the wire, Russ."

"I hope I don't close down. My larynx feels like it's in a vise."

"This is radio, buddy. Can't close down. Think of what's out there. They are hugging their little portables."

"You're not making me feel any better."

"They are goddamn crouched over the wireless. You're like Murrow from London."

"Thank you, Al."

"Save the voice."

"I am trying mightily."

"This game is everywhere. Dow Jones tickers are rapping out the score with the stock averages. Every bar in town, I guarantee. They're smuggling radios into boardrooms. At Schrafft's I hear they're breaking into the Muzak to give the score."

"All those nice ladies with their matched sweater sets and genteel sandwiches."

"Save the voice," Al says.

"Do they have tea with honey on the menu?"

"They're eating and drinking baseball. The track announcer at Belmont's doing updates between races. They got it in taxicabs and barbershops and doctors' offices."

They're all waiting on the pitcher, he's a faceful of boding, upper body drawn forward, glove hand dangled at the knee. He's reading and reading the sign. He's reading the sign. Hitter fidgeting in the box. This son of a buck can bring it.

The shortstop moves his feet to break the trance of waiting.

It's the rule of confrontation, faithfully maintained, written across the face of every slackwit pitcher since there were teams named the Superbas and the Bridegrooms. The difference comes when the ball is hit. Then nothing is the same. The men are moving, coming out of their crouches, and everything submits to the pebble-skip of the ball, to rotations and backspins and airstreams. There are drag coefficients. There are trailing vortices. There are things that apply unrepeatably, muscle memory and pumping blood and jots of just, the narrative that lives in the spaces of the official play-by-play.

And the crowd is also in this lost space, the crowd made over in that one-thousandth of a second when the bat and the baseball are in contact. A rustle of murmurs and curses, people breathing soft moans, their faces changing as the play unrolls across the grassy scan....

Look at the man in the bleachers who's pacing the aisles, a neighborhood crazy, he waves his arms and mumbles, short, chunky, bushy-haired—could be one of the Ritz Brothers or a lost member of the Three Stooges, the Fourth Stooge, called Flippo or Dummy or Shaky or Jakey, and he's distracting the people nearby, they're yelling at him to siddown, goway, meshuggener, and he paces and worries, he shakes his head and moans as if he knows something's coming, or came, or went—he's receptive to things that escape the shrewdest fan....

Gleason is shouting down a vendor, trying to order beers. People on their feet, shaking off the tension and fret. A man slowly wiping his glasses. A staring man. A man flexing the stiffness out of his limbs.

"Get me a brandy and soda," Toots says.

Jackie tells him, "Don't be a clamhead all your life."

"Treat the man nice," Frank says. "He's come a long way for a Jew who drinks. He's best buddies with world leaders you never even heard of. They all roll into his joint sooner or later and knock back a brandy with Toots. Except maybe Mahatma Gandhi. And *him* they shot."

Gleason flares his brows and goggles his eyes and shoots out his arms in a nitwit gesture of revelation.

"That's the name I couldn't think of. The midget that pinch-hits."

People around them, hearing part of this and reacting mainly to inflection and gesture—they've seen Jackie physically building the remark and they knock together laughing even before he has finished the line.

Edgar is also laughing despite the return of the midget business. He admires the rough assurance of these men. It seems to flush from their pores. They have a size to them, a natural stamina that mocks his own bible-school indoctrination even as it draws him to the noise. He's a self-perfected American who must respect the saga of the knockabout boy emerging from a tenement culture, from back-streets slant with danger. It makes for gusty egos, it makes for appetites. The pussy bandits Jackie and Frank have a showy sort of ease around women. And it's true about Toots, he knows everybody worth knowing and can drink even Gleason into the carpeting. And when he clamps a sympathetic paw on your shoulder you feel he is some provident force come to guide you out of old despond.

Frank says, "This is our inning."

And Toots says, "Better be. Because these shit-heel Dodgers are making me nervous."

Jackie is passing beers along the row.

Frank says, "Seems to me we've all made our true loyalties known. Shown our hearts' desire. We got a couple of old-timey Giant fans. And this porpoise with a haircut from Brooklyn. But what about our friend the G-man. Is it G for Giants? Fess up, Jedgar. Who's your team?"

J. Edgar. Frank calls him Jedgar sometimes and the Director likes the name although he never lets on—it is medieval and princely and wily-dark.

A faint smile creeps across Hoover's face.

"I don't have a rooting interest. Whoever wins," he says softly. "That's my team." ...

Look at the four of them. Each with a hanky neatly tucked in his breast pocket. Each holding his beer away from his body, leaning forward to tease the high scud from the rim of the cup. Gleason with a flower in his lapel, a damp aster snatched from a vase at Toots' place. People are still after him to do lines from the show.

They want him to say, "Harty har-har."

The plate umpire stands mask in hand, nearly blimpish in his outfitting. He is keeping the numbers, counting the pitcher's warm-up tosses. This is the small dogged conscience of the game. Even in repose he shows a history thick with embranglement, dust-stomping men turning figures in the steep sun. You can see it in his face, chin thrust out, a glower working under his brow. When the number reaches eight he aims a spurt from his chaw and prepares to take his whisk-broom to the rubber slab.

In the stands Bill Waterson takes off his jacket and dangles it length-wise by the collar. It is rippled and mauled and seems to strike him as a living body he might want to lecture sternly. After a pause he folds it over twice and drops it on his seat. Cotter is sitting again, surrounded by mostly vertical people. Bill looms above him, a sizable guy, a one-time athlete by the look of him, getting thick in the middle, his shirt wet under the arms. Lucky seventh. Cotter needs a measly run to keep him from despairing—the cheapest eked-out unearned run ever pushed across. Or he's ready to give up. You know that thing that happens when you give up before the end and then your team comes back to perform acts of valor and you feel a queasy shame stealing over you like pond slick.

Bill says down to him, "I take my seventh-inning stretch seriously. I not only stand. I damn well make it a point to stretch."

"I've been noticing," says Cotter.

"Because it's a custom that's been handed down. It's part of
something. It's our own little traditional thing. You stand, you
stretch—it's a privilege in a way."

Bill has some fun doing various stylized stretches, the body-
builder, the pet cat, and he tries to get Cotter to do a drowsy kid in
a classroom.

"Did you ever tell me your name?"

"Cotter."

"That's the thing about baseball, Cotter. You do what they did
before you. That's the connection you make. There's a whole long
line. A man takes his kid to a game and thirty years later this is what
they talk about when the poor old mutt's wasting away in the
hospital."

Bill scoops his jacket off the seat and puts it on his lap when he
sits down. Seconds later he is standing again, he and Cotter watching Pafko chase down a double. A soft roar goes up, bushy and dense,
and the fans send more paper sailing to the base of the wall. Old
shopping lists and ticket stubs and wads of fisted newsprint come
falling around Pafko in the faded afternoon. Farther out in left field
they are dropping paper on the Dodger bullpen, on the working figure of Labine and the working figure of Branca and the two men
who are catching them and the men sitting under the canted roof
that juts from the wall, the gum-chewing men with nothing to say.

Branca wears the number thirteen blazoned on his back....

Lockman squares around to bunt.

There's a man in the upper deck leafing through a copy of the
current issue of *Life*. There's a man on 12th Street in Brooklyn who
has attached a tape machine to his radio so he can record the voice
of Russ Hodges broadcasting the game. The man doesn't know why

he's doing this. It is just an impulse, a fancy, it is like hearing the game twice, it is like being young and being old, and this will turn out to be the only known recording of Russ' famous account of the final moments of the game. The game and its extensions. The woman cooking cabbage. The man who wishes he could be done with drink. They are the game's remoter soul. Connected by the pulsing voice on the radio, joined to the word-of-mouth that passes the score along the street and to the fans who call the special phone number and the crowd at the ballpark that becomes the picture on television, people the size of minute rice, and the game as rumor and conjecture and inner history. There's a sixteen-year-old in the Bronx who takes his radio up to the roof of his building so he can listen alone, a Dodger fan slouched in the gloaming, and he hears the account of the misplayed bunt and the fly ball that scores the tying run and he looks out over the rooftops, the tar beaches with their clotheslines and pigeon coops and splatted condoms, and he gets the cold creeps. The game doesn't change the way you sleep or wash your face or chew your food. It changes nothing but your life.

The producer says, "At last, at least, a run."

Russ is frazzled, brother, he is raw and rumpled and uncombed. When the teams go to the top of the eighth he reports that they have played one hundred and fifty-four regular season games and two play-off games and seven full innings of the third play-off game and here they are tied in a knot, absolutely deadlocked, they are stalemated, folks, so light up a Chesterfield and stay right here.

The next half inning seems to take a week. Cotter sees the Dodgers put men on first and third. He watches Maglie bounce a curve in the dirt. He sees Cox bang a shot past third. A hollow clamor begins to rise from the crowd, men calling from the deep reaches, an animal awe and desolation.

In the booth Russ sees the crowd begin to lose its coherence, people sitting scattered on the hard steps, a priest with a passel of boys filing up the aisle, paper rolling and skittering in the wind. He hears the announcer from St. Louis on the other side of the blanket, it is Harry Caray and he sounds like his usual chipper self and Russ thinks of the Japanese term for ritual disembowelment and figures he and Harry ought to switch names about now.

Light washing from the sky, Dodgers scoring runs, a man dancing down the aisle, a goateed black in a Bing Crosby shirt. Everything is changing shape, becoming something else.

Cotter can barely get out the words.

"What good does it do to tie the score if you're going to turn around and let them walk all over you?"

Bill says, "They're going into that dugout and I guarantee you they're not giving up. There's no quit in this team. Don't pull a long face on me, Cotter. We're buddies in bad times—gotta stick together."

Cotter feels a mood coming on, a complicated self-pity, the strength going out of his arms and a voice commencing in his head that reproaches him for caring. And the awful part is that he wallows in it. He knows how to find the twisty compensation in this business of losing, being a loser, drawing it out, expanding it, making it sickly sweet, being someone carefully chosen for the role.

The score is 4–1.

It should have rained in the third or fourth inning. Great rain drenching down. It should have thundered and lightning'd.

Bill says, "I'm still a believer. What about you?"

The pitcher takes off his cap and rubs his forearm across his hairline. Big Newk. Then he blows in the cap. Then he shakes the cap and puts it back on.

Shor looks at Gleason.

"Still making with the mouth. Leave the people alone already. They came here to see a game."

"What game? It's a lambasting. We ought to go home."

"We're not going home," Toots says.

Jackie says, "We can beat the crowd, clamhead."

Frank says, "Let's take a vote."

Toots says, "You're tubercular in the face. Sit back and watch the game. Because nobody goes until I go and I ain't going."

Jackie waves down a vendor and orders beer all around. Nothing happens in the home half of the eighth. People are moving toward the exit ramps. It is Erskine and Branca in the bullpen now with the odd paper shaving dropped from the upper deck. Dodgers go down in the top of the ninth and this is when you sense a helpless scattering, it is tastable in the air, audible in the lone-wolf calls from high in the stands. Nothing you've put into this is recoverable and you don't know whether you want to leave at once or stay forever, living under a blanket in the wind....

The closeness in the booth, all this crammed maleness is making Russ a little edgy. He lights another cigarette and for the first time all day he does not reproach himself for it. He hears the solitary wailing, he hears his statistician reciting numbers in fake French. It is all part of the same thing, the feeling of some collapsible fact that's folded up and put away, and the school gloom that traces back for decades—the last laden day of summer vacation when the range of play tapers to a screwturn. This is the day he has never shaken off, the final Sunday before the first Monday of school. It carried some queer deep shadow out to the western edge of the afternoon.

He wants to go home and watch his daughter ride her bike down a leafy street.

Dark reaches for a pitch and hits a seeing-eye bouncer that ticks off the end of the first baseman's glove....

Russ is thinking base hit all the way but glances routinely at the clubhouse sign in straightaway center to see if the first E in CHESTERFIELD lights up, indicating error.

Robinson retrieves the ball in short right....

Mueller stands in, taking the first pitch low.

In the Dodger dugout a coach picks up the phone and calls the bullpen for the eighteenth time to find out who's throwing good and who ain't.

Mueller sees a fastball belt-high and pokes a single to right....

Russ describes Dark going into third standing up. He sees Thomson standing in the dugout with his arms raised and his hands held backwards gripping the edge of the roof. He describes people standing in the aisles and others moving down toward the field.

Irvin dropping the weighted bat....

Maglie's already in the clubhouse sitting in his skivvies in that postgame state of disrepair and pit stink that might pass for some shambles of the inner man, slugging beer from the bottle.

Irvin stands in.

Russ describes Newcombe taking a deep breath and stretching his arms over his head. He describes Newcombe looking in for the sign....

Fastball high and away.

The crowd noise is uncertain. They don't know if this is a rally in the works or just another drag-tail finish that draws out the pain. It's a high rackety noise that makes Russ think of restive waiting in a train station.

Irvin tries to pull it, overeager, and Russ hears the soul of the crowd repeat the sorry arc of the baseball, a moaned vowel falling softly to earth. First baseman puts it away.

Decent people out there. Russ wants to believe they are still assembled in some recognizable manner, the kindred unit at the radio, old lines and ties and propinquities.

Lockman stands in, the towhead from Caroline.

How his family used to gather around the gramophone and listen to grand opera, the trilled *r*'s of old Europe. These thoughts fade and return. They are not distractions. He is alert to every movement on the field.

A couple of swabbies move down to the rail near third base.

How the records were blank on one side and so brittle they would crack if you looked at them cross-eyed. That was the going joke.

He is hunched over the mike. The field seems to open outward into nouns and verbs. All he has to do is talk.

Saying, "Carl Erskine and fireballer Ralph Branca still throwing in the bullpen."

Pitch.

Lockman fouls it back into the netting.

Now the rhythmic applause starts, tentative at first, then spreading densely through the stands. This is how the crowd enters the game. The repeated three-beat has the force of some abject faith, a desperate kind of will toward magic and accident.

Lockman stands in once more, wagging the yellow bat.

How his mother used to make him gargle with warm water and salt when he complained of a sore throat.

Lockman hits the second pitch on a low line over third. Russ hears Harry Caray shouting into the mike on the other side of the blanket. Then they are both shouting and the ball is slicing toward the line and landing fair and sending up a spew of dirt and forcing Pafko into the corner once again.

Men running, the sprint from first to third, the man who scores coming in backwards so he can check the action on the base paths. All the Giants up at the front of the dugout. The crowd is up, heads weaving for better views. Men running through a slide of noise that comes heaving down on them.

The pitch was off the plate and he wrong-wayed it and Harry started shouting.

The hit obliterates the beat of the crowd's rhythmic clapping.

They're coming into open roar, making a noise that keeps enlarging itself in breadth and range. This is the crowd made over, the crowd renewed.

Harry started shouting and then Pafko went into the corner and Russ started shouting and the paper began to fall.

One out, one in, two runs down, men on second and third. Russ thinks every word may be his last. He feels the redness in his throat, the pinpoint constriction. Mueller still on the ground at third, injured sliding or not sliding, stopping short and catching his spikes on the bag, a man in pain, the flare of pulled tendons.

Paper is falling again, crushed traffic tickets and field-stripped cigarettes and work from the office and scorecards in the shape of airplanes, windblown and mostly white, and Pafko walks back to his position and alters stride to kick a soda cup lightly and the gesture functions as a form of recognition, a hint of some concordant force between players and fans, the way he nudges the white cup, it's a little onside boot, completely unbegrudging—a sign of respect for the sly contrivances of the game, the patterns that are undivinable.

The trainer comes out and they put Mueller on a stretcher and take him toward the clubhouse. Mueller's pain, the pain the game exacts—a man on a stretcher makes sense here.

The halt in play has allowed the crowd to rebuild its noise. Russ keeps pausing at the mike to let the sound collect. This is a rumble of a magnitude he has never heard before. You can't call it cheering or rooting. It's a territorial roar, the claim of the ego that separates the crowd from other entities, from political rallies or prison riots—everything outside the walls.

Russ nuzzles up to the mike and tries to be calm although he is very close to speaking in a shout because this is the only way to be heard.

Men clustered on the mound and the manager waving to the

bullpen and the pitcher walking in and the pitcher leaving and the runner for Mueller doing kneebends at third.

They are banging on the roof of the booth.

Russ says, "So don't go way. Light up that Chesterfield. We're gonna stay right here and see how big Ralph Branca will fare."

Yes. It is Branca coming through the dampish glow. Branca who is tall and stalwart but seems to carry his own hill and dale, he has the aura of a man encumbered. The drooping lids, leaden feet, the thick ridge across the brow. His face is set behind a somber nose, broad-bridged and looming.

The stadium police are taking up posts.

Look at the man in the upper deck. He is tearing pages out of his copy of *Life* and dropping them uncrumpled over the rail, letting them fall in a seesaw drift on the bawling fans below. He is moved to do this by the paper falling elsewhere, the contagion of paper—it is giddy and unformulated fun. He begins to ignore the game so he can waft pages over the rail. It brings him into contact with the other paper throwers and with the fans in the lower deck who reach for his pages and catch them—they are all a second force that runs parallel to the game.

Not far away another man feels something pulling at his chest, arms going numb. He wants to sit down but doesn't know if he can reach an arm back to lower himself to the seat. Heart, my heart, my god.

Branca who is twenty-five but makes you think he exemplifies ancient toil. By the time he reaches the mound the stretcher bearers have managed to get Mueller up the steps and into the clubhouse. The crowd forgets him. They would forget him if he were dead. The noise expands once more. Branca takes the ball and the men around the mound recede to the fringes.

Shor looks at Gleason.

He says, "Tell me you want to go home. What happened to let's go home? If we leave now, we can beat the crowd."

He says, "I can't visualize it enough, both you crumbums, you deserve every misery in the book."

Jackie looks miserable all right. He loosens his necktie and undoes the top button of his shirt. He's the only member of the quartet not on his feet but it isn't the shift in the game that has caused his discomfort. It's the daylong booze and the greasy food.

Shor says, "Tell me you want to go home so I can run ahead and hold the car door open and like *usher* you inside."

Paper is coming down around the group, big slick pages from a magazine, completely unremarkable in the uproar of the moment. Frank snatches a full-page ad for something called pasteurized process cheese food, a Borden's product, that's the company with the cow, and there's a color picture of yellowish pressed pulp melting horribly on a hot dog.

Frank deadpans the page to Gleason.

"Here. This will help you digest."

Jackie sits there like an air traveler in a downdraft. The pages keep falling. Baby food, instant coffee, encyclopedias and cars, waffle irons and shampoos and blended whiskeys. Piping times, an optimistic bounty that carries into the news pages where the nation's farmers record a bumper crop. And the resplendent products, how the dazzle of a Packard car is repeated in the feature story about the art treasures of the Prado. It is all part of the same thing. Rubens and Titian and Playtex and Motorola. And here's a picture of Sinatra himself sitting in a nightclub in Nevada with Ava Gardner and would you check that cleavage. Frank didn't know he was in this week's *Life* until the page fell out of the sky. He has people who are supposed to tell him these things. He keeps the page and reaches for another to stuff in Gleason's face. Here's a Budweiser ad, pal. In a country that's in a hurry to make the future, the names attached to the products are an enduring reassurance. Johnson & Johnson and Quaker State and RCA Victor and Burlington Mills and Bristol-Myers and General Motors. These are the venerated emblems of the burgeoning economy, easier to identify than the names of battlefields or dead presidents. Not that Jackie's in the mood to scan a magazine. He is sunk in deep inertia, a rancid sweat developing, his mouth filled with the foretaste of massive inner shiftings.

Branca takes the last of his warm-up tosses, flicking the glove to indicate a curve. Never mind the details of manner or appearance, the weight-bearing body at rest. Out on the mound he is strong and loose, cutting smoothly out of his windup, a man who wants the ball.

Furillo watching from right field. The stone-cut profile.

The bushy-haired man still pacing in the bleachers, moaning and shaking his head—call the men in the white suits and get him outta here. Talking to himself, head-wagging like a street-corner zealot with news of some distant affliction dragging ever closer. Siddown, shaddap, they tell him.

Frank keeps putting pages in Gleason's face.

He tells him, "Eat up, pal. Paper clears the palate."

When in steps Thomson.

The tall fleet Scot. Reminding himself as he gets set in the box. See the ball. Wait for the ball.

Russ is clutching the mike. Warm water and salt. Gargle, said his mother.

Thomson's not sure he sees things clearly. His eyeballs are humming. There's a feeling in his body, he's digging in, settling into his stance, crowd noise packing the sky, and there's a feeling that he has lost the link to his surroundings. Alone in all this rowdy-dow. See the ball. Watch and wait. He is frankly a little fuddled is Bobby. It's like the first waking moment of the day and you don't know whose house you're in.

Russ says, "Bobby Thomson up there swinging."

Mays down on one knee in the on-deck circle half leaning on his cradled bat and watching Branca go into a full windup, push-pull click-click, thinking it's all on him if Thomson fails, the season riding on him, and the jingle plays in his head, it's the radio embrace of the air itself, the mosaic of the air, and it will turn itself off when it's ready.

There's an emergency station under the stands and what the stadium cop has to do is figure out a way to get the stricken man down there without being overrun by a rampant stomping crowd. The victim looks okay considering. He is sitting down, waiting for the attendant to arrive with the wheelchair. All right, maybe he doesn't look so good. He looks pale, sick, worried and infarcted. But he can make a fist and stick out his tongue and there's not much the cop can do until the wheelchair arrives, so he might as well stand in the aisle and watch the end of the game.

Thomson in his bent stance, chin tucked, waiting.

Russ says, "One out, last of the ninth."

He says, "Branca pitches, Thomson takes a strike called on the inside corner."

He lays a heavy decibel on the word strike. He pauses to let the crowd reaction build. Do not talk against the crowd. Let the drama come from them.

Those big rich pages airing down from the upper deck.

Lockman stands near second and tries to wish a hit onto Thomson's bat. That may have been the pitch he wanted. Belt-high, a shade inside—won't see one that good again.

Russ says, "Bobby hitting at two ninety-two. He's had a single and a double and he drove in the Giants' first run with a long fly to center."

Lockman looks across the diamond at home. The double he hit is still a presence in his chest, it's chugging away in there, a body-memory that plays the moment over. He is peering into the deltoid opening between the catcher's knees. He sees the fingers dip, the blunt hand make a flapping action up and left. They'll give him the fastball high and tight and come back with the curve away. A pretty two-part scheme. Seems easy and sweet from here.

Russ says, "Brooklyn leads it four to two."

He says, "Runner down the line at third. Not taking any chances."

Thomson thinking it's all happening too fast. Thinking quick hands, see the ball, give yourself a chance.

Russ says, "Lockman without too big of a lead at second but he'll be running like the wind if Thomson hits one."...

Russ says, "Branca throws."

Gleason makes a noise that is halfway between a sigh and a moan. It is probably a sough, as of rustling surf in some palmy place. Edgar recalls the earlier blowout, Jackie's minor choking fit. He sees a deeper engagement here. He goes out into the aisle and up two steps, separating himself from the imminent discharge of animal, vegetable and mineral matter.

Not a good pitch to hit, up and in, but Thomson swings and tomahawks the ball and everybody, everybody watches. Except for Gleason who is bent over in his seat, hands locked behind his neck, a creamy strand of slime swinging from his lips.

Russ says, "There's a long drive."

His voice has a burst in it, a charge of expectation.

He says, "It's gonna be."

There's a pause all around him. Pafko racing toward the left-field corner.

He says, "I believe."

Pafko at the wall. Then he's looking up. People thinking where's the ball. The scant delay, the stay in time that lasts a hairsbreadth. And Cotter standing in section 35 watching the ball come in his direction. He feels his body turn to smoke. He loses sight of the ball when it climbs above the overhang and he thinks it will land in the upper deck. But before he can smile or shout or bash his neighbor on the arm. Before the moment can overwhelm him, the ball appears again, stitches visibly spinning, that's how near it hits, banging at an angle off a pillar—hands flashing everywhere.

Russ feels the crowd around him, a shudder passing through the stands, and then he is shouting into the mike and there is a surge of color and motion, a crash that occurs upward, stadium-wide, hands and faces and shirts, bands of rippling men, and he is outright shouting, his voice has a power he'd thought long gone—it may lift the top of his head like a cartoon rocket.

He says, "*The Giants win the pennant.*"

A topspin line drive. He tomahawked the pitch and the ball had topspin and dipped into the lower deck and there is Pafko at the 315 sign looking straight up with his right arm braced at the wall and a spate of paper coming down.

He says, "*The Giants win the pennant.*"

Yes, the voice is excessive with a little tickle of hysteria in the upper register. But it is mainly wham and whomp. He sees Thomson capering around first. The hat of the first-base coach—the first-base coach has flung his hat straight up. He went for a chin-high pitch and coldcocked it good. The ball started up high and then sank, missing the facade of the upper deck and dipping into the seats below—pulled in, swallowed up—and the Dodger players stand looking, already separated from the event, staring flat into the shadows between the decks.

He says, "*The Giants win the pennant.*"

The crew is whooping. They are answering the roof bangers by beating on the walls and ceiling of the booth. People climbing the dugout roofs and the crowd shaking in its own noise. Branca on the mound in his tormented slouch. He came with a fastball up, a pitch that's tailing in, and the guy's supposed to take it for a ball. Russ is shouting himself right out of his sore throat, out of every malady and pathology and complaint and all the pangs of growing up and every memory that is not tender.

He says, "*The Giants win the pennant.*"

Four times. Branca turns and picks up the rosin bag and throws it down, heading toward the clubhouse now, his shoulders aligned at a slant—he begins the long dead trudge. Paper falling everywhere. Russ knows he ought to settle down and let the mike pick up the sound of the swelling bedlam around him. But he can't stop shouting, there's nothing left of him but shout.

He says, "Bobby Thomson hits into the lower deck of the left-field stands."

He says, "The Giants win the pennant and they're going crazy."

He says, "They're going crazy."

Then he raises a pure shout, wordless, a holler from the old days—it is fiddlin' time, it is mountain music on WCKY at five-thirty in the morning. The thing comes jumping right out of him, a jubilation, it might be *heyyy-ho* or it might be *oh-boyyy* shouted backwards or it might be something else entirely—hard to tell when they don't use words. And Thomson's teammates gathering at home plate and Thomson circling the bases in gamesome leaps, buckjumping—he is forever Bobby now, a romping boy lost to time, and his breath comes so fast he doesn't know if he can handle all the air that's pouring in. He sees men in a helter-skelter line waiting at the plate to pummel him—his teammates, no better fellows in the world, and there's a look in their faces, they are stunned by a happiness that has collapsed on them, bright-eyed under their caps.

He tomahawked the pitch, he hit on top of it and now his ears are ringing and there's a numbing buzz in his hands and feet. And Robinson stands behind second, hands on hips, making sure Thomson touches every base. You can almost see brave Jack grow old.

Look at Durocher spinning. Russ pauses for the first time to catch the full impact of the noise around him. Leo spinning in the coach's box. The manager stands and spins, he is spinning with his arms spread wide—maybe it's an ascetic rapture, a thing they do in mosques in Anatolia.

People make it a point to register the time.

Edgar stands with arms crossed and a level eye on Gleason folded over. Pages dropping all around them, it is a fairly thick issue—laxatives and antacids, sanitary napkins and corn plasters and dandruff removers. Jackie utters an aquatic bark, it is loud and crude, the hoarse call of some mammal in distress. Then the surge of flannel matter. He seems to be vomiting someone's taupe pajamas. The waste is liquidy smooth in the lingo of adland and it is splashing freely on Frank's stout oxford shoes and fine lisle hose and on the soft woven wool of his town-and-country trousers.

The clock atop the clubhouse reads 3:58.

Russ has got his face back into the mike. He shouts, "I don't believe it." He shouts, "I don't believe it." He shouts, "I do *not* believe it."

They are coming down to crowd the railings. They are coming from the far ends of the great rayed configuration and they are moving down the aisles and toward the rails.

Pafko is out of paper range by now, jogging toward the clubhouse. But the paper keeps falling. If the early paper waves were slightly hostile and mocking, and the middle waves a form of fan commonality, then this last demonstration has a softness, a selfness. It is coming down from all points, laundry tickets, envelopes swiped from the office, there are crushed cigarette packs and sticky wrap from ice-cream sandwiches, pages from memo pads and pocket calendars, they are throwing faded dollar bills, snapshots torn to pieces, ruffled paper swaddles for cupcakes, they are tearing up letters they've been carrying around for years pressed into their wallets, the residue of love affairs and college friendships, it is happy garbage now, the fans' intimate wish to be connected to the event, unendably, in the form of pocket litter, personal waste, a thing that carries a shadow identity—rolls of toilet tissue unbolting lyrically in streamers.

They are gathered at the netting behind home plate, gripping the tight mesh.

Russ is still shouting, he is not yet shouted out, he believes he has a thing that's worth repeating.

Saying, "Bobby Thomson hit a line drive into the lower deck of the left-field stands and the place is going crazy."

Next thing Cotter knows he is sidling into the aisle. The area is congested and intense and he has to pry his way row by row using elbows and shoulders. Nobody much seems to notice. The ball is back there in a mighty pileup of shirts and jackets. The game is way behind him. The crowd can have the game. He's after the baseball now and there's no time to ask himself why. They hit it in the stands, you go and get it. It's the ball they play with, the thing they rub up and scuff and sweat on. He's going up the aisle through a thousand pounding hearts. He's prodding and sideswiping. He sees people dipping frantically, it could be apple-bobbing in Indiana, only slightly violent. Then the ball comes free and someone goes after it, the first one out of the pack, a young guy in a scuttling crawl with people reaching for him, trying to grab his jacket, a fistful of trouser-ass. He has wiry reddish hair and a college jacket—you know those athletic jackets where the sleeves are one color and leathery looking and the body is a darker color and probably wool and these are the college colors of the team.

Cotter takes a guess and edges his way along a row that's two rows down from the action. He takes a guess, he anticipates, it's the way you feel something will happen and then you watch it uncannily come to pass, occurring almost in measured stages so you can see the wheel-work of your idea fitting into place.

He coldcocked the pitch and the ball shot out there and dipped and disappeared. And Thomson bounding down on home plate mobbed by his teammates, who move in shuffled steps with hands extended to keep from spiking each other. And photographers edging near and taking their spread stances and the first of the fans appearing on the field, the first strays standing wary or whirling about to see things from this perspective, astonished to find themselves at field level, or running right at Thomson all floppy and demented, milling into the wedge of players at home plate.

Frank is looking down at what has transpired. He stands there hands out, palms up, an awe of muted disgust. That this should happen here, in public, in the high revel of event—he feels a puzzled wonder that exceeds his aversion. He looks down at the back of Jackie's glossy head and he looks at his own trouser cuffs flaked an intimate beige and the spatter across his shoe tops in a strafing pattern and the gumbo puddle nearby that contains a few laggard gobs of pinkoid stuff from deep in Gleason's gastric sac.

And he nods his head and says, "My shoes."

And Shor feels offended, he feels a look come into his face that carries the sting of a bad shave, those long-ago mornings of razor pull and cold water.

And he looks at Frank and says, "Did you see the homer at least?"

"I saw part and missed part."

And Shor says, "Do I want to take the time to ask which part you missed so we can talk about it on the phone some day?"

There are people with their hands in their hair, holding in their brains.

Frank persists in looking down. He allows one foot to list to port so he can examine the side of his shoe for vomit marks. These are handcrafted shoes from a narrow street with a quaint name in oldest London.

And Shor says, "We just won unbelievable, they're ripping up the joint, I don't know whether to laugh, shit or go blind."

And Frank says, "I'm rooting for number one or number three."

Russ is still manning the microphone and has one last thing to say and barely manages to get it out.

"The Giants won it. By a score of five to four. And they're picking Bobby Thomson up. And carrying him off the field."

If his voice has an edge of disquiet it's because he has to get to the clubhouse to do interviews with players and coaches and team officials and the only way to get out there is to cross the length of the field on foot and he's already out of breath, out of words, and the crowd is growing over the walls. He sees Thomson carried by a phalanx of men, players and others, mostly others—the players have run for it, the players are dashing for the clubhouse—and he sees Thomson riding off-balance on the shoulders of men who might take him right out of the ballpark and into the streets for a block party.

Gleason is suspended in wreckage, drained and humped, and he has barely the wit to consider what the shouting's about.

The field streaked with people, the hat snatchers, the swift kids who imitate banking aircraft, their spread arms steeply raked.

Look at Cotter under a seat.

All over the city people are coming out of their houses. This is the nature of Thomson's homer. It makes people want to be in the streets, joined with others, telling others what has happened, those few who haven't heard—comparing faces and states of mind.

And Russ has a hot mike in front of him and has to find someone to take it and talk so he can get down to the field and find a way to pass intact through all that mangle.

And Cotter is under a seat handfighting someone for the baseball. He is trying to get a firmer grip. He is trying to isolate his rival's hand so he can prise the ball away finger by finger.

It is a tight little theater of hands and arms, some martial test with formal rules of grappling.

The iron seat leg cuts into his back. He hears the earnest breathing of the rival. They are working for advantage, trying to gain position.

The rival is blocked off by the seat back, he is facedown in the row above with just an arm stuck under the seat.

People make it a point to read the time on the clock atop the notched facade of the clubhouse, the high battlement—they register the time when the ball went in.

It is a small tight conflict of fingers and inches, a lifetime of effort compressed into seconds.

He gets his hands around the rival's arm just above the wrist. He is working fast, thinking fast—too much time and people take sides.

The rival, the foe, the ofay, veins stretched and bulged between white knuckles. If people take sides, does Cotter have a chance?

Two heart attacks, not one. A second man collapses on the field, a well-dressed fellow not exactly falling but letting himself down one knee at a time, slow and controlled, easing down on his right hand and tumbling dully over. No one takes this for a rollick. The man is not the type to do dog tricks in the dirt.

And Cotter's hands around the rival's arm, twisting in opposite directions, burning the skin—it's called an Indian burn, remember? One hand grinding one way, the other going the other, twisting hard, working fast.

There's a pause in the rival's breathing. He is pausing to note the pain. He fairly croons his misgivings now and Cotter feels the arm jerk and the fingers lift from the ball.

Thomson thrusting down off the shoulders of the men who carry him, beating down, pulling away from grabby hands—he sees players watching intently from the clubhouse windows.

And Cotter holds the rival's arm with one hand and goes for the ball with the other. He sees it begin to roll past the seat leg, wobbling

on the textured surface. He sort of traps it with his eye and sends out
a ladling hand.

The ball rolls in a minutely crooked path into the open.

The action of his hand is as old as he is. It seems he has been
sending out this hand for one thing or another since the minute he
shot out of infancy. Everything he knows is contained in the splayed
fingers of this one bent hand.

Heart, my heart.

The whole business under the seat has taken only seconds. Now
he's backing out, moving posthaste—he's got the ball, he feels it hot
and buzzy in his hand.

A sense of people grudgingly getting out of his way, making way
but not too quickly, dead-eye sidewalk faces.

The ball is damp with the heat and sweat of the rival's hand.
Cotter's arm hangs lank at his side and he empties out his face,
scareder now than he was when he went over the turnstile but determined to look cool and blank and going down the rows by stepping over seat backs and fitting himself between bodies and walking
on seats when it is convenient.

Look at the ushers locking arms at the wrists and making a
sedan seat for the cardiac victim and hauling him off to the station
under the grandstand.

One glance back at the area above, he allows himself a glance
and sees the rival getting to his feet. The man stands out, white-
shirted and hulking, and it's not the college boy he thought it might
be, the guy in the varsity jacket who'd been scrambling for the ball.

And the man catches his eye. This is not what Cotter wants, this
is damage to the cause. He made a mistake looking back. He allowed
himself a glance, a sidewise flash, and now he's caught in the man's
hard glare.

The raised seams of the ball are pulsing in his hand. . . .

———

With advancing dark the field is taking on a deeper light. The grass is incandescent, it has a heat and sheen. People go running past, looking half ablaze, and Russ Hodges moves with the tentative steps of some tourist at a grand bazaar, trying to hand-shuffle through the crowd.

Some ushers are lifting a drunk off the first-base line and the man warps himself into a baggy mass and shakes free and begins to run around the bases in his oversized raincoat with long belt trailing.

Russ makes his way through the infield and dance-steps into an awkward jog that makes him feel ancient and extraneous and he thinks of the ballplayers of his youth, the men with redneck monickers whose endeavors he followed in the papers every day, Eppa Rixey and Hod Eller and old Ivy Wingo, and there is a silly grin pasted across his face because he is a forty-one-year-old man with a high fever and he is running across a ball field to conduct a dialogue with a pack of athletes in their underwear. . . .

Al shouts, "Do you believe it?"

"I do not believe it," says Russ.

They shake hands on the run.

Al says, "Look at these people." He is shouting and gesturing, waving a Cuban cigar. "It's like I-don't-know-what."

"If you don't know what, then I don't know what."

"Save the voice," says Al.

"The voice is dead and buried. It went to heaven on a sunbeam."

"I'll tell you one thing's for certain, old pal. We'll never forget today."

"Glad you're with me, buddy."

The running men shake hands again. They are deep in the outfield now and Russ feels an ache in every joint. The clubhouse windows catch the flash of the popping bulbs inside. . . .

Russ Hodges stands on an equipment trunk trying to describe the scene in the clubhouse and he knows he is making no sense and the players who climb up on the trunk to talk to him are making no sense and they are all talking in unnatural voices, failed voices, creaturely night screaks. Others are pinned to their lockers by reporters and family members and club officials and they can't get to the liquor and beer loaded on a table in the middle of the room. Russ holds the mike over his head and lets the noise sweep in and then lowers the mike and says another senseless thing.

Thomson goes out on the clubhouse veranda to respond to the sound of his chanted name and they are everywhere, they are on the steps with stadium cops keeping them in check and there are thousands more spread dense across the space between jutting bleacher walls, many arms extended toward Thomson—they are pointing or imploring or making victory fists or stating a desire to touch, men in suits and hats down there and others hanging over the bleacher wall above Bobby, reaching down, half falling over the edge, some very near to touching him.

Al says, the producer, "Great job today, Russ buddy."

"We did something great just by being here."

"What a feeling."

"I'd smoke a cigar but I must die."

"But what a feeling," Al says.

"We sure pulled something out of a hat. All of us together. Damn I just realized."

"What's a ball game to make us feel like this?"

"I have to go back. Left my topcoat in the booth."

"We need a walk to settle us down."

"We need a long walk."

"That's the only coat you've ever loved," says Al.

They leave by way of the Dodger clubhouse and there's Branca all right, the first thing you see, stretched facedown on a flight of six steps, feet touching the floor. He's still in uniform except for shirt and cap. He wears a wet undershirt and his head is buried in his crossed arms on the top step. Al and Russ speak to a few of the men who remain. They talk quietly and try not to look at Branca. They look but tell themselves they aren't. Next to Branca a coach sits in full uniform but hatless, smoking a cigarette. His name is Cookie. No one wants to catch Cookie's eye. Al and Russ talk quietly to a few more men and all of them together try not to look at Branca.

The steps from the Dodger clubhouse are nearly clear of people. Thomson has gone back inside but there are fans still gathered in the area, waving and chanting. The two men begin to walk across the outfield and Al points to the place in the left-field stands where the ball went in.

"Mark the spot. Like where Lee surrendered to Grant or some such thing."

Russ thinks this is another kind of history. He thinks they will carry something out of here that joins them all in a rare way, that binds them to a memory with protective power. People are climbing lampposts on Amsterdam Avenue, tooting car horns in Little Italy. Isn't it possible that this midcentury moment enters the skin more lastingly than the vast shaping strategies of eminent leaders, generals steely in their sunglasses—the mapped visions that pierce our dreams? Russ wants to believe a thing like this keeps us safe in some undetermined way. This is the thing that will pulse in his brain come old age and double vision and dizzy spells—the surge sensation, the leap of people already standing, that bolt of noise and joy when the ball went in. This is the people's history and it has flesh and breath that quicken to the force of this old safe game of ours. And fans at the Polo Grounds today will be able to tell their grandchildren—they'll be the gassy old men leaning into the next century and trying to convince anyone willing to listen, pressing in with medicine breath, that they were here when it happened.

The raincoat drunk is running the bases. They see him round first, his hands paddling the air to keep him from drifting into right field. He approaches second in a burst of coattails and limbs and un-tied shoelaces and swinging belt. They see he is going to slide and they stop and watch him leave his feet.

All the fragments of the afternoon collect around his airborne form. Shouts, bat-cracks, full bladders and stray yawns, the sand-grain manyness of things that can't be counted.

It is all falling indelibly into the past.

THE RECORD
ALMOST BROKE HIM

A cautionary tale that suggests that a considerable triumph does not lend itself to a sense of well-being.

⚾

S UNDAY, OCT. 1, 1961, Yankee Stadium, Bronx, N.Y. Bottom of the fourth, nobody on, one out, no score. Roger Maris of the Yankees steps to bat for the second time in the final game of the season. Tracy Stallard, a 24-year-old righthander for the Boston Red Sox, delivers a fastball—"a strike, knee-high on the outside of the plate," he would say later.

Maris swings and everybody knows the ball is gone. In the melee in the right-field stands, Sal Durante, a teen-ager from Brooklyn, emerges with the home-run ball and becomes a footnote to history. Maris slowly circles the bases to a standing ovation from the crowd. Yogi Berra, the next batter, shakes his hand, as does the bat boy and an ecstatic fan who has leaped out of the stands. Maris disappears into the dugout, comes out again, doffs his cap and smiles. On the last possible day he has broken Babe Ruth's "unbreakable" record and hit 61 home runs in a season.

Wednesday, March 23, 1977, Perry Field, Gainesville, Fla. Roger Maris, beer distributor and 42-year-old father of six, stands in the Yankee dugout watching his old teammates prepare to play a spring-training game against the University of Florida. George Steinbrenner, the owner of the Yankees, approaches. "Hey, Rog," he says, "where's the beer?" Maris laughs and shrugs his shoulders. "You should have asked me earlier," he says.

Steinbrenner chuckles, but then his smile fades a bit. "You know, you're a hard guy to get a hold of, Roger," he says. "You're hard to get to New York for just one day."

There is a pause. Maris' smile continues, but it is artificial now, as though propped up with toothpicks. Steinbrenner is referring to the annual Old Timers' Game, an event Maris has never attended since he left the Yankees in 1966. Maris has refused to visit Yankee Stadium for any reason.

"Why don't you come?" Steinbrenner says in a softer voice.

Maris stares out at the field. "They might shoot me," he says.

Steinbrenner's voice becomes solemn. "I'm telling you, Roger, you won't ever hear an ovation like the one you'd get if you'd come back to Yankee Stadium."

Maris looks at the ground. "Maybe," he says without conviction, and the conversation is over.

After all these years, the man who hit more home runs in a season than anyone else still has not recovered from the emotional turbulence of the summer of '61. Hounded ceaselessly by an aggressive sporting press and by fans who lusted for the long ball, Maris proved himself inadequate to the vast demands of public relations. It is uncertain whether anyone could have been adequate.

At times, 50 or more reporters so packed the Yankee clubhouse to interview Maris that some of his teammates could not reach their lockers. Rather than clarifying his image, many of the reporters garbled it, filling their copy with adjectives as diverse as their own natures. At various times in 1961 Maris was described as "shy," "decent," "hot-headed," "low-key," "easily agitated," "devout and home-loving," "surly," "cooperative," "unselfish," "reticent," "talkative," "trite," "choleric," "self-pitying," "sincere," "wonderful," "sensible," "petulant," "honest," "literate," "straightforward" and "morose."

When it became apparent that Maris had a real shot at Ruth's record, the barrage of home-run questions intensified. A hundred times a day he was asked if he thought he could break the record, how soon, what had he done to his swing, what did he think of all this. "You can believe me or not—I don't care—but I honestly don't know," he would answer, when thinking became unbearable.

Never a patient man, Maris told reporters that if they thought he was surly, it was just too bad, because that was how he was going to stay. In one away game, angered by catcalls, he made obscene gestures to the crowd. In every road park, and frequently at Yankee Stadium, he was booed. He was, after all, chasing the immortal Babe, who hit his 60 home runs in 1927, before TV coverage and routine mass postgame interviews.

Autograph seekers grew vicious. "People would elbow up to Rog and yell, 'Give me your John Hancock!'" recalls teammate Moose Skowron, "so sometimes Rog would sign 'John Hancock.' Sometimes they'd say, 'Gimme yer X!' So he'd sign X. I mean, how many hours can you put up with that garbage?"

Though he admitted to having a short fuse, Maris resented being labeled a redneck by the press. He stopped smiling. His mouth always seemed set in a tight line. His hair began to fall out. His wife, visiting New York from Kansas City after giving birth to their fourth child, told him he looked like a molting bird. A private person, Maris found he could never be alone, and his statements became less and less printable. The needs of the public were not his needs, and the chasm of misunderstanding widened. In 1963 a reporter wrote that the trouble with Maris was not that he had problems with the press but that "he has proved to be such an unsatisfactory hero."

As a final dig at Maris' authenticity, Baseball Commissioner Ford Frick, an old friend of Babe Ruth's and a former sportswriter who once ghosted articles under Ruth's byline, decreed that Maris' record must go into the books accompanied by an asterisk. This, explained Frick, was because Maris played in a 162-game season, while Ruth played a 154-game schedule; 1961 was the year that baseball expanded its schedule to 162 games, and Maris' feat was the first baseball record thus qualified.

Since finishing his playing days in 1968, Maris has had little to do with baseball. He came to Perry Field this spring only because he has a few friends on the Yankees and because the team was now on his turf. "Baseball is just like a kid with a train," he told a reporter not long ago. "You got to outgrow it sometime." But there have been signs that Maris has not outgrown baseball, that very cautiously he is coming back to the game he never really wanted to leave. This year when he took his sons to a spring training game in Fort Myers, he even stepped into the batting cage to help the Royals' John Mayberry work on his swing.

Nonetheless, long distance, over the phone, he had still been wary about being interviewed. "I don't know," he said. "I don't need publicity anymore."

Would it help if the conversation has nothing to do with baseball, with the 61 homers or old times? "Well, see, that's another thing they've gotten wrong," he said. "I don't mind talking about baseball. It's just that every now and then I give another interview, and when it doesn't turn out right, I back off again."

Now, several days later, having agreed to talk, Maris sits behind his desk at the Maris Distributing Company near the Gainesville airport, taking business calls and feeling chipper. Judging from the furnishings, it is apparent that discussing baseball does not disturb him. In the foyer, a glass case holds several large trophies, including a metal crown presented to Maris by the Maryland Professional Baseball Players' Association for the most outstanding batting achievement of 1961. Across the front are engraved the words, "Sultan of Swat."

Numerous photographs, plaques and game mementos are on the walls of his office. One photograph shows Maris with President Kennedy. Another shows him and Mickey Mantle with President Truman. A framed blowup of a cartoon depicting Maris in quest of his 61 homers includes an inset of Ruth, looking heroic and somewhat sad. The caption at the bottom makes reference to the 154-game, 162-game controversy and ends with Ford Frick's quote in defense of the asterisk: "You can't break the 100-meter record in a 100-yard dash."

Next to the cartoon is a color photograph of the 1968 World Champion St. Louis Cardinals, Maris smiling in the front, flanked by Tim McCarver, Bob Gibson, Lou Brock and Orlando Cepeda, among others. Maris played two twilight years for St. Louis—1967 and 1968—and he was much happier there than in New York. The team did well, the press eased off and the home fans did not boo. Cardinal President August A. Busch Jr. approved Maris for ownership of the Anheuser-Busch distributorship in Gainesville at the end of the '67 season. Maris, who had intended to retire, showed his gratitude by playing one more season. A valuable property in a thirsty college town, the distributorship (which handles Busch, Budweiser and Michelob) enables Maris to maintain his independence, to stay away from anything to do with organized baseball.

Rumors once had it that Cepeda, another Cardinal slugger, was slated for a Busch outlet when his baseball days were over. Cepeda never got it, and recently ran afoul of the law. Maris, seeing Cepeda's picture on the wall, recalls his teammate.

"I heard there were some people in Boston who were supposed to help him, to try and get him off or something," Maris says. "He was from Puerto Rico, you know. Most of those guys could speak English, but communication can still be tough. I still remember this one Latin kid who played with me in the Three-I League. He couldn't speak a word of English. When he first came up, everybody ordered hamburger steaks for a meal. And, you know, that poor kid ate hamburger steak for I don't know how many months—for breakfast, lunch and dinner. It was the only word he knew for food. I went over to the Dominican Republic to play winter ball one year, and I really got mad when I couldn't get things across. I can imagine what it must be like for them up here."

Paunchier, fuller-faced and less hawk-eyed than the blond, crew-cut young athlete who, it was said, could have posed for a Marine recruiting poster, Maris seems at ease now, but somehow misplaced in his role as small-town businessman. He fidgets with his tie, pulls at the tight sleeves of his blue blazer. He is a man of action at a sit-down job.

His hair is now dark and long. When he leans forward it falls over his forehead and he pushes it back. "This hair in my eyes, this long stuff, it bothers me," he says with the irritation of someone who grew up believing in barber shops. "I'm about this close to getting a crew cut again. I really am. You know, it's hard these days when athletes and professors and everybody has long hair—it's hard for me to tell my kids to get theirs cut."

Maris looks at the family photos on the back wall of his office, the snapshots of his six blond children, aged 11 to 19, and his infant grandson. Always fiercely protective of his family, Maris never considered moving them to New York during his years with the Yankees. "Never, ever," he says quickly. "I knew it wasn't my permanent home. I don't like big cities. I don't like hustle and bustle." Patricia Maris and the kids lived instead in a suburb of Kansas City where Maris returned as soon as each season ended.

"It can be rough on you having five adolescent kids," Maris adds. "I shudder to think what would happen if they got up in the morning with nothing to do. Fortunately, we belong to a country club, and the boys are pretty interested in golf. Oh, they like baseball, too, but the private school they go to is too small to have a team. The only other thing around here is American Legion ball, and that can be rough when you have all those older boys to compete with.

"I don't push my kids into anything, but I think golf is a good clean sport—no broken bones or anything like that. And if you ever make the pro tour, why, you don't even have to win. You can do fine just finishing near the top.

"Roger Jr., my oldest boy, is going to sign a basketball scholarship next week with a junior college north of here. He's 6' 4" and he loves basketball. Of course, he loves baseball, too, but the thing is. . . ." Maris hesitates, his voice becoming harder, his gray eyes taking on a steely look. "Well, some of those coaches are different, and just because he's Roger Maris Jr., some of them started getting on him. And I think he just got tired of it and said the hell with baseball. I'll tell you, if I had it to do all over again I never would have named him that."

Maris spins the large World Series ring he wears on his right hand, one of three championship rings he got during his 12-year career. "The thing is," he says with a shrug, "how would you know?"

It would have been hard to predict that the name Roger Maris would someday be famous. Raised in Fargo, N. Dak., the son of a railroad man, Maris was a star football and basketball player at a school that did not field a baseball team. "I'd have played college football if I'd been smart enough to get into school," Maris told a reporter in 1960. Trying to make a career of baseball, instead, he was told after a tryout with the Chicago Cubs that he was too small for the game. At the time Maris was 5' 11½" and 190 pounds, and the judgment made no sense. But Maris has always looked smaller than he is. Later, managers would say he "undressed big."

After several years of American Legion ball, Maris was finally signed by Cleveland, and in 1957, his first big league season, he hit 14 home runs and batted .235. In 1958 he was traded to Kansas City and hit 28 home runs while batting .240. In 1959 he raised his average to .273, but he hit only 16 homers.

In 1960 he and two lesser A's were traded to the Yankees for Don Larsen, Marv Throneberry, Hank Bauer and Norm Siebern, and he gave the first real indication that power was his specialty. On Opening Day he hit two home runs, a double and a single and drove in four runs. That year he had 39 homers and 112 RBIs and was voted the American League's Most Valuable Player, even though a sore rib caused him to slump badly in August and September.

At the beginning of 1961 even bigger things were expected of him. Before his rib injury in '60, Maris had been ahead of Ruth's pace, and his compact, lashing swing seemed custom-made for Yankee Stadium's short right-field fence. But in April of '61, Maris hit only one homer; by mid-May he had only three. Then he loosened up with the heat, and his production rose dramatically. He had 20 by June 11, 30 by July 2, 40 by July 25. In August, against Washington and Chicago, Maris all but burst into flames, belting seven home runs in six games.

The last two—Nos. 47 and 48—came off Billy Pierce, the Chicago lefthander. Those were significant blows because Maris supposedly could not hit lefthanders. In 1953, while playing Class C ball, he had been struck in the head by a pitch from a lefty, and for a long time afterward he had a tendency to bail out on the close ones. "Getting hit is scary," he says. "The last thing you remember is collapsing over the place, and the next thing you remember is riding in the ambulance. I can still feel the imprint of that ball on my temple, it's still tender. In '53 we didn't even wear batting helmets."

Pierce claims Maris' home-run total never entered his mind when he was pitching to him in 1961. "To tell you the truth," he says, "I don't even remember giving up those two homers. I do remember that you usually tried to pitch Roger inside. Or if you went outside, you wanted it way outside. And of course, you didn't walk Roger to get to Mantle."

Mickey Mantle, the affable golden boy contrasting with the brooding Maris, was in the midst of an outstanding year himself in 1961. Together the "M & M Boys" blasted 115 homers—61 for Maris, 54 for Mantle—a major league record for teammates. It soon became part of the skeptics' argument that were it not for Mantle's batting cleanup, Maris never would have seen the pitches he did, never would have approached even 50 home runs. (In fact, all the Yankees aided one another. Six different players hit 20 or more home runs in 1961, and the team total of 240 is by far the most ever hit by one club in a season.)

In the team's 159th game Maris finally hit his 60th homer, tying Ruth's record. Five days later he hit the 61st, and as the dust cleared, he said that he was immensely—exhaustedly—relieved, that he could never go through the same experience again. But instead of the public nightmare dissipating, as Maris hoped, it reappeared in a different form. Now everyone wanted to know if Maris could repeat his feat. There were many—fans, reporters, players—who felt he had to, to prove his legitimacy. But in 1962 Maris hit only 33 home runs, and after that he never hit more than 26 in a season. In his last four years he averaged slightly less than nine.

The notion that Maris was a fluke, that he was not in Ruth's class in anything—skill, endurance, personality, charisma—gained credence. He was, to many, not worthy of being considered Ruth's equal. He would never make the Hall of Fame, they said. (He hasn't.) Forgotten were Maris' outstanding arm, his fielding skills, his baserunning, his three years of 100 or more RBIs, his two MVP trophies—he got his second, of course, in 1961—his many debilitating injuries, the fact that he never claimed to be anything more than a man "just doing my job."

After 1961 fans booed him as routinely as they ordered hot dogs. Some sportswriters gloated over his failings, crediting themselves for much of his fame. "If it weren't for sportswriters," said

Tommy Devine of the Miami *News* in 1962, "Roger Maris would probably be an $18-a-week clerk in the A&P back in Missouri." On a "home-run derby" tour in the South after the '61 season, Maris reached one of the low points of his career. Playing before almost deserted stands, he was jeered by children each time he took a pitch or hit a ball that did not clear the fence.

In New York the press continued to pursue him. Though Maris had informed reporters that he led "the most boring existence you can imagine," that he didn't read, didn't drink, didn't go out, that world events held no interest for him, that he tried to get 10 hours of sleep a night, they would not quit.

"Some of the questions they asked me!" says Maris, his eyes narrowing again. "I remember one writer asked what I did on the road. I said, 'What do you mean?' He said, 'Well, do you go out with girls, fool around, anything like that?' I said, 'I think I'm married, if I remember correctly.' He said, 'Well, so am I, but I still go out and fool around.' I said, 'You do whatever you want. I don't do it.' I mean, that's an intelligent question, isn't it? Especially with about a hundred reporters around me. Then another brilliant guy asks, 'What would you rather do, bat .300 or hit 61 home runs?' That's a hell of a question. How many guys hit .300 and how many hit 61 home runs? Doesn't common sense tell you what you answer to something like that?"

Maris shakes his head. "I tried to get along with them, but it just didn't work. I think the problem was that at a certain point the baseball writers got to be gossip columnists. I'm not speaking of some of the old, polished writers—I mean this new breed that came in around 1961. They weren't there to write what happened on the field. And the Yankees, with the experience they'd had, they should have been able to see the whole thing coming. But they did nothing. They just let you stew in your own brew, baby.

"I used to sit at the Stadium for three and four hours after games, until the last reporter was gone. That's wrong. I know there was competition among the writers, and I guess there were times when I got things going, too. Like for years, Willie Mays said that he'd play for nothing. I always maintained I was playing for my family and my bread and butter, and when the bread or butter's not there, I'm not there. So the headlines come out that I'm playing strictly for money, which wasn't true, because I loved the game, too. The press was making me a—what do you call it?—a whipping boy.

"What's funny is that when I first came to the Yankees everybody was giving Mantle a bad time. Why, I don't know. But when I got there, all of that stuff just sort of slid off him and came onto me. I was the one assaulting baseball, apple pie, Chevrolet, the whole works. That's when Mickey got to be the golden boy."

Though the potential for conflict between the two stars was there, it never materialized. Maris and Mantle liked each other, even shared an apartment for a time. When the going got particularly rough for Maris, Mantle would often try to soothe his friend, telling him he would have to get used to the pressure.

"I saw Mickey about two weeks ago," says Maris. "The first time in a while. He was in Florida for a golf tournament. Did the papers get any pictures of us together? No, I don't get along too well with the local press. There's a sports editor here who hammered me in a column a while back, so I told him to do me a favor and just leave me completely out of the paper. Now I even see wire stories in the other papers that the Gainesville paper doesn't run." Maris chuckles with glee over the turnabout.

Leaning back, he furrows his brow and thinks for a moment. "Did you happen to see that book Joe Pepitone wrote?" he asks. He whistles softly, obviously pleased the book isn't his own autobiography. "There's stuff about Joe's wife before their wedding and about Joe and other girls and all that. I mean, his children have to read that someday. Joe just wasn't that bad a guy. He had talent. He could sing on stage—when we were at a bar he'd get up there and sing. I thought he was good. He could dance, too. And he was funny. I don't know, I just think you can go to confession without the whole world knowing it."

The subject turns to another athlete-writer, Jim Bouton, the former Yankee pitcher and author of *Ball Four*. In the book Bouton took several shots at Maris, alluding, among other things, to his alleged shallowness and lack of hustle.

"Jim Bouton," says Maris. "Now there's a guy I never had anything to do with. I didn't like him. He had ability, too, but his head was more his problem. He was the kind of guy who, if somebody made an error behind him, would come up with, 'It's all your fault,' instead of just pitching harder. He couldn't get on me, though, because I didn't want him around. In his book he called me the biggest loafer he'd ever seen, which was a compliment compared to what he wrote about the other guys.

"It's strange, but nobody's interested in anything nowadays unless you're knocking people. Sour grapes. Everytime somebody interviews me, that's all they say—Maris is sour about this, bitter about that. I personally have no interest in ever doing a book. All the things that happened, it's water down the drain, right? I don't think anybody is interested in what I have to say now."

Later in the day Maris drives to the Gainesville Hilton to await the arrival of the Yankees for their night game with the University of Florida. In the hotel restaurant he orders a sandwich and a Budweiser Natural Lite beer. The beer is a new low-calorie brew that Anheuser-Busch is test-marketing in Maris' district, and he is certain it will be a success. "Everybody's on a diet, now," Maris says. "I'm up to 230, though people still guess my weight at around 185 or 190." He pats his ample belly. His hands are large and strong, and his wrists are as thick as a blacksmith's.

"I was always a wrist hitter," he says. "Mickey had a hard and big swing, but mine was short and quick. And I always pulled the ball—I hit only one left-field home run the whole time I played in Yankee Stadium. Most of my home runs were line drives, too, but I did hit some towering ones. My 57th and 58th hit the roof of Tiger Stadium in Detroit, and in Kansas City I hit one out onto the street. I think only seven or eight players had ever done that."

The waitress returns and informs Maris that they are out of Natural Lite beer. He drinks water instead, and mentions that he'll have to get on the manager about this. Then the conversation, perhaps inevitably, drifts back to 1961.

"People say '61 was a fluke," Maris says. "But it wasn't. It was *unusual* in that most of the balls I hit hard went out that year. In '62 I hit the ball even better, but they all seemed to be sinking line drives. I mean 'fluke'—what's a 'fluke'? Babe Ruth only hit 60 home runs once, so was that a fluke? How many times do you have to do something?"

A few minutes later the Yankee bus arrives, and Maris stands just inside the lobby doors, eagerly watching the procession of players entering the hotel. He has visibly perked up, now paces back and forth, looking for faces. Dock Ellis, Roy White and Lou Piniella file through the door, and Maris greets each of them. He says hello to Catfish Hunter and then pumps hands excitedly with Yogi Berra and Manager Billy Martin.

Still watching the doorway, Maris' eyes abruptly light up and a large smile spreads over his face. "Well, look who did make it!" he shouts.

Tanned, with an open-necked shirt, young-man blond bangs and blue eyes set in a craggy, weathered face, Mantle walks into the lobby. The two old teammates greet each other warmly and within minutes are comfortably seated in the hotel bar. Martin joins them, and the stories spill out. Drinking stories, golf stories, women stories—locker-room talk. Mantle is traveling with the Yankees as a special batting coach, and Maris is delighted to learn they will be able to sit together in the Yankee dugout.

In the locker room before the game, Mantle dresses in a Yankee uniform. He is 45 now and, despite his broad shoulders and big biceps, he looks ludicrous in the uniform of a young man. "Look at this, Rog," he says, handing his new glove to Maris. "Ain't that just too big?"

Maris inspects the cavernous mitt and agrees that, yes, it is too large. The conversation turns to the old days.

"When did you quit playing?" Mantle asks.

"I was 34. It was long enough, Mick."

"You could've kept playing."

"Naw. In 1968, when they saw my hand was hurt and I couldn't hit the fastball, I was through." Maris grabs a beer from the cooler and follows Mantle into the restroom, never once stopping the chatter. Later, in the dugout, Maris looks at Mantle, who is leaning back eating peanuts. "Hey, Mick," he says. "After signing all those autographs, you gonna take a shower?" They both burst into laughter. Maris stands against the wall, his arms around his youngest son, Richard, enjoying himself hugely. Earlier he had said that one of his biggest pleasures since moving to Gainesville was being able to remain anonymous. But this is different.

In the fifth inning, Centerfielder Mickey Rivers hits a home run over the right-field fence. Maris turns to Reggie Jackson, who is selecting a bat from the rack. Like Ruth and Maris, Jackson is a left-handed-hitting outfielder whose specialty is home runs. Pressure will seek him out, too. Maris points to the fence. "That's what I want, Reggie," he says.

In the eighth Jackson hits a sizzling 360-foot line-drive double that isn't high enough to clear the fence. Later, when he scores, he trots over to Maris. "Rog, that was for you," he says. "I want you to remember me for something. I want to at least get mentioned in the same paragraph with you some day." Reggie Jackson is smiling, but his voice is filled with deference.

After the game Jackson sits on a stool in the locker room and explains how he feels about Maris. "I have so much admiration for the man," he says solemnly. "For the mental part almost more than the physical. I mean, can you imagine what it's like to hit 61 home runs in a season? In New York? It's like hitting .400. With the way the press is today, it would take a new breed of man to do it again, a deaf and dumb man would have the best chance. People don't know what Roger had to go through—he *had* to act the way he did to maintain his sanity. Believe me, people just don't understand."

Maris stands in the center of the locker room, drinking a beer, swapping jokes, rehashing the ball game, relishing the reunion with his old game. If someone were to ask him if he cared anymore whether people understood or not, he would certainly say no. But that would not be the case. He hasn't forgotten the boos. But after more than a decade, it might be time he went back to Yankee Stadium. He would never forget the sound he would hear there now, either.

A MATTER OF RECORD

This collection gives me the chance to commemorate Henry Aaron's breaking Babe Ruth's home-run record by including an edited version of an "instant" book that I was commissioned to finish within days of the event. Originally, *Sports Illustrated* assigned me to follow Aaron as he chased Babe Ruth's great record of 714 home runs which had stood for 39 years. I traveled to Houston at the end of the 1973 season where I missed watching him hit number 712—a ferocious line drive that I was told went between the hands of a guy reaching for it, hit an iron railing, and bounced practically back into the infield, but I saw him hit number 713 on the second-to-last day. I went to Cincinnati for the first day of the 1974 season, and incredibly enough, Aaron came to the plate for the first time and on the first swing of his bat, the first swing of the *season,* tied Ruth's record with a ball that rose on a line for the center-field seats. Jack Billingham was the Reds' pitcher. When he got to the dugout after the inning he commented: "I didn't waste any time, did I?"

That home run set the stage for what was to happen in Atlanta.

My plan was to focus on the principals in the drama—the pitcher, the batter, the fan who would catch the ball, and the announcer who would break the news in words he hoped would become immortal.

Against my wishes, the publisher entitled the book *One for the Record.* I preferred *A Matter of Record,* which has a nice ring to it, and there it stands.

I T WAS A SIMPLE ACT by an unassuming man which touched an enormous circle of people, indeed an entire country. It provided an instant which people would remember for decades—exactly what they were doing at the time of the home run that beat Babe Ruth's great record of 714 home runs which had stood for 39 years, whether they were watching it on a television set, or heard it over the car radio while driving along the turnpike at night, or whether a neighbor leaned over a picket fence and told them about it the next morning.

Its effect was far-reaching, and more powerful than one would expect from the act of hitting a ball over a fence. The Mexico sports correspondent from *El Sol de Mexico*, almost overcome with emotion, ended his piece on the Aaron 715th home run with thanks to God. "We lived through this historic moment, the most fabulous in the world. Thanks to God we witnessed this moment of history."

In Japan the huge headlines in Tokyo's premier sports daily read haikulike: WHITE BALL DANCES THROUGH ATLANTA'S WHITE MIST and under the subhead I SAW IT the correspondent began: "In my Atlanta hotel room I now begin writing this copy. I know I have to be calm. But I find it impossible to prevent my writing hand from continuing to shake..."

It caused tragedy. In Jacksonville, Florida, a taxicab driver shot himself when his wife pulled him out of his chair in front of the television to send him out to work just as he was settling down to the game. He died before the home run was hit....

Almost everyone in baseball was in front of a television set. In Kansas City the ancient black pitcher Satchel Paige had seventeen of his family crowded around ("all these sisters-in-law of mine") and when they saw the ball hit they began shouting and they could hear the people next door carrying on the same way.

For those who sat in the stadium in Atlanta their recollections would be especially intimate—the sharp cork-pop sound of the bat hitting the ball, startlingly audible in that split second of suspense before the crowd began a roar that lasted for more than ten minutes. Perhaps that is what they would remember—how people stood in front of their seats and sucked in air and bellowed it out in a sustained tribute that no other athlete has ever received. Or perhaps they would remember the wonder at how easy and inevitable it seemed—that having opened the season in Cincinnati by hitting the tying home run number 714 with his first swing of the year, it was obviously appropriate that the man called "Supe" by his teammates (for Superman) was going to duplicate the feat in Atlanta with his first swing of *that* game to break the record. That was why 53,775 had come. Or perhaps they would remember the odd way the stadium emptied after the excitement of the fourth inning, as if the crowd felt that what they had seen would be diluted by sitting through any more baseball that night.

But finally there were those few in the core of that immense circle—the participants themselves—who would be the ones most keenly touched: the pitcher, in this case a gap-toothed pleasant veteran named Al Downing who of the more than one hundred National League pitchers happened to be the one who threw a fast ball at a certain moment that did not tail away properly; the hitter, Henry Aaron himself, for whom the event, despite his grace in dealing with it, had become so traumatic that little in the instant was to be relished except the relief that it had been done; the Braves' sports announcer, whose imagination for months had been working up words to describe the event to the outside world; and a young bullpen pitcher who would reach in the air and establish contact with a ball whose value as baseball's greatest talisman had been monetarily pegged at $25,000 and whose sentimental value was incalculable....

THE HITTER

On occasion, as Henry Aaron sits in the Braves' dugout, he takes off his baseball cap and holds it close against his face. He moves it around until he is able to peer through one of the ventholes in the crown of the cap at the opposing pitcher on the mound. The practice, like focusing through a telescope, serves to isolate the pitcher, setting him apart in a round frame so that Aaron can scrutinize him and decide how he will deal with him once he reaches the plate.

The thought process he goes through during this is to decide what sort of pitch during his stand at the plate he will almost surely see... engraving this possibility in his mind's eye so that when the pitch comes (almost as if dictating what he wants) he can truly rip at it. Home-run hitters must invariably be "guessers," since their craft depends on seeing a pitch come down that they *expect*—so they have time to generate a powerful swing. More than one pitcher had said that Aaron seems to hop on a pitch as if he had called for it. Ron Perranoski, an ex-Dodger relief pitcher who in his first six seasons against Aaron held him to an .812 average (13 for 16), once said: "He not only knows what the pitch will be, but *where* it will be."

Aaron describes his mental preparation as a process of elimination. "Suppose a pitcher has three good pitches—a fast ball, a curve, and a slider. What I do, after a lot of consideration and analyzing and studying, is to eliminate two of those pitches, since it's impossible against a good pitcher to keep all three possibilities on my mind at the plate. So in getting rid of two, for example, I convince myself that I'm going to get a fast ball down low. When it comes, I'm ready. Now I can have guessed *wrong*, and if I've set my mind for a fast ball it's hard to do much with a curve, short of nibbling it out over the infield. But the chances are that I'll eventually get what I'm looking for."

The procedure of "guessing" has many variants. Roger Maris, for one, went up to the plate always self-prepared to hit a fast ball, feeling that he was quick enough to adjust to a different sort of pitch as it flew toward the plate. Most "guess" hitters play a cat-and-mouse game with the pitcher as the count progresses. What distinguishes Aaron's system is that once he makes up his mind what he will see during a time at bat he never deviates. He has disciplined himself to sit and wait for one sort of pitch whatever the situation.

One might suppose that a pitcher with a large repertoire of stuff would trouble Aaron—and that indeed turns out to be the case. He shakes his head when he thinks of Juan Marichal. "When he's at the prime of his game he throws a good fast ball, a good screwball, a good change-up, a good slider, a good you-have-it...and obviously the elimination system can't work; you can't throw out five or six different pitches in the hope of seeing one; the odds of seeing it would be too much against the batter."

What to do against a Marichal then? "It's an extra challenge," Aaron says. "I've just got to tune up my bat a little higher. It's a question of confidence, *knowing* that the pitcher cannot get me out four times without me hitting the ball sharply somewhere."

It is this confrontation between pitcher and hitter that fascinates Aaron, and indeed it is what he likes best about baseball—what he called "that damn good guessing game."

"So much of it has to do with concentration," Aaron explained to me. "On the day of a night game I begin concentrating at four in the afternoon. Just before I go to bat, from the on-deck circle, I can hear my little girl—she's 12 now—calling from the stands, 'Hey daddy! Hey, daddy!' After the game she says to me, 'Hey, you never look around, daddy, to wave.' Well, sometimes I look at her, I can't help it, but not too often. I'm looking at the pitcher. I'm thinking very hard about him."

His discipline is so extreme that not only does Aaron not hear anything when he gets to the plate, simply sealed in his vacuum of concentration, but his habits are so strictly adhered to that over the years he has never seen one of his home runs land in the stands. He is too busy getting down the first-base line.

I said I couldn't believe him. I must have sounded petulant about it because his brown eyes looked at me quickly.

"What I mean is," I said, "that I can't imagine denying oneself the pleasure of seeing the results of something like that. I mean it's like finishing a painting with one grand stroke of the brush and not stepping back to look at it."

I knew that most players do watch the home runs drop, at least the long ones, dawdling just out of the batter's box on that slow trot, the head turned. In the films of Bobby Thomson's Miracle home run in 1951 against the Dodgers in the playoffs at the Polo Grounds, it is quite apparent, his face in profile, that he glories in the drive going in; in fact, he does a small hop of delight halfway down the first-base line.

"Well, that's not what I'm supposed to do," Aaron was saying. "I've seen guys miss first base looking to see where the ball went. My job is to get down to first base and touch it. Looking at the ball going over the fence isn't going to help. I don't even look at the home runs in batting practice. No sense to break a good habit."

The odd thing about Aaron's attitude at the plate is that there is nothing to suggest any such intensity of purpose. His approach is slow and lackadaisical. He was called "Snowshoes" for a time by his teammates for the way he sort of pushes himself along. He carries his batting helmet on his way, holding two bats in the other hand. He stares out at the pitcher. He drops the extra bat. Then, just out of the batting box, resting his bat on the ground with the handle end balanced against his thighs, he uses both hands to jostle the helmet correctly into position. He steps into the box. Even here there is no indication of the kinetic possibility—none of the ferocious tamping of his spikes to get a good toehold that one remembers of Willie Mays, say, and the quick switching of his bat back and forth as he waits. Aaron steps into the batter's box as if he were going to sit down in it somewhere. His attitude is such that Robin Roberts, the Phillies pitcher, once explained, "That's why you can't fool Aaron. He falls asleep between pitches."

Jim Brosnan, ex-pitcher and author of the fine baseball chronicle *The Long Season*, once told me, "It was odd pitching to him. I always had a lot of confidence—perhaps because he walked up the way he did and because he stood so far away from the plate, just as far away as he could. That made you think that he wasn't fearless, which is good for a pitcher's morale. It looked as though he was giving away the outside of the plate to the pitcher, like he didn't want to stand in there and protect it. Still, I gave up two home runs to him. Funny, I don't remember one of them at all. I must have made a mistake, which I have made so many of that I tend to forget. But the other I remember because it was made off a perfect pitch, right in that classic spot where you're supposed to pitch to him, and he reached over, and those wrists of his snapped, and it was gone. I was so startled that I thought I'd thrown a bad pitch. When I got back to the dugout, I asked Hal Smith, who was my catcher, and he said right off that it could not have been improved on.

"I'm sure there're all sorts of stories like that. I remember once that Dick Sisler, the pitcher, came over to us from the American League in a winter trade and he sort of scoffed at those Aaron tales we told him. When you have someone like Aaron in your league you spend a lot of time bragging about him—perhaps so that when he hits a home run you can slough it off: 'I told you so; see?' Well, Sisler didn't believe any of this stuff. He kept telling us what it was like to pitch to Mickey Mantle, how *he* was the sort of guy who really scared you when he stood in the batter's box. Finally, in the exhibition season, Sisler got a chance to pitch to Aaron. The game was in Bradenton, Florida, and on Sisler's first pitch to him, a breaking ball, Aaron hit a foul line drive over the clubhouse, which is 450 feet away. It went out there on the line—just a terrible thing for any pitcher to see, even if it was foul. At the end of the inning Sisler came back to the dugout and he was saying, 'All right. All right. OK. OK'—like you say when you're convinced and you don't want to hear about it no more."

Dixie Walker, who was a Braves' batting coach at one time, and National League batting champion in 1944, used to stand in the shower and gaze at Aaron, his body glistening in the steam across the room, to try to figure out where this sort of power came from. "There's nothing you can tell by his size," he once said. "All I know is that he has the best wrists I've ever seen on a batter. He swings the bat faster than anyone else, it's as simple as that, and that's why the ball *jumps* the way it does."

That was what the baseball people marveled at when they talked about Aaron's batting—his wrists, the strength and quickness of them which produced a home-run trajectory like that of a good four-iron shot in golf—line drives quite unlike the towering lofty shots of a Mantle or Babe Ruth, whose blasts very often were coming straight down when they dropped out of the sky into the seats.

Bob Skinner, who coaches the Pittsburgh Pirates in the National League, once described the trajectory of an Aaron home run with convincing clarity: "The ball starts out on a line and the shortstop jumps for it, just over his fingertips, and then the left fielder jumps for it, just over *his* glove, and the ball keeps rising on that line and whacks up against the slats of a seat in the stands. The two fielders both figured they had a chance of catching that ball, except none of them realized how fast it was rising."

This reminds one, of course, of the famous hyperbolic description of a Rogers Hornsby home run which went between the pitcher's legs and kept on rising in a line over second base and then the center fielder and, for all I know, out over the center-field clock. But I have heard any number of players say they have seen infielders leap for an Aaron hit powered by those incredible wrists that went out on a line and landed beyond the wall.

THE PITCHER

The pitcher most usually identified with a personal disaster on the mound is Ralph Branca, the Dodger pitcher who gave up the famous Miracle home run to Bobby Thomson in the 1951 playoff game that won the Giants the pennant. He is an insurance salesman now, in Binghamton, New York, and I was able to reach him by phone up there. He didn't appear to mind talking about what had happened.

"In fact if you asked me if I could strike that home run out of my life, I would say No. I'd rather have been involved with that thing. It's been beneficial." He began talking about the instant itself. He told me that Thomson had hit a fast ball thrown high and in-side—what he intended as a waste pitch—hitting it with overspin, topping the ball slightly, and Branca kept crying inwardly, "Sink! Sink! Sink!" as he turned and watched the ball head for the seats. The motion pictures show him picking up the rosin bag behind the pitching rubber and throwing it down in disgust. Branca doesn't re-member doing this. He recalls the long walk to the clubhouse steps in deep center field, being hardly aware of the commotion going on around him as his inner voice blared in horror at what he had done.

"It's a long walk. I don't think anyone walked with me."

I said that I remembered an extraordinary photograph taken of him in the clubhouse in which he was lying in his uniform face down on a flight of steps as if his grief had laid him out stiff as a length of cordwood.

"Yes," he said. "Those were the steps in the locker room that led up to a sort of alcove with lockers along the wall. The picture was taken by Barney Stein, who was a *New York Post* photographer. He was a great Dodger fan. All the other photographers had rushed over to the Giants locker room but he had stayed. The picture he took *before* the one you've remembered won him a big award—the Pulitzer prize, I think. It showed me sitting on the steps with my head down and my hands up and my fingers laced like I was trying to shut it all out. One reporter was still behind with Barney and when he asked some bugging question, I rolled over to get away from him, flat out, and Barney snapped the picture. It looks like I've stumbled on the bottom step and fallen full length on the steps."

"All this time—what was going on in your mind?" I asked somewhat tentatively—it seemed like such an excruciating experience to lead him through despite the twenty-odd years' lapse...

"I've described it, of course..." he said wearily.

"Yes."

"I kept wondering why it had happened to *me.* 'Why me? Why me?' I kept asking. I was a gung-ho all-American boy then. I lived the best life I could. I didn't drink or mess around. So I sat there and said to myself that there was no justice in life. I remember dressing finally and walking out to the parking lot where my fiancée was waiting in the car with Father Pat Rawley, who was a dean at Fordham University. My fiancée saw me coming and burst into tears. I got into the car and I said, 'Why me? Why did it have to happen to me?' I really was frantic to know. Father Rawley leaned over the back seat and reminded me what Christ had realized from God: that He had been given the cross because He had a strong enough faith to bear it.

"That was quite a dramatic moment, the three of us in that car in that enormous empty parking lot. It made me feel better, of course, but it took a time. That night we went out for dinner with Rube Walker and his wife at the Derby Steakhouse, up past the Concourse, and I remember we had a helluva good steak, but not much conversation. It lasted for a while. Crazy people called up my family and shouted into the phone, why hadn't they taught their son how to pitch."

"And nothing now? It hasn't marked you?"

"Oh, every once in a while in a bar somebody'll say, 'Hell, there's Ralph Branca,' and some other guy will come up with a grin, 'Hey, how's Bobby Thomson?' Now what the hell am I supposed to do about that? Fall over in a faint?"

He went on to say that he felt others—not only fans, but fellow ballplayers—were far more affected by what had happened in the Polo Grounds than he was. The reverberation of the disaster resulted in a near-paranoid reaction in the Dodger organization. Branca, who wanted to wear number 13 the following spring, a number he had always been partial to, was not allowed to use it. The front office came up with all sorts of strange computations. They pointed out that the Thomson home run had been hit off him on the third day of the tenth month, which added up to thirteen, and no sirree, he wasn't going to be allowed to wear *that* number. But the main thing, according to Branca, was that he was *stared* at by everyone as if they half expected him to collapse in his tracks under the weight of what he had gone through. The result was that he began to press on the mound under this sort of scrutiny, and his confidence waned. His back began to hurt him; he tried to pitch through the pain; then his arm began to give him trouble and quickly his skills suffered, never to recover. He left baseball at the age of 31 in 1957 after mediocre turns with the Detroit Tigers (where he wore number 35) and with the Yankees (where he wore number 25).

"Wherever I went I asked for 13," he told me. "But they always said no. If I had my druthers I'd still want 13. Or 44."

"Aaron's number."

"Yup. I always liked that number."

I said that I could not understand how he felt that the Thomson home run had been beneficial in any way—he had just recited a most melancholy saga.

"It was an albatross for a long time," he said. "But on the other hand I'm recognized. Why if I walked down the street with Bobby Thomson I think more people would recognize me."

I asked him why.

"Well, I think they're more interested in me," he said. "They look at me and wonder if I'm all right. I went through that terrible thing. What did it do to me? It's not that they appreciate a loser. But they're curious about how a man's difficulties affect him—it's awfully close to their own lives, and it makes them feel better to see that someone can go through that and walk around and smile and function. They want reassurances.

"And of course it's good for my business, which is with the Security Mutual Life here in Binghamton. When I pick up the phone and say, 'I'm Ralph Branca,' the person on the other end says, 'Oh?' and he'll want me to drop around and talk about baseball. That's fine with me. After a while I can get the talk shifted around to insurance. Sometimes it takes quite a while."

When we'd finished talking, I remembered sitting back and thinking what a taxing profession baseball was—never forgiving its major sinners, or forgetting them. Their reputations were stamped irrevocably with their misfortune—as if a debt to society had been incurred which could never, under any circumstances, be absolved. Just as the Cincinnati series got underway, an obituary about an old ballplayer appeared in the *New York Times* under the headline FRED SNODGRASS DIES: BALLPLAYER MUFFED 1912 FLY. The article began "Fred Carlisle Snodgrass, who muffed an easy fly ball that helped cost the New York Giants the 1912 World Series, died Friday at the age of 86." Snodgrass had gone on to great things after he retired from baseball: he was a successful banker and rancher, the mayor of Oxnard, California—which was related in the obituary for sure, but unrelentingly the obituary writer came back to dwell on the indiscretion committed during the course of a second or so on a summery afternoon some sixty years before. "Mr. Snodgrass made a two-base muff of pinch hitter Clyde Engle's easy [note that Snodgrass is not let off with an unmodified "fly"—it is an "easy" chance] pop fly to set up the tying run. One man walked and another singled, driving in Mr. Engle to tie the game and put the winning run on third. A long outfield fly scored the winning run. He is survived by his widow, Josephine; two daughters," etc. . . .

Al Downing had realized during the Cincinnati series that he was to pitch the opener in Atlanta, that he would be providing the model for Thomas Wolfe's grand description: ". . . the pitcher who stands out there all alone, calm, desperate, and forsaken in his isolation." The notion did not bother Downing overly. Now a veteran of long service, he is not an overpowering pitcher, but he has great confidence, relying on perfect control and a good change of pace.

Watching him pitch in his early days with the New York Yankees a lot of people were reminded of Whitey Ford—"Blackie Ford," the press sometimes called him. He had an easy motion out of which flashed a tremendous whippy fast ball and he led the league in strikeouts in 1964. Then, throwing a curve ball to Andy Etchebarren of the Baltimore Orioles, something popped in his arm, and at the age of 27 he sagged back into the New York farm system to try to get his arm in shape. He was finally traded to Oakland, then Milwaukee, who traded him to the Los Angeles Dodgers for a player named Andy Kosco. With the Dodgers he found his form, a different kind of pitcher, but a very effective one. His teammates call him "Ace"— an encomium for winning 20 games in 1971. He is also called "Gentleman Al" for his bearing not only off the field but around the mound where he behaves, as Vince Scully, the Los Angeles announcer, has pointed out, "like a man wearing a bowler hat." He is very much his own boss, shaking off his catcher's signs as many as 25 pitches a game, and relying on his own concepts, and always on his sense that much of pitching is "feel." ("If you don't 'feel' you can throw a curve at a particular time, there's not much point in trying.") He is such a student of his craft that he always made it a point to room with a hitter, rare in a society in which there is such a confrontation between the two specialists.

We got talking about it in the locker room before the game. He said, "It helps a pitcher to be exposed to the enemy camp. For years I roomed with Maury Wills and it helped my pitching considerably just listening to him talk about hitting. At the very best I knew if I ever had to pitch to him—if either of us was traded away—that I knew something of his thought process as a batter and might be able to take advantage of it.

"Aaron? Well, I'm not sure that rooming with him for ten years would really help. You can have all the know-how, but if you make one small mistake there's no one in the league who can take advantage of it like he does. He knows what I can throw. He hit two home runs off me last year. But I'm not going to change my pattern. I mustn't go against what I've been successful with...I shouldn't re-arrange pitches that complement each other."

"You mean you'd never try to fool him with something different?" I asked.

"Well, sometimes you throw a pitch just in the hope of getting some idea of what the hitter is thinking...like an off-speed pitch out of the strike zone...just to see how he reacts. By the way the batter anticipates, the pitcher can tell if he's looking for a fast ball—he'll be way out in front of it. And that tells the pitcher something, and he can go on from there. Of course, sometimes the batter will purposefully fool you, 'decoy' you, we call it. Willie Mays was very good at this. He'd look completely fooled by an off-speed pitch, practically fall *down* he'd be so far out in front; so the pitcher'd think, 'Well, now, maybe I can throw him another.' But this time Mays, who was praying he'd fooled the pitcher into doing it, well, his face'd light up to see that ball drifting up to him, and he'd time it right and spank it out of there. Mays was very good at that.

"My theory is that you *have* to go with what the best is that you have. Aaron knows what I know. He knows what I'd *like* to throw to him, and perhaps he'll dig in and wait for it. Now I can change speeds and move the ball around, but both he and I know that the sinking ball, low and outside, is what is going to give him the most trouble. I cannot throw that out of the arsenal because he expects it of me. I'm going to challenge him with it."

Some pitchers had come up with extreme notions of how to pitch to Aaron. Sal Maglie, who was a pitcher of blazing malevolence, had said, "The only way I could handle Aaron was to get his face in the dirt. Then he'd be edgy and I could work on him. Not always, but sometimes. It was the only way I could pitch to him."

Downing, of course, didn't have the disposition of a Maglie. He was going to meet Aaron on his own terms, and I was reminded of the latter's confident dictum that he felt he ultimately had the advantage over the pitcher. "I've got a bat, and all *he's* got is a ball. I figure that gives me the edge."

So I asked Downing if he had any superstitions.

"Six runs," he said. "Six runs in the first inning." The gap between his two front teeth showed as he grinned. "That's the best one. Look," he said more seriously, "if I throw 715 I'm not going to run and hide. There's no disgrace in that. On the other hand I'm not going to run into the plate to congratulate him. It's a big home run for him, for the game, for the country, but not for me!"

THE RETRIEVER

There was hardly a fan who turned up in the Atlanta Stadium left-field seats that night who did not firmly believe that he was going to catch the Aaron home run. Many of them brought baseball gloves. A young Atlantan from the Highway Department had established himself in the front row wielding a 15-foot-long bamboo pole with a fishnet attached. He was proficient with it, sweeping it back and forth over the Braves' bullpen. He had started coming to the ball park the previous season. He told me that at home his stepsister tossed up baseballs over the winter for him to practice on. The closest he had come to catching anything in the ball park with his gear had been a batting-practice home run hit into the bullpen enclosure the year before by a catcher named Freddie Valasquez. He missed sweeping it in by a couple of feet.

The left-field stands of Atlanta Stadium contain the cheapest seats in the ball park and perhaps its more knowledgeable and intractable fans. They have a close affinity with Aaron. He stands immediately in front of them when the Braves are in the field, and they look down at the big red-trimmed blue 44 on the back of his uniform and watch the way he rests his oversized glove ("These days I need all the glove I can get") on his hip between pitches. They rise and cheer him when he walks out to his position, and he lifts his throwing hand in an awkward, shy gesture to acknowledge them.

The Braves' outfield is bordered by a high wire-mesh fence which runs around the perimeter of the grass. In the space between it and the high wall of the stands are the two bullpens. The visitors' bullpen is in the right-field corner. The Braves' mascot, Chief Nok-A-Homa, sits in his tepee on the left-field foul line, adjacent to the Atlanta bullpen, and when a Braves' batter hits a home run he steps out in his regalia and does a war dance. The Braves' bullpen is immediately under the left-field wall; the fans with front-row seats can look down and see the catchers resting their right knees on towels to keep their pants legs from getting dusty as they warm up the relief pitchers.

The Braves' bullpen array was the weakest in either league last year (the reason that the Braves, despite a Murderers' Row of Darrell Evans, Aaron, Dusty Baker, Mike Lum, and Dave Johnson, who last year broke Rogers Hornsby's home-run record for second basemen, were not pennant contenders), and the left-field fans have the same sort of despairing affection for the relievers that Mets fans had for their team in its early bleak days. "We *know* the pitchers out here," one fan told me. "In the expensive part of the stadium they never see them long enough to get acquainted. They go in and they're bombed and they're on their way to the showers which are kept going full and heavy. They never turn off the showers once the starting pitcher is knocked out."

The main reason, of course, for sitting in the left-field corner is that the majority of Aaron's home runs are pulled toward there, either to reach the stands, or to land in the enclosure where a denizen of the bullpen or Chief Nok-A-Homa will retrieve it. Nok-A-Homa says he has seen every home run Aaron has hit in Atlanta Stadium since 1969 with the exception of number 698, which he missed because he was trying to find a chair for one of the bullpen pitchers. He has not retrieved an Aaron home run since 671, being too busy doing his celebratory foot-stomping dance, but being brisk of foot himself and outfitted with a lacrosse stick for additional reach he saw himself as a possible retriever should 715 drop in the enclosure.

Chief Nok-A-Homa's true name is Levi Walker. His Indian blood is Ottawa-Chippewa. He gets paid $8,500 a year by the Braves for what he does—his personal appearances around Georgia on their behalf, his war dance on the pitcher's mound before each game, his whooping exhortations, echoing loonlike among the empty blue seats, and for driving the bullpen pitchers through a gate in the outfield fence to the mound in a 1929 Model A Ford equipped with a modern 283 Chevelle engine with automatic transmission ("It's not a bad car though the front end is a little squirrelly"). A year or so back someone (undoubtedly a member of the bullpen crew) put a smoke bomb under the hood which went off halfway to the pitcher's mound and enveloped the car in such a thick cloud that Chief Nok-A-Homa revolved in it a few times before a gust of wind blew enough away so he could get straightened out.

It was not his first experience at the hands of saboteurs. In 1969 his tepee caught fire during a game against the St. Louis Cardinals. Nok-A-Homa has always suspected Joe Torre, the Cardinals' first baseman. The fire was a brisk one and burned out about a third of the tepee despite Nok-A-Homa's desperate attempts to stamp it out with a horsehide shield and then a broom as a helpful rain of beer, Coke and grape was poured down from the ledge above by fans.

His tepee was quite well appointed before the fire. It had a carpet, a small air conditioner, a portable radio, and a folding chair for the chief to relax in when his limbs were weary from supporting him in a semilotus position in front of the tepee door, or he was tired of war-crying.

He is constantly hollering at the opposing left fielder in the hope of causing a lapse of some sort. He told me that he felt he had finally succeeded with one outfielder, Ken Henderson of the San Francisco Giants. "The physical signs are there," he told me. "You can see by the crick in the neck and the way he kicks little stones that he is very aware of someone behind him."

I asked him how he felt he had a chance at catching the ball.

He said that he felt that his chances for the ball were excellent. "I've got my old lacrosse stick. Now, I don't want to hurt none of them, but I'll guarantee I'll be among them. I'm *tall* with that stick."

"Are you frightened that someone might topple down on you from the stands?"

"That's a possibility," Nok-A-Homa said. "A couple of years back we had some drunken fan from Chicago who took a wild leap from the stands trying to get a ball. He broke his back."

There was little doubt there would be mayhem if the ball landed up in the stands. Last year, the Braves' officials told me, a man named A. W. Kirby from Old Hickory, Tennessee, sprinted down an aisle, dove over a chair, and after suffering a broken fingernail and lacerated wrists and ankles in a tremendous scuffle came up with home run 693. He thought the ball was worth $1,700. His son had misinformed him.

The abrasions and thumps suffered in the pileup over 715 would be worth it. The official high was $25,000 (the anonymous Venezuelan fan had been matched by Sammy Davis, Jr., though rumors abounded that even higher offers had come in). The retriever would be photographed giving it back to Aaron, and his or her face would shine out of the country's sports pages, and even if on the periphery, he would know something of the excitement of being touched by the moment.

Eventually the prize would go to the Hall of Fame at Cooperstown, New York (even the big-money bidders had promised this, though no one was positive about the Venezuelan), to join other great talismans of baseball history under their domes of glass—among others Roger Maris's 61st and Babe Ruth's 714th, each with the name of the retriever included.

There are a couple of astonishing things about Ruth's last home run—among others, that it was ever recovered at all. I looked it all up. It was the *third* he hit on that day (May 25, 1935), and it was the first hit completely out of Forbes Field since its construction in 1909, an accomplishment which stood until the 1950s when Ted Beard, a Pirate outfielder, was the first of a select few, including Willie Stargell who did it a couple of times, to join him.

The Pirate pitcher on the mound that day against the Boston

Braves (with whom Ruth was finishing his career as a ballplayer) was Guy Bush, who had come in to relieve the starter, Red Lucas, off whom Ruth had hit the first of his trio. Bush now lives on a farm in Mississippi. I managed to find his phone number and called him up to chat about Ruth.

It turned out he had pitched to Ruth twice before—both times in the 1932 Yankees-Cubs World Series (the one in which Ruth hit his fabled "called-shot" home run into the center-field bleachers). In the opener of that series Bush said that he had retired Ruth (he referred to him as "the Big Bamboo") on his first two times at bat. He got him to hit soft ground balls. But then George Sewall ("a lil' ol' fellah raised down here in the South") hit a drive back through the pitcher's box that busted open the index finger of Bush's right hand and forced his removal from the game.

So it was not until late in the series that he faced Ruth again. This time Bush decided to start off by low-decking him.

"Why did you want to do that?" I asked.

"I had no respect for *any* batter," Bush told me. In the background, over the phone, I could hear the murmur of what sounded like a local television news broadcast. Bush raised his voice: "I wanted no part of any of them, Ruth included. I never spoke to an opposing player for the ten years I played in the major leagues 'cept to shout at 'em from the top step of the dugout. None of them liked me, sir, if you want to know the truth about it."

"So you knocked Ruth down?"

"I throwed to *scare* him. He couldn't get out of the way and I hit him on the arm. I'm sorry of it now. I'd like to take that pitch back."

"He didn't react in any way?"

"Well, he got to second base on an infield out. There was some sort of time-out and he walked halfway to the pitcher's mound. He called to me, 'Hey, *Bush*'—and he said 'Bush' like he was referring to a bush-league player—'if you're going to *hit* anyone, put something on it.'"

A dry chuckle rose from that distant TV set, a man's hollow-sounding laugh at some unheard joke.

"I never answered him," Bush was saying. "Like I told you, sir, I never spoke to anyone on an opposing team—all those years."

"How did one pitch to him?" I asked.

"The book was to keep moving the ball around the plate and you might be lucky. In Pittsburgh, there in Forbes Field that last game in 1935, I threw him a screwball the first time he came up against me, low and outside. He swung and missed it by 18 inches. Well, sir, he missed it by so much that I thought maybe he had a blind spot and that maybe he couldn't *see* a ball thrown there. Well, that was very exciting. So I threw the same pitch in the same spot and he swung and came very near killing my second baseman.

"The next time I decided to throw a slow curve. Well, sir, I threw the slow curve and he hit this little Chinese home run down the right-field line which was no distance at all, 20 feet back into the stands for his second of the day. He'd hit his first off Lucas. That made me so mad that when he came up again at the back end of the game I called Tommy Padden, my catcher, out to the mound, and I said, 'Tommy, I don't think the Big Bamboo can hit my fast ball.' I *didn't* think so, sir. He had a stance at the plate where he near had his back to the pitcher; he was so far turned around that I could see the number 3 on his uniform; I didn't think the monkey could come around quick enough on my fast ball to get his bat on it. So I told Tommy that I was going to challenge him with the fast ball. In fact, I told Tommy to go back and *tell* the Big Bamboo what I was going to do, that I was going to *damn* him to hit my fast ball. That's how confident I was. Now Tommy Padden has passed away, poor soul, and I can't tell you for sure whether he told the Bamboo what I was going to do. But I can tell you this, sir, that I threw two fast balls and he hit the second one for the longest ball I ever saw. It cleared those whole three decks, and I was too surprised to be mad anymore."

As for Roger Maris's 61st home run, that was caught by a young truck driver named Sal Durante. He saw the ball begin its ride, and he hopped up on his seat (number 3 in box 163D in section 33 of Yankee Stadium) and made a one-hand grab. He shouted, "I got it! I got it!" and was immediately engulfed by a tide of fans trying to wrest the ball away. The ball was worth $5,000 to him, put up by a West Coast restaurateur to buy the ball for Maris. It was a pleasant windfall for Durante (who was going to present the ball to Maris anyway) and made his stadium seat, according to the *New York Times* the next day, the most "profitable in baseball history."

Durante got married soon after he caught the ball. The $5,000 proceeds came in very handy. He had to deliver the ball to the Sacramento restaurateur in person to pick up his money. He was so petrified he might lose the ball that he thought of sending it to Sacramento by registered mail.

"If I lose the ball, it's all over for us," he said at the time.

I had found his phone number through the Yankees (who sent him season tickets for a couple of years after the event) and called him up to see how he had fared since. He told me that catching Maris's home run ranked along with his marriage and the births of his children (he has three) as the most exciting moment of his life. It hadn't marked him with much good luck though (he'd tried to make a go of it in Florida, but hadn't, and was out of work when I called him), but the home run was good to think back on, and sometimes things came of it. When the Seattle Exposition opened in 1962, the promoters asked him to come out and try to catch a ball dropped from the Space Needle by Tracy Stallard, who had given up the home run to Maris and was there playing for a minor-league club called the Seattle

Rainiers. Durante was to get $1,000 if he caught the ball. Dropping it from the Space Needle proved to be too dangerous; speculation was that Durante might be driven into the ground like a spike. So Tracy Stallard went up in a Ferris wheel about 100 feet or so, and after five practice drops which Durante caught cleanly, the circle of photographers got their gear set and the official toss was signaled.

Durante dropped it!

"I blew it and couldn't believe it," he told me. "The glove they gave me wasn't the best and the ball bounced off the heel. Of course, you must realize," he said, "that I hadn't had much practice..."

THE ANNOUNCER

The NBC crew was on hand (Curt Gowdy, Tony Kubek, and Joe Garagiola) and so was Vince Scully, the Dodger announcer for the past 25 years, broadcasting the game back to Los Angeles. Through their combined media, over 35 million people would see or hear the instant but now had a more personal involvement than Milo Hamilton; being with the Braves he was the only broadcaster in the country who had known for months that at some point he would be describing Aaron's historic home run—which made his situation enviable for a sports broadcaster. While he had to verbalize instantly into a microphone what he saw, in the case of Aaron's great home run, since it was inevitable, Hamilton had a chance to prepare a sentence so perfect that if it worked, if enough people heard it and commented on it, it had a fine chance to slip into Bartlett's Quotations alongside "One small step..." etc.

I was intrigued by the possibility. We talked about it quite a lot. Hamilton told me that he wasn't going to work at anything very ornate, but that he certainly had something planned. He wouldn't tell me what it was. I asked him if he would write the sentence down and slip it into an envelope which I wouldn't open until after the home run had been hit. No, he said, he'd as soon keep it to himself.

I looked into Bartlett's Quotations myself to see if I could find anything that might inspire Hamilton in his search. As phrases to drop into the general hubbub of exaltation I rather liked Cicero's "What a time! What a civilization!" and Horace's "This day I've lived!" My favorite was an extension of William Wordsworth: "There's not a man who lives who hath not known his godlike hours—and here is Aaron's!" I resisted handing them on to Hamilton.

Milo Hamilton has a small cherubic face out of which one might expect a choirboy's voice; instead, he rumbles in the orotund throatal tones of the true broadcaster, which a friend of mine in the television industry refers to as a "four-ball" voice. It was hard not to be solemn, equipped with such a voice. His earliest idol as he grew up in Iowa was Bob Elson, who broadcast the Chicago White Sox games for almost 40 years—a span which had seen (Hamilton felt) a drift from straight reporting to showmanship. "I like to think of myself as a meld of the professionalism of Bob Elson and the enthusiasm of Harry Caray, the sportscaster for the White Sox." He had told me that he had especially hoped that 715 would be hit in Atlanta. "We have a television blackout for home games, so I'll be on radio. On radio a sportscaster really has to paint a picture, and it's always been one of my great rewards that I get a lot of praise from blind people."

The other man on the broadcast team was Ernie Johnson—a former pitcher for the Braves during the "good" years in the mid-fifties, a New Englander with a somewhat more folksy, down-to-earth quality than Hamilton. By chance he was on the radio when Aaron hit home runs 500, 600, and 700—much to Hamilton's dismay. The regular procedure on radio had been for Hamilton to hand over the microphone for the third and seventh innings, and it was during these innings that Aaron hit those monumental home runs.

It was a cause of considerable merriment among the Braves' management, and indeed with listeners, to note Hamilton's care not to be caught short again. Since the 700th home run, if Aaron happened to come to bat in the third or seventh inning, Ernie Johnson's voice would suddenly give way to Milo Hamilton's familiar oratory. One could imagine a struggle up in the booth between the two of them over the microphone, hauling it back and forth between them, but Johnson was not only the junior partner but resigned, and rather phlegmatic about the situation.

Hamilton, on the other hand, feels that his entire career has been building toward the instant of Aaron's 715th. He has already had some climactic games to describe. They include a pair of no-hitters, one by Toothpick Sam Jones in May 1955, who walked the first three Pirate batters he faced in the ninth inning and had to talk manager Stan Hack, who stood on the pitcher's mound reaching for the ball, out of removing him; he stayed in to strike out the side. The other no-hitter was pitched by the Braves' knuckleballer, Phil Niekro; Hamilton still remembers his exact wording over the air as the last man up grounded a ball into the infield: "If he gets the man at first, it's a no-hitter *(pause)*. And it *is!*"

I asked him if that had been prearranged—if he had decided on that conceit if it happened he should describe a no-hitter.

He said not at all—that spontaneity was always the key to sports-casting. "It's very much my cup of tea. It has to be everybody's."

A consideration of important moments in sports reporting would bear him out. The most common characteristic, since the description is made under pressure and against the crowd noise, is that key sentences are often repeated, such as the flurry of repetitions when Russ Hodges, ordinarily a somewhat low-keyed sportscaster, gave his on-the-spot report of Bobby Thomson's "miracle of Coogan's Bluff" home run in the Dodger-Giant play-off game in 1951: "The Giants win the pennant! The Giants win the pennant!

The Giants win the pennant! The Giants win the pennant! I don't believe it! I don't believe it! I DO NOT BELIEVE IT!"

Describing the extraordinary home run of Ted Williams in his last time at bat in the majors (as neat a punctuation to his career as an exclamation point) Curt Gowdy had a brace of repeated sentences: "It's got a chance! It's got a chance! And it's gone..." all of this, in fact, in somewhat restrained fashion since in an earlier inning Williams had hit a long fly ball which Gowdy described as if it were going into the seats; he did not want to be fooled again.

Phil Rizzuto, the Yankee sportscaster, had a quasi-opportunity much like Hamilton's to prepare for Roger Maris's 61st home run, which was a strong possibility though hit on the last day of the season. Obviously, he did not do so, since his radio commentary, utilizing his favorite epithet, was absolutely predictable. "Holy cow!" he cried. "That's gonna be it."

Red Barber remembers that when he was broadcasting the famous Cookie Lavagetto double that destroyed Yankee Bill Bevens's no-hitter in the 1947 World Series, he described the high drive and how it hit the fence, and here came the tying run and now the winning run, and here was Lavagetto being mobbed by his own teammates, and near beaten-up, and then Barber gave a sigh, worn out by all the drama, and he said memorably, "Well, I'll be a suck-egg mule."

Television broadcasting, obviously, gives the announcer a better chance to drop in a *bon mot,* since the picture on the set, if the technicians are on their toes, portrays so much. When Barber was the television commentator on the day that Roger Maris broke Ruth's 60-home-runs-in-a-year record, he started out, "It's a high fly ball..." and he paused, noting on the TV monitor that the flight of the ball was clearly shown, and then remembering that a Los Angeles restaurateur had offered a large sum of money for the ball, he announced when it dropped into the stands: "It's 61 and $5,000!"

I spoke to a number of sportscasters about describing the Aaron home run. Joe Garagiola was in Atlanta. He said what he felt many announcers would do: let the crowd take over. He told me about broadcasting Mickey Mantle's 500th home run, over which there had been considerable buildup and hoopla. When he heard the "awful" sound of the ball hitting the bat (as a former catcher Garagiola was acutely responsive to that doom-ridden sound—"awful" was how he described it) he cried "It's gone!" and backed off the microphone and let the huge crowd roar dramatize the moment. Afterward people came up to tell him to his astonishment, "Boy, what a great job you did on that home run. Wow!"

I asked him about Milo Hamilton's thought of preparing a deathless phrase.

"I don't see how you can prepare anything... 'a giant step for the horsehide'... No, I don't think so."

Howard Cosell said it was not his method either. When I telephoned him, I started by asking him if he ever constructed a dramatic scene in his mind, a superlative round in a heavyweight championship, say, and practiced by pretending to be on hand doing the play-by-play announcing. He said that no, he didn't. Frankly he never thought of himself as a play-by-play announcer. He spoke with some testiness, as if I had irked him by suggesting that he had anything to do with play-by-play. He was what he referred to as a "reporter-commentator."

"The play-by-play announcer is a parrot," he went on. "He performs only slightly more of a function than the public-address announcer. 'A bouncing ball to short... the throw across to first...' what else is there to say. In television the play-by-play announcer is becoming obsolete."

"If you were broadcasting on radio, how would you describe the Aaron home run?" I asked.

"The noise and excitement of the crowd will carry that instant," Cosell replied, affirming what Garagiola had said. "What I would probably do—of course it depends on the *feel* of the moment—is to comment on the growth of Aaron the man as well as Aaron the baseball player. I'd splice in my memories—Aaron's relationship with his managers—Bobby Bragan and Eddie Mathews, and how riding back from Ebbets Field with Jackie Robinson one day, I heard him say that number 44 would one day be a greater player than he or Willie Mays but that he had no feeling for him as a *man*. Finally, before he died, he *did*, you know—Robinson could see that Aaron was coming out of the shell, the shyness which was really the reason he was so obscure despite his brilliance... and beginning to *try*, at least, to deal with the issues that Robinson felt every black was compelled to. The growth of Aaron as a person—that's the sort of thing I would have dealt with."

The other broadcaster I talked to in the pressroom on the evening of the game was Vince Scully. He is the Los Angeles Dodgers' "voice" and has been so for the last 25 years... in fact so long that he said as we sat down over coffee that he felt like a man who's observed everything, seen Halley's comet—at least as far as baseball was concerned, and was running out of records to watch set.

"I've seen Maury Wills beat Ty Cobb's base-stealing record; Don Drysdale's 56 consecutive scoreless innings streak. Every time I saw Hoyt Wilhelm pitch he was extending Cy Young's old record of number of pitching appearances. Larsen's perfect game..."

"What did you say when he threw the final pitch?" I asked.

"Larsen? Yes. To Dale Mitchell. A called strike. I cried out: 'Perfect game!!'"

"Was that the most dramatic?"

Scully shook his head. "The only time I ever got carried away and became rather ultraformal was in 1955 when the Dodgers finally won the World Series." Scully leaned back. "'Pee Wee Reese straightens up to throw... ladies and gentlemen, the Brooklyn Dodgers are the champions of the world!'"

A number of the press craned around to look at us. His voice had boomed out into the room.

"But that wasn't prepared," he told me, leaning in across the table. "That was pure emotion."

Curt Gowdy, the head of the NBC broadcast crew, had a different reason for not cluttering up the mind with key phrases.

"What every sportscaster is truly scared of is anticipating something that doesn't happen," he said. "Why, suppose the Aaron homer starts going out and the guy unleashes the great sentence he's been working on for two months and the ball ends up in an outfielder's glove. It happens more than you think. I won't ever be *allowed* to forget a tremendous hit that was slugged by Hoot Evers with the bases loaded in Shibe Park in Philadelphia in 1952...just soaring for the upper deck, and I could see Gus Zernial, the outfielder, watching it go with his hands on his hips practically, and that's the way you tell— watch the fielder—and I shouted, 'There it goes! A grand slammer!'

"Something happened to it up there—a gust of wind, perhaps, that knocked it down like a dying bird, and Gus Zernial, who told me later that he was almost as surprised as I was, put his glove up and hauled it in. Well, I had to retract. I told them, 'Fans, I really blew it,' and Tom Yawkey, who owned the Red Sox, kidded me for five years about that.

"Well, that's the sort of thing that absorbs the mind of the sportscaster. He hasn't got the capacity to carry prepared phrases around in his mind if he's got that sort of responsibility to worry about."

All the broadcasters seem to have had disasters of this sort. Mel Allen once told me about describing a tremendous drive Mickey Mantle hit out over the bleachers which he felt had been slugged hard enough to carry out of Yankee Stadium—for the first time ever—and losing sight of it as it started to drop from its enormous height he watched to see if the people in the bleachers scrambled for it. Nobody moved. Heads were looking back. That was enough for Allen. He cried: "It's out of the ball park—first time in history!!"

But it turned out that a man sitting with his back to the wall had caught the ball as he sat there—catching it cleanly (and with considerable aplomb, one would assume, without moving a jot on his bleacher seat) so that the quick rush of scramblers which would indicate to Allen that the ball was still in the park never occurred.

Sometimes the reverse happens. Charley Jones, who is the chief Cincinnati Reds announcer, once got caught on what he described as a routine fly ball ("there's a fly ball to right field") which suddenly landed deep in the pavilion and Jones was forced to shift gears abruptly in his commentary.

I told Milo Hamilton about these conversations—that all his peers felt that prearranging anything was *suspect,* to say the least. Hamilton said that he was certainly tempted to agree with them, and *would* ordinarily, but that on his speaking tour that past winter he realized that so much curiosity was being generated by what he was going to say at the climactic moment that he felt bound to work something up.

In the evenings he would sit around and let his imagination take over; as he watched the Aaron home run arch into the seats, his lips murmured; the sentences formed; the facts crowded his mind, especially the similarities between Aaron and Babe Ruth...that both were born just a day apart in February, both hitting the 714th home run at the same age (40) and both as members of the Braves' organization. He had toyed with the idea of announcing much of this material as Aaron circled the bases after hitting 715, using each base as marker along the way ("...he steps on *second*...and the Babe's great record, nearly twoscore years old...and he steps on *third*...a great day for Aquarians! Both Henry and the Babe...").

"And the big sentence?" I asked. "Just as he whacks it."

"I'm not going to tell you. You'll have to wait and see."

THE HITTER

Aaron came up for the second time in the fourth inning. He had yet to swing the bat off his shoulder at a ball. Downing's first pitch was a change-up that puffed in the dirt in front of the plate. The umpire, Satch Davidson, looked at it suspiciously through the bars of his mask and tossed it out. He signaled to Frank Pulli, the first-base umpire, to throw in another of the specially marked balls, this one identified with a 12, stamped twice in invisible ink, and two 2's. Downing polished it up a bit, turned, and as the clock on the scoreboard showed 9:07 he wheeled and delivered a fast ball, aiming low and expecting it to tail away on the outside corner.

The ball rose off Aaron's bat in the patented trajectory of his long hits, ripping out over the infield, the shortstop instinctively bending his knees as if he could leap for it, and it headed for deep left center field.

From behind the plate Satch Davidson leaned over the catcher Joe Ferguson's shoulder, and as the two stood up to watch the flight of the ball going out, the umpire said, "Fergie, that might be it." The catcher said, "I think so too."

Out in left center field Jimmy Wynn, who often plays with a toothpick working in his mouth, and Bill Buckner converged on the ball. The pair of them had a vague hope that if the ball was going over, somehow Buckner was going to scale the fence and get to the ball before anyone else; he would toss it back over the fence, and the two of them were going to split the reward. Afterward, his toothpick whisking busily in his mouth, Wynn admitted that the two of them would doubtless have given the ball to Aaron: "We wanted him to get it over with, so he could be a human being again."

At the time, though, Buckner made a leap up the fence, scaling up it with his spikes in the wire mesh until, spread-eagled for an instant like a gigantic moth against a screen door, he saw that he had no chance, and he dropped back down.

Aaron never saw the ball clear the fence. As he had done those countless times, he looked toward first base as he ran, dropping his bat neatly just off the base path, and when he saw the exultation of the first-base coach, Jim Busby, he knew for sure that the long chase was over.

THE ANNOUNCER

I found Milo Hamilton the next day in the ball park. That morning the *Atlanta Constitution* had published a transcript of Curt Gowdy describing the home run over NBC television. It ended:

> ... There's a long drive... the ball's hit deep... deep... and it's gone! He did it. Henry Aaron is the all-time home-run leader now.

I had looked through the paper but could not find any transcript of Hamilton's words. I thought Gowdy's were fine, if somewhat functional. Of course, on television he would be letting the picture speak for the event.

"Well, what was it?" I asked Hamilton. "You promised to tell me."

We sat in his office with its window that looked down on the diamond—what Thomas Wolfe had called "the velvet and unalterable geometry of the playing field." What a good phrase *that* was.

"It didn't work out quite the way I'd planned," Hamilton said. "First of all, the sequence of comparing Ruth and Aaron as Henry circled the bases was wiped out. I'd wanted to use the bases as touchstones in his career..."

"I remember," I said.

"But it was obviously going to be impossible. There wasn't time.

Aaron circled the bases too quickly! He's not one to slow down and glory in his occasion. And then there was the tremendous crowd noise and the burst of fireworks above the center-field rim. Pretty hard to do much with that going on."

"What about the big sentence at the moment of impact?" I asked.

"Well, for home run number 714 I decided on 'Henry has tied the Babe!' That's what I said in Cincinnati. As for 715, the tie breaker, I came up with..."

"Yes?"

"'Baseball has a new home-run king! It's Henry Aaron!'"

"Oh."

"You look disappointed."

"Well, not really," I said, admitting to myself that while the phrase was not earthshaking (or in the case of the latter, especially grammatical) anything else would have sounded hollow and forced.

"The fact is I didn't even say what I wanted to say. The tapes show that I said, 'It's 715! There's a new home-run *champion*...'"

"I thought it was going to be a 21-gun-salute kind of thing, '*mirabile dictu!*'—something like that."

"Say again."

What would be remembered about the instant? I asked.

Hamilton said he had been startled during his commentary by something he had never seen before in his 9 years of describing the Braves in action: as Aaron turned third base, his solemn face suddenly broke into a bright grin, as surprising to see considering his usual mien as if he had started doing an Irish jig coming down the base path toward the plate. Hamilton was struck by it, but he never had time to describe it to his audience; by the time he recovered, Aaron was running into the pack of players and dignitaries with more streaming from both benches and the grandstand. "I had those things to describe to the listeners. But it's the one sight I'll particularly remember of that day..."

I talked to the other broadcasters afterward and was surprised that each of them, like Hamilton, had a special image of what they had seen which they had not described to their listeners, almost as if there was something of the day they wished to take away and secrete somewhere up in the attic.

For Tony Kubek, of the NBC crew, who had seen Mantle belt home-run balls out of stadiums and who batted in front of Roger Maris when he hit 61 home runs—all of that suddenly seemed obscure beside Aaron's feat. Never had he had such an odd feeling in a ballpark—everyone there for a weird *happening,* that's what it reminded him of, with not a person there not convinced that he was going to watch Aaron perform. They settled down to see it, somewhat chilled by the wind sifting in through the gate openings. The weird aspect was heightened by what came *after*—that once Aaron had fulfilled his function, the stadium emptied, TV sets across the country were undoubtedly turned off by the millions, and even the ballplayers themselves stumbled around for the rest of the game as if in a trance. Everyone seemed to be saying, It's been done—let's shut down the shop—let's pack up and go home. The Dodgers made 6 errors, and though this was by no means a record (the Detroit Tigers made 12 errors against the Chicago American League team in 1901), Walter Alston, their manager, could not remember a game as sloppily played. Even in the broadcast booth an astonishing number of mistakes cropped up—"the sort of errors we rarely make," Kubek said. "We goofed on Aaron's records; we spent a lot of time correcting each other. We just didn't seem to care."

Curt Gowdy remembered of the instant: "Of course, I think I'll always remember the swing itself, the arc of the bat, and then seeing that the ball had enough loft to go a long way. And also the drama of *when* he did it—out goes 715 with the first swing of his bat in his home park... after hitting 714 with his first swing of the *season.* The superstars seem to have a knack for this sort of improbability. Everyone remembers that Ted Williams finished his career in Fenway Park with a home run on that gray day. But then the astonishing thing is that he hit a home run off Dizzy Trout the last time he came to bat before going into the service in Korea. His first time up on his return was as a pinch hitter against Mike Garcia. Damned if he didn't hit a homer off *him*. But what I'll truly remember about the night in Atlanta is the odd presentiment I felt when he spoke during the pregame ceremonies of 'getting this thing over with.' I remember thinking back to what Joe Louis said before that famous Louis-Conn fight... that 'he can run but he can't hide.' Aaron said his phrase with that same sense of finality—so that the home run seemed almost inevitable. Well, Mr. Aaron 'obliged,' didn't he?"

THE HITTER

Aaron himself does not remember very much about that run around the bases. The tension, the long haul, the discomfiture of the constant yammering, the hate mail—perhaps all of that was symbolized by 715, and to hit it produced a welcome mental block. Aaron had always said that the most important home run in his life was number 109, an undistinguished number, but it was a home run hit in the 11th inning of a 2–2 tie which defeated the St. Louis Cardinals and gave the Braves—the Milwaukee Braves, then—the 1957 pennant. Aaron has a very clear memory of his reaction as he circled the base paths in the enormous tumult of rejoicing. He suddenly remembered Bobby Thomson's Miracle home run of the 1951 play-off and how he had heard about it over somebody's radio as he was coming home from school in Mobile, Alabama; he had begun running as if coming down from third toward his teammates waiting at an imaginary plate. "That had always been my idea of the most important homer," Aaron said in 1957. "Now I've got one for myself. For the first time in my life I'm excited."

But about 715 he remembered only his relief that it was over with, and the vague happiness, that a weight "like a stove" had been lifted from his back, and that his legs seemed rubbery as he took the tour of the bases, the Dodger second baseman and shortstop sticking out their hands to congratulate him. "I don't remember the noise," he said as he tried to recall. "Or the two kids that ran on the field. My teammates at home plate, I remember seeing them. I remember my mother out there and she hugging me. That's what I'll remember more than anything about that home run when I think back on it. I don't know where she came from, but she was there..."

THE OBSERVER

I watched 715 go over the fence while sitting back in the left-field corner. I had taken a quick look to either side—at the rows of faces in perfect profile, poised in expectation, jaws slightly dropped, a gallery leaning slightly forward off their seats in the ashen light of the arcs. Then, almost as one, everybody stood up.

I'd never heard a sound like that. My notes show that a seismograph scribble was the best I could do to describe that sustained pitch—absolutely constant, so that after a while it seemed caught inside the head, like a violent hum in the ears.

While this uproar was going on, all around I saw arms raised in every form of salute...clenched fists, V's for victory, arms pumped up and down. Below in left field, I could see Jimmy Wynn, the Dodgers' left fielder. He had his glove off and he was clapping. In center field Bill Buckner was shaking his fist in triumph.

In the distance Downing headed for the dugout. He sat down and looked out on the festivities as detached as an old man watching children play from his park bench. No one seemed to cluster around, or even look at him. Motionless, the bills of the Dodgers' baseball caps pointed out to the field.

After the ceremonies at home plate, Downing came back out. His control problems, which had gotten him into the mess, had not been helped by the layover, and he walked the first two batters. Walter Alston relieved him. It seemed proper somehow—that the small lefthander, having supplied the dramatic moment (almost as if he and Aaron had breakfasted together to mastermind this engineering feat), should be allowed to depart to the wings.

THE PITCHER

Downing went to the empty Dodger locker room and dressed. A taxi was ordered for him and he stood out in the stadium tunnel waiting for it. The game was still on and Milo Hamilton's voice murmured from the amplifying system in the visiting-team locker room. I was coming along the tunnel and I happened to spot him. He was in a coal black jump-suit outfit, with a black felt belt looped around his waist, and he was wearing black shoes polished to a glisten. I went up and said I was sorry that it had happened to him. He has a very cheery voice which seems to belie the gravity of any situation one might connect him with...

"Well, that's that," he said. "I didn't have the rhythm and the fast ball wasn't doing what it was supposed to, which is to drop slightly. I threw a change-up, low, and then I threw a fast ball right down the middle—the best possible pitch if it had done what it was supposed to. There was a man on base. Since my fast ball sinks—usually!— there was every reason to believe he would bang it along the ground for a double-play possibility. That's what Satchel Paige always said: 'With men on base, throw the ball low and let the infielders do the work for you.' What did I think when he hit it? 'Damn, there goes our lead!' So I went and sat in the dugout. Nobody said anything about the home run. Why should they? We're all grown men. We don't have to console each other. One or two people came by and said, 'We'll get the runs back for you.'"

It was awkward talking to him—one wanted to commiserate and assure him that the whole thing was nonsense, and yet one had the notebook that flipped back on itself, and the pencil poised.

"What about the catcher?" I asked merrily. "I mean he was the guy who called for the pitch."

Downing laughed. "I'm the guy who's going to have to live with the ramifications. It was a fine call—a good idea." ...

A photographer appeared with a small souvenir placard handed out by the Braves testifying that the bearer had been on hand to see the record home run hit. It had a picture of Aaron and the number 715. The photographer wanted Downing to pose with it, hold it up, and smile.

Downing shook his head quickly. "I don't think that would prove anything." He looked up and down the tunnel for his taxi.

"Is it going to bother you much?" I asked.

"I've been around too many great athletes, and observed them, to kick the water cooler and throw things," he said. "If Whitey Ford had a bad day, he never made excuses or made life embarrassing for others. A lot of players think that if they throw a bat, they're showing that they're competitive. But that's not what I think. A pitcher has to maintain composure. I'm more concerned about my next start," he went on. "This thing is over. It's history. It won't bother me. There's only one home run hit off me that's ever stayed in my mind. That was the grand-slam home run that Ken Boyer hit off me in the sixth inning of the 1964 World Series that beat the Yankees 4–3 and turned the whole series around. I threw him a change-up, and there was a lot of second-guessing that I had thrown him the wrong pitch, that I should have challenged him. I thought about that

for a long time. I was 23 at the time. It was a technical consideration. This one? It's more emotional. Well, pitchers don't ever like to
give up home runs. But," he said in the cheery voice, "I'm not giving myself up to trauma. People will be calling to see if I've jumped
out the window yet. I'm not going to wake up in the middle of the
night and begin banging on the walls, and looking over the sill down
into the street. The next time I pitch against him I'll get him out."

A distant roar went up from the crowd. The Braves were having
a good inning.

"Your team has made six errors."

"That so? They must be pressing," Downing said. "Everybody's
edgy tonight." He craned his head, looking for his taxi.

THE RETRIEVER

The last man in line up along the fence toward center field had been
the lefthander Tommy House, one of the staff's "short" relievers. He
is called "Puma" by his teammates for the way he bounces around
during the pepper games and thumps down cat-like on the ball.

The ball came right for him. When he caught it, he raised both
his arms in triumph, the white of the ball glistening in his left hand,
an enormous bright grin flashed on his face, and he ran for the infield where Aaron was circling the bases.

I tried to see him after the game. His cubicle was banked solid
with reporters trying to get a word with him. . . . I went over to talk
to him. He was sitting on his stool, a slight figure, his face still cheerful with excitement. He took off his baseball shoes and placed them
with studied neatness by the side of his cubicle. Behind him I noticed
that his locker was fastidiously kept—each hanger evenly spaced,
each article on the shelf placed just so. I remarked on it, and he said
Yes, it bothered the locker-room boys, who were mother hens and
liked to pick up after the ballplayers.

"Quite a day for you," I said. "Did you ever think you might drop the ball out there—I mean muff it?"

"The whole thing blew my mind. The ball came right at me, just rising off the bat on a line. If I'd frozen still like a dummy the ball would have hit me right in the middle of the forehead. Drop the ball?" He shook his head and laughed. "It never occurred to me. It wouldn't to anyone who's been catching fly balls since he was a kid. The only vague problem was someone directly above me who had a fishnet on a pole; he couldn't get it operating in time." ...

"Did you ever think of keeping the ball for yourself?" I asked.

"All of us had agreed to turn it in," he said. "I remember going up to Henry and saying that I would give the ball to him if I caught it. He said, 'I appreciate it.' Since then I've been getting a lot of kidding, particularly from the other people out in the bullpen, because I'm studying to get my master's degree in marketing and I don't suppose my professors would give me high marks for opportunism, what with so much being offered for the ball. But I'm not at all sorry. What made it worthwhile was what I saw when I ran in with the ball, holding it in my gloved hand, running really fast—in fact my teammates joked afterward that it was the fastest I'd run in a couple of years—really just wanting to get rid of it, to put it in Henry's hand. In that great crowd around home plate I found him looking over his mother's shoulder, hugging her to him, and suddenly I saw what many people have never been able to see in him—deep emotion. *I'd* never seen that before in my two years with the club. He has such cool. He never gets excited. He's so *stable*. And I looked and he had tears hanging on his lids. I could hardly believe it. 'Hammer, here it is,' I said. I put the ball in his hand. He said, 'Thanks, kid,' and touched me on the shoulder. I kept staring at him. And it was then that it was brought home to me what his home run meant, not only to him, but to all of us..."

SADAHARU OH (WITH DAVID FALKNER)

● ●

A ZEN WAY OF BASEBALL

Sadaharu Oh, born in Tokyo in 1940 (he survived the firebombing of the city), became the most significant player in the history of Japanese baseball: in the course of a 27-year career he hit 868 home runs, far eclipsing Babe Ruth's 714 and Henry Aaron's 755. He never played in other countries (he admits that his totals would have been considerably less had he played in the United States where the fences are longer and the pitching more formidable) but he was known world-over for his peculiar batting style in which he lifted his foreleg far off the ground in a stance he referred to as "dog-lifting-his-leg-at-the-hydrant." He was taught this one-legged stance by a *sensei,* Arakawa-san, to get rid of a hitch he had developed early on in his swing. Arakawa-san explained to him: "Standing in this position, if you hitch, you will fall flat on your ass." At first, Sadaharu Oh laughed at the exercise ("I laughed myself off balance") but after three years of instruction he was able to use the unique batting style to remarkable effect. What follows are excerpts from Sadaharu Oh's memoir (with David Falkner).

⚾

And so we resumed our work on a daily basis. I could no longer say it was fear or love of the game or even the presence of Nagashima-san, but I seemed to put more and more of myself into what I was doing. It was not so much a question of hours but of feeling. I wanted to swing the bat, I wanted what standing on one foot brought to me. More and more I came to see that when I stood on one foot, my sense of things changed. On one foot, I became hungry for hitting. On two feet, I was just another hitter. I loved the contest between myself and the pitcher, the struggle of wills that, miraculously, could be resolved in this unity of movement that was the home run.

AS A YOUNG BALLPLAYER

My uniform number was One—all the years I was in high school and all the years I was a major league ballplayer. Number One. People made something of that. BIG ONE the press blurbs read. Big One! What is a "big one"? I don't put that down. I enjoyed it too much. But I know who I am—or who I have been. I am ordinary. No larger, no smaller than life-size. But my number matters to me. In my mind's eye, I see my number on my uniform jersey in the only way that it has ever been important—showing toward the pitcher as I assume my batting stance. What I was at my best, I turned my back almost ninety degrees toward the pitcher. I felt like a rough Japanese sea. My number suddenly rose toward the pitcher like a dark wave just before I struck.

In the middle of all this was baseball. Baseball was everywhere in those years following the war. You could no more avoid baseball as a boy in Japan than a Canadian child could avoid skates. Even though we had no real fields to play on, though our equipment was handmade and very crude—balls fashioned from wound string and strips of cloth, bats made from tree limbs and discarded sticks—baseball seemed to grow from the very rubble itself, like some mysterious blossom of renewal. There were pickup teams from the neighborhoods, sandlot teams, school teams, and the reemergence of the pro teams. Baseball had always been popular in Japan (an American missionary, so the story goes, introduced the game here in 1873; pro baseball began in Japan in 1936, although it was suspended during the war). But now, in the ruins of the Occupation, streets and alleyways became meeting places for sudden games of catch, eruptions of ground ball, and pop-fly drills. I was a very typical Japanese boy. From the earliest time, I simply loved baseball. The country was baseball crazy, and so was I!

Don Larsen *did* serve as an inspiration for me—but not in the way it was reported. The real story is far more curious. On New Year's Day that winter, Mr. Kubota said that he wanted me to watch a film of Larsen's perfect game. I went to a house in Toshima Ward to see it. There was nothing special about the house. It was small, unpretentious, typical of many in that area of Tokyo. But it belonged to Arakawa-san!

I could scarcely believe it when I saw this shadowy figure of my boyhood dreams standing there in the doorway to greet us. What did this mean? Did he remember who I was? Was this only the wildest coincidence, or had Arakawa-san all the while remembered me and been keeping tabs on me at Waseda? I bowed to him and shook his hand.

"We meet again," he said with a smile.

No coincidence at all!

But I could not bring myself to speak or to ask questions. I was there because it was determined that I should see this film, and that was all I permitted myself. The film, obviously, confirmed the correctness of what I had been working on. I saw what was possible at the highest level of professional play using this style of delivery, and it immediately compelled my attention. I watched Larsen's motion very carefully, making notes as I went. I studied the position of hand and glove at the waist, the way in which the turn of his body helped hide the ball till the last moment before the whip of the arm, how the stride forward left him balanced and in perfect fielding position. All the while I tried to see this in a kind of reverse mirror, checking each of these points against the movements I made as a left-hander. Yes, of course, it could be done. More than that, just because it eliminated so much excess motion, it might be the ideal counterfoil to the destructive effects of my nervous system. I was full of hope for the new year and the new season, which was shortly to begin.

I felt tremendous gratitude to Mr. Miyai and Mr. Kubota for helping me. But toward Arakawa-san I felt something I could not begin to explain. It was as though, in re-entering my life at this point, he had all along been a kind of invisible helping spirit, watching me from afar, interceding just at those moments when I needed help the most. I wanted to say some of this to him, but it was all too confusing.

I bowed deeply to him when I said goodbye. I wondered if he saw what was in my heart. I did not want to embarrass him, and yet I wanted to convey some sense of this powerful upsurge of thankfulness. He smiled and nodded, and the glint in his eye, whether a glimmer of recognition or the simplest light of good feeling, was enough to send my spirits soaring.

At any rate, it was my impression then that this meeting was a kind of circle closing on a magical story. I knew I would be all right now. But I still had no idea at all that the story had not yet even begun.

One night I woke up and wrote this: "There are three ways to get rid of a slump. One is to drink and change the feeling you are walking around with. Another one is to get involved in some sort of hobby so you can forget for a while. The third is just to practice and practice again. In order to get rid of uneasiness, the first two ways should be considered. The last way sometimes deepens the feeling of uneasiness.

However, the first two have nothing to do with progress. If the monster called slump requires improvement in technique and skill then there is only the road of practice and practice and practice...."

THE TRAINING

Arakawa-san and I, as any other students, sat at the far edges of the room, on our heels in the proper position, toe touching toe. All of the fledgling warriors wore combinations of white or white and black blouses with *hakama*. Ueshiba Sensei alone was dressed in a full-flowing black kimono. The time I first saw him, he was approaching eighty. His appearance and manner, though, were vigorous. He had a long, wispy, snow-white beard and moustache along with bushy white eyebrows. Severity and kindliness both seemed etched into his features. He looked more like a fifteenth-century village elder than a master of the martial arts—that is, until he began to perform the movements he had perfected over a lifetime. The beauty and power of these movements were astonishing. Trained athletes or dancers could not easily have duplicated them. They were the fruits of unparalleled accomplishment. When he finished his session, we spoke to him. It was Arakawa-san's turn to play the straight man.

"What is *ma*?" he asked, deliberately echoing Kikugoro. But the Sensei answered him differently.

"*Ma* exists because there is an opponent."

"I understand," Arakawa-san said. This seemed to jibe with something he was thinking. He took me by the elbow.

"You see," he said to me, "in the case of baseball it would be the pitcher and the batter. The one exists for the other; they are caught, both, in the *ma* of the moment. The pitcher tries in that instant of time and space to throw off a batter's timing; the batter tries to outwit the pitcher. The two are struggling to take advantage of the *ma* that exists between them. That's what makes baseball so extraordinarily difficult."

As long as I live, I'll never forget how lovely that day was. The sun on the sidewalk was like the first sun of the world. I have never seen such a sight! I stared like a man who has taken leave of his senses. My mother certainly was startled, because she prodded me to get a move on. I was late for the game! But I wanted nothing more than to drink in this sudden perfect beauty. There was a particular way the pavements shone with the rain of the night before; the color of the sky was so pure. I wondered, if Fortune had first put me in the way of Arakawa-san, was it not Fortune also at work in this moment? Not Fortune in any sense I had known before, but Fortune as a trickster, glazing my eyes and soul with the romance of things, so that I would be blind to the certain sorrows that awaited me. What was my answer?

The rain glistened on the pavements. The noon sun warmed the world. The sky was a painter's curve of blue.

"Get a move on, don't be so lazy! Move!"

Yes, I had to move. I had to leave, what choice had I? The beautiful aftermath of a storm. But you see, if it had rained that day, I would never have become a top batsman. For it was out there, under that lovely blue sky, just an hour or two away, that the idea of hitting on one foot came about.

"Look," he said, "it's time we faced up to something. That hitch of yours looks like it's here to stay. We are going to have to get a little extreme, I think."

"Extreme?"

"Very," he said. "Remember one day in Miyazaki we returned from camp and I had you take different poses with the bat in your hands? Do you remember?"

I vaguely remembered trying to experiment with different batting poses as a way of getting myself to stop hitching, but I didn't remember specifically what Arakawa-san was referring to.

"The one-legged one, remember that? The one where you bring your right foot up and hold it there?"

"Yes, yes." It came back to me.

I was at first not sure Arakawa-san was really being serious. Perhaps this was just another bit of shock therapy to make a point. But, no, he was quite in earnest. He picked up a bat and coiled himself into the pose to demonstrate.

It looked *so* peculiar. I could not imagine how a batter could survive more than a few seconds in such a position, let alone react to any kind of pitch. But what I saw in front of me was a man standing on one foot, who told me, as he stood there, that the time had now come for me to try that in a game.

I didn't know whether to laugh or cry. I sat there bewildered. Arakawa-san winked and smiled. And continued standing on one foot.

I was miserable. Why was he playing with me? What was he trying to do? I finally decided that all this was just an attempt to psych me up for the game, so I tried as politely as I could to shrug it off and gear my thoughts to the afternoon's work. But Arakawa-san did not budge. Only now the smile left his face. I turned, finally, and began to go off toward my locker.

"*Oh!*" he called; his voice snapped like a whip. I turned around. He was glaring at me.

"I order you to do it."

I stood frozen for a moment, terrified. All I could do was bow my head.

And thus commenced the biggest gamble of my life. The tens of thousands of fans in Kawasaki Stadium witnessed my first attempts at "flamingo batting" in the game that followed. I had no chance to try it beforehand, because the team had omitted batting practice; even in the on-deck circle before my first at-bat in the game there was no chance to do anything but kneel and wait.

"Batting for the Giants, number one, Sadaharu Oh," boomed the loudspeaker. I approached the plate, stepped into the batter's box, and then assumed my pose. The crowd buzzed, then chattered, then hooted and roared as the first pitches to me were thrown. With the count two and two, I flicked out my bat and hit a clean single into center field. The roaring of the crowd suddenly dropped away. I was standing on first. The first trial was done.

I came up again two innings later, and this time the crowd was ready for me. They whistled and stomped and called out to me as I moved to the plate. When I coiled myself into the flamingo position, they roared—I didn't know whether they were enjoying this or viewing it as an insult of some sort. I tried to concentrate. I held my leg as steady as I could. I took one pitch. Then, on the next pitch, an inside fastball, I stepped forward, bringing my curled leg forward and toward the mound, snapping my bat through in the shortest possible arc. I hit the ball on the sweetest part of the bat. It rose on a low trajectory and kept going, far over the right-field wall. I circled the bases, wondering how in the world I could ever have done that standing in that position. But who was I to argue with Fortune, who had indeed smiled on us that day?

"Yes," Arakawa-san said, beaming with satisfaction, "yes. You have passed the 'dog-lifting-his-leg-at-the-hydrant' test. Now all that remains is for you to become what you secretly are."

"Look," Ueshiba Sensei said, "the ball comes flying in whether you like it or not, doesn't it? Then all you can do is wait for it to come to you. To wait, this is the traditional Japanese style. Wait. Teach him to wait."

———

"This business of standing on one leg," Arakawa-san purred, "we discover is a matter of life and death. Accordingly, when you step into the batter's box, you may never do it casually. Too much is at stake. The center in your lower abdomen prepares you for any contingency just as if you were a warrior awaiting the moves of a deadly opponent. Likewise, when you are good enough to have mastered *ma*, you bring your opponent into your own space; his energy is then part of yours. Together you are one. This is what concentration can bring, why it is so crucial. So you must locate it properly, in the one point, and be conscious of it at all times, even when you're walking down the street or sitting at a meal. Once your concentration is thus focused, you automatically begin to see things better. In a state of proper concentration, one is ready for anything that comes along. Even a baseball hurtling toward you at ninety miles an hour!"

As I have mentioned, you cannot be "merely technical" when you swing a sword. If it is possible to fall into the habit of a harmless game when you repeatedly swing a baseball bat, that can never happen with a sword. The feel of a sword in your hands will prevent this; the knowledge of what gleams on the edge of the blade compels your attention. It is also impossible to swing a sword without in some way risking injury to yourself. A slip, an off-balance move, going too far in a follow-through, and you run the very real risk of slashing yourself. Practice with the sword demands intensity. As your mind must be concentrated when you face an opponent, so, too, your practice must include this mental effort.

Because Arakawa-san forbade me any kind of combat in my training, he was forced to find other means to challenge me. The challenge of an opponent is, of course, the ultimate test in any martial arts practice. In baseball, just as much as in Aikido, success against an opponent is fundamentally bound up with timing. Our goal, "acquiring the Body of a Rock," literally meant having the discipline to wait. This implied far more than balance. To train one's entire being to hold back from the tricks and feints of a pitcher, no less than from an enemy with a sword, is finally the single most important step in harmonizing one's *ki* with the opponent's. *Ma,* the interval or distance between you, is eventually that which you rather than the other create by the strength of your waiting.

Arakawa-san and I had reached the point where there were no tricks in what I was doing. And consequently no tricks used against us would get in our way. Nothing could stop me from hitting. I longed to hit as a starving man longs for food. The ball coming toward me was a rabbit, and I was a wolf waiting to devour it. I attacked a baseball as though it were no longer a question of hitting it but of crushing it totally. The home runs rocketed off my bat almost as though a power beyond my own was responsible. I was fascinated by the runs I got all by myself. My head, my mind—quite literally—became a void. I went to the plate with no thought other than this moment of hitting confronting me. It was everything. And in the midst of it, in the midst of chanting and cheering crowds, colors, noises, hot and cold weather, the glare of lights, or rain on my skin, there was only this noiseless, colorless, heatless void in which the pitcher and I together enacted our certain, preordained ritual of the home run.

BREAKING THE HOME RUN RECORD

When I left my locker and headed for the field, I had no feeling of tiredness. I could feel in my bones that this indeed was the night. I came upon the lights and noise of Korakuen almost as if they didn't exist. The quietness my mother had brought me surrounded me like a spell. It was not going to be broken. I hit in the first inning and then in the third. The third inning. One out, no one on base. The pitcher's name, in this twenty-third game of the year against the Swallows, was Kojiro Suzuki. The goal, Arakawa-san had always said, was oneness of mind, body, and skill. You and the opponent together create the moment. The *ma* is the one you create but in which you are not at all separate from your opponent. The pitcher and I, the ball—and the silence my mother gave me—these were all one. In the midst of whatever was going on, there was only this emptiness in which I could do what I wanted to do. The count went full. Mr. Kojiro Suzuki threw a sinker on the outside part of the plate. I followed the ball perfectly. I could almost feel myself waiting for its precise break before I let myself come forward. When I made contact, I felt like I was scooping the ball upward and outward. The ball rose slowly and steadily in the night sky, lit by Korakuen's bright lights. I could follow it all the way, as it lazily reached its height and seemed to linger there in the haze, and then slowly began its descent into the right-field stands.

The crowd erupted, almost as a single voice. A huge banner was suddenly unfurled that read, "Congratulations, World Record!" Everywhere—but on the diamond—people were running and lights were flashing. For me, it was the moment of purest joy I had ever known as a baseball player.

No one can stop a home run. No one can understand what it really is unless you have felt it in your own hands and body. It is different from seeing it or trying to describe it. There is nothing I know quite like meeting a ball in exactly the right spot. As the ball makes its high, long arc beyond the playing field, the diamond and the stands suddenly belong to one man. In that brief, brief time, you are free of all demands and complications. There is no one behind you, no obstruction ahead, as you follow this clear path around all the bases. This is the batsman's center stage, the one time that he may allow himself to freely accept the limelight, to enjoy the sensation of every eye in the stadium fixed on him, waiting for the moment when his foot will touch home plate. In this moment he is free.

REGGIE JACKSON'S THREE HOMERS

Reggie Jackson used to refer to a fast ball down the middle of the plate as a "mattress pitch" because (as he said) "if you're feeling right you can lay all over 'em." Red Smith writes about Jackson's four consecutive swings of the bat. After the last of them, Jackson (according to his autobiography) "floated home on the noise."

⚾

1977

It had to happen this way. It had been predestined since November 29, 1976, when Reginald Martinez Jackson sat down on a gilded chair in New York's Americana Hotel and wrote his name on a Yankee contract. That day he became an instant millionaire, the big honcho on the best team money could buy, the richest, least inhibited, most glamorous exhibit in Billy Martin's pin-striped zoo. That day the plot was written for last night—the bizarre scenario Reggie Jackson played out by hitting three home runs, clubbing the Los Angeles Dodgers into submission and carrying his supporting players with him to the baseball championship of North America. His was the most lurid performance in 74 World Series, for although Babe Ruth hit three home runs in a game in 1926 and again in 1928, not even that demigod smashed three in a row.

Reggie's first broke a tie and put the Yankees in front, 4–3. His second fattened the advantage to 7–3. His third completed arrangements for a final score of 8–4, wrapping up the championship in six games.

Yet that was merely the final act of an implausible one-man show. Jackson had made a home run last Saturday in Los Angeles and another on his last time at bat in that earthly paradise on Sunday. On his first appearance at the plate last night he walked, getting no official time at bat, so in his last four official turns he hit four home runs.

In his last nine times at bat, this Hamlet in double-knits scored seven runs, made six hits and five home runs and batted in six runs for a batting average of .667 compiled by day and by night on two seacoasts three thousand miles and three time zones apart. Shakespeare wouldn't attempt a curtain scene like that if he was plastered.

This was a drama that consumed seven months, for ever since the Yankees went to training camp last March, Jackson had lived in the eye of the hurricane. All summer long as the spike-shod capitalists bickered and quarreled, contending with their manager, defying their owner, Reggie was the most controversial, the most articulate, the most flamboyant.

Part philosopher, part preacher and part outfielder, he carried this rancorous company with his bat in the season's last fifty games, leading them to the East championship in the American League and into the World Series. He knocked in the winning run in the twelve-inning first game, drove in a run and scored two in the third, furnished the winning margin in the fourth and delivered the final run in the fifth.

Thus the stage was set when he went to the plate in last night's second inning with the Dodgers leading 2–0. Sedately, he led off with a walk. Serenely, he circled the bases on a home run by Chris Chambliss. The score was tied.

Los Angeles had moved out front, 3–2, when the man reappeared in the fourth inning with Thurman Munson on base. He hit the first pitch on a line into the seats beyond right field. Circling the bases for the second time, he went into his home-run glide—head high, chest out. The Yankees led, 4–3. In the dugout, Yankees fell upon him. Billy Martin, the manager, who tried to slug him last June, patted his cheek lovingly. The dugout phone rang and Reggie accepted the call graciously.

His first home run knocked the Dodgers' starting pitcher, Burt Hooton, out of the game. His second disposed of Elias Sosa, Hooton's successor. Before Sosa's first pitch in the fifth inning, Reggie had strolled the length of the dugout to pluck a bat from the rack, even though three men would precede him to the plate. He was confident he would get his turn. When he did, there was a runner on base again, and again he hit the first pitch. Again it reached the seats in right.

When the last jubilant playmate had been peeled off his neck, Reggie took a seat near the first-base end of the bench. The crowd was still bawling for him and comrades urged him to take a curtain call but he replied with a gesture that said, "Aw, fellows, cut it out!" He did unbend enough to hold up two fingers for photographers in a V-for-victory sign.

Jackson was the leadoff batter in the eighth. By that time, Martin would have replaced him in an ordinary game, sending Paul Blair to right field to help protect the Yankees' lead. But did they ever bench Edwin Booth in the last act?

For the third time, Reggie hit the first pitch but this one didn't take the shortest distance between two points. Straight out from the plate the ball streaked, not toward the neighborly stands in right but on a soaring arc toward the unoccupied bleachers in dead center, where the seats are blacked out to give batters a background. Up the white speck climbed, dwindling, diminishing, until it settled at last halfway up those empty stands, probably 450 feet away.

This time he could not disappoint his public. He stepped out of the dugout and faced the multitude, two fists and one cap uplifted. Not only the customers applauded.

"I must admit," said Steve Garvey, the Dodgers' first baseman, "when Reggie Jackson hit his third home run and I was sure nobody was listening, I applauded into my glove."

ROGER ANGELL

· ·

HOMERIC TALES

In the introduction to his first collection of baseball pieces, entitled *The Summer Game*, Roger Angell wrote as follows: "When I began writing sports pieces for the *New Yorker*, it was clear to me that the doings of big league baseball—the daily happenings on the field, the managerial strategies, the celebration of heroes, the medical and financial bulletins, the clubhouse gossip—were so enormously reported in the newspapers that I would have to find some other aspect of the game to study. I decided to sit in the stands—for a while at least—and watch the baseball from there. I wanted to pick up the feel of the game as it happened to people around me."

He went on to describe his progression from there to the press box and eventually to summoning up "the nerve to talk to some ballplayers face-to-face."

Thank goodness! The home run, while memorable to those who watch the ball arch into the stands, is of unique importance to the two personages most closely involved—the hitter and his victim on the mound, now turning away in disgust at what has happened to him. Indeed, many pitchers will simply turn away from writers who bring up the subject of home runs. But Angell has gone to the principals (even some pitchers) to discuss this most dramatic of consequences.

There is one interesting sidelight to Roger Angell's *Homeric Tales*. After reading it, Fay Vincent, baseball's commissioner at the time, decreed that the asterisk that accompanied Roger Maris's 61 home-run total in the record books (to indicate that his season was longer than Babe Ruth's) should be dropped.

W HERE I WAS WAS in Boston, at my mother-in-law's. We'd stopped off for a couple of days on our way back from a vacation in Maine. I was in the living room (view of the Charles River), intently watching via black-and-white television (view of Clint Hartung leading off third and Whitey Lockman leading off second; awareness of the Harlem River, somewhere offscreen), and when it became plain that the Dodgers weren't going to walk the batter to set up a possible double play, I gestured urgently to my wife, just then passing from kitchen toward bedroom with a jar of Gerber's in her hand. "You might not want to miss this," I said, unable to lift my gaze from the screen. "It could just be—"

"Be right back," she said, disappearing from the room.

Too late. Several other things now disappeared as well—in rough succession: the ball, into the lower grand-stand seats at the Polo Grounds, above the left-field wall; self-control ("They did it! They did it! My God, they did it!" I yelled, rushing distractedly from room to room, bumping into walls and dogs and relatives); Bobby Thomson, the batter (who had just written the meaty portion of the first sentence of his obituary, whenever that would be), into embraces of his teammates around home plate; the Dodgers (severally, slowly, slumpingly, across the littered outfield and up the steep stairway to their clubhouse); and—soon thereafter, it seems—all further memory of the day and the game and my own succeeding emotions and remarks and celebratory gestures and exclamations on this the greatest moment of my life as a deep-dyed, native-born Giants fan, fan of baseball, fan of fable, *fan*. My mind goes blank, I mean, with me more or less in midair there in the Back Bay, possibly trying to invent the high-five some thirty years before its time. The four-run ninth-inning rally, capped by Bobby Thomson's killing homer against the Dodgers' Ralph Branca, not only won that 1951 National League pennant for the Giants (the two teams had finished the regular season in a tie, and split the first two games of their best-of-three playoff) but stands as the most vivid single moment, the grand exclamation point, in the history of the pastime. So we believed then—*knew* it, on the instant—and so I believe to this day, and it's funny that I can remember nothing else about that afternoon.

Homers will do that to you. Even when one goes out in midgame, it stops the story. Nothing *ensues,* for the connective tissue of the game—the men on base, the defensive deployments, the pitcher's struggles, the count, the score—has been snipped, and all our attention falls upon the hero. In the stands, we yell or groan and, a little distanced, observe his tour of the bases and the home-plate ceremonials. The cheering dies away and we resume our seats, waiting for the game to show its face once again. Game-winning homers really slam the door. Bang go the cymbals: wow, it's over. The curtain drops, the houselights come up, and, numbered, we grope around under the seats for our wraps as the long night's drama and the soaring sudden moment go rushing off arm in arm into the past. Kids love this ending, but the rest of us, greedy for context, are a fraction let down, much as we hate to admit it. Home runs are non-participatory; home runs, as Crash Davis might have said, are fascist. In the clubhouse after the game, the slugger is smiling, his face still alight, but he hasn't got much to say. "I've been seein' the ball pretty good lately. It was a slider, a little up, and it went out." He shrugs, almost apologetically, and the writers go off to talk to the batter and the base runner and the third-base coach about that double in the sixth, with a man on base. The manager isn't much help, either. "You saw it," he says in his office, his hands in the air, and the talk shifts to the next day's starter. Home runs are terrific fun—jaw-dropping, preposterous, grandiloquent, outta here—but the strange thought obtrudes that we fans may not always appreciate them as much as we should.

The 1951 Thomson classic will be seen often on our home

screens this summer—Bobby, in that grainy black-and-white, prancing around third (where Eddie Stanky suddenly runs into the picture from the left and tackles manager Leo Durocher, there in the coach's box), and his swan dive into the jovial sea of teammates at home plate—for it is part of a triple jubilee for baseball this year: a celebration of three seasons, now thirty, forty, and fifty years gone, that were all illuminated by extraordinary offensive feats. In 1961, Mickey Mantle and Roger Maris launched their conspicuous double assault on Babe Ruth's hallowed (the word inserts itself here like a cab-meter drop) record of sixty home runs in a season, which ended when Maris knocked No. 61 against Tracy Stallard, of the Red Sox, in his second at-bat of the final day of the schedule, at Yankee Stadium. Mantle, who was ill or injured through most of September that year, had fallen back near the end, and wound up with fifty-four. He is not much mentioned nowadays in connection with the Maris exploit, but his lurking switch-hitting presence immediately behind Roger in the Yankee batting order had a great deal to do with the outcome. The two M's, in any case, batted in a total of two hundred and seventy runs that summer.

Maris pulled off his coup, it should be recalled, in spite of a summer of tormenting publicity and distraction. He had wafted twenty-seven home runs by the end of June, forty by the beginning of August, and fifty-one by the time September came along—each stage well ahead of Ruth's level in his record year, 1927, when the Babe finished up with an amazing rush of seventeen homers in September—but long before he uncoiled on Stallard's fastball that final afternoon he knew that the new mark, if it came along, would be tainted in the books by an appended demeaning explanation that his sixty-one had been achieved over the course of a hundred-and-sixty-two-game season, as against Ruth's sixty in a hundred and fifty-four games. The famous asterisk (in truth, it has always been an annotation—a parenthetical "162 G/S" just after the number) remains in place in the game's two accepted record books, kept by the Elias Sports Bureau and by *The Sporting News,* although numerous other records established since that time (including stolen bases, at-bats, pitchers' strikeouts, saves, etc.) do not bear the ugly tick. The instigator was Commissioner Ford Frick, who brought forth the edict in July and then lobbied busily through the summer with repeated explanations to the vestals of the Baseball Writers Association that the holy Ruthian total would be "cheapened" by an unexplained larger figure established over an additional week of play—not quite a disinterested campaign, since Frick, a former sportswriter himself, had been a coeval and an adulating biographer of the Babe. It should also be recalled that the American League had added two new teams that selfsame summer, in the first major-league expansion of the century—the Los Angeles Angels and a reconstituted Washington Senators club—and "cheapening the game" was much in the minds of the columnists and the fans. When the thunderbolt of sixty-one homers arrived, moreover, it was launched by a player who had been a Yankee for only two seasons. If Mickey Mantle, a Yankee hero almost from his first days as a pinstriped rookie, had swatted the magic blow, many old-timers still believe, the New York front office would have raised an ungodly fuss over any diminishment of the new record, and it would have stood unsmirched, as it deserved. There is no wish here to revive the shoutings and buzzings that accompanied the Maris achievement thirty years back, but I think the present commissioner and some brave committee should meet one of these days and quietly wield an eraser, instead of waiting for some young slugger to come along and do it for them with his bat.

In baseball's arithmetic, 1941 will always be the sum of fifty-six and .406: Joe DiMaggio's record fifty-six-game hitting streak that summer, coupled with Ted Williams' season's batting average, which he gloriously nailed up for all to see by choosing to play both ends of a doubleheader on the final day of the regular schedule. His option could have been to sit safely on the bench, nursing his .3996 average to date, which would have translated into an official .400—a platform unascended by any major-leaguer since Bill Terry batted .401 for the Giants, in 1930. The Kid, as every schoolboy from Presque Isle to Pelham used to know, went six for eight for the afternoon, against the Philadelphia Athletics: four singles, a double, and a home run. (The double, in the fourth inning of the nightcap, partly demolished a loudspeaker high on the wall in right center and fell back onto the playing field.) Both the DiMaggio and the Williams marks stand untouched to this day, a half-century later, although several gallant expeditions toward the .400 peak have been mounted in the interim, including Williams' own .388 in 1957, when he was thirty-nine years old. The DiMaggio streak looks safer: the premier one-season offensive record in the game.

Bobby Thomson's homer, the middle trophy on the shelf, is probably the least of the anniversary deeds—a single swing of the bat, as against the excruciating labors of two months (DiMaggio's fifty-six games stretched from May 15th to July 16th) or a full season's hacking—but its clarity and finality invite us wonderfully. Or invite *me*, I should say. Thinking about it this winter and trying to bring that day to mind called back other home runs as well—a couple at first, then ten or a dozen or more, some celebrated, some shrouded—which I had seen down the years and which had stayed with me, awaiting this nudge, it seemed, to sail into view once again. If these memoirs felt like short stories, for the reasons I have been suggesting here, they were also vivid and cheerful, and could all be told in the great lexicon of swat.

HOME RUN (nouns, verbs):

Homer, rough-tripper, four-bagger, four-ply blow, clout, circuit clout, blast, dinger, downtowner, tater, long tater, shot, moon shot, slam (on occasion), grand slam, park one, lose one, crank one, clean the bases, gone, goner, outta here, going deep, took him (take him/ took me) deep, Chinese homer, Ruthian wallop, Ballantine Blast, 800 number, Dial 8, day-tripper, still circling the airport, had a full crew and stewardesses (etc.), Federal Express, Dome-dong (Kingdome HR), Chicken on the Hill (Stargell HR at Three Rivers Stadium), street piece (out of the park, in Dennis Eckersley's language), walk-off piece (also Eckersleyesque, meaning pitcher has nothing else to do but walk off the field), etc., etc.

With these exclamatory sounds filling my head, I travelled about in Arizona and Florida this spring, and, once the season began, in some Northern parks, talking to baseball people, past and present, and asking them the same thing: "Tell me a homer." Then I would say that I was not just in search of monuments—all-timers like the Thomson or Maris pokes, Gabby Hartnett's ancient homer in the gloaming, Bill Mazeroski's Series winner against the 1960 Yankees, Carlton Fisk's Game Sixer in 1975, or Kirk Gibson's ninth-inning stunner against the Oakland Athletics three years ago, and the rest—or even the longest homers my deponents had witnessed. Any homer would do—whatever came to mind. (I talked to a lot of writers and media people, too; beat people have seen as much baseball as anyone, and they like to talk about it sometimes, once their deadlines have gone by.) As it turned out, we always seemed to get around to the historic pokes and the monsters in due course, but there were plenty of others, of every degree and distance, ready at hand. And each tale, I noticed (getting out my notebook), began with a smile.

"Any homer?" said Tracy Ringolsby, the Dallas *Morning News* national baseball writer. "Bo Jackson's against Nolan, two years ago. I think it was during the Royals' first swing south, probably in May. Ryan had struck him out the first five or six times he'd faced him, and the first time Bo ever makes contact he hits the longest home run in Arlington Stadium history."

We were standing in the bright sunlight in front of the Giants' dugout, before a game in Scottsdale, along with another writer friend, Vern Plagenhoef, of the Booth papers.

"Mine is Kirk Gibson's in the last game of the '84 Series, against the Padres," Plagenhoef said when his turn came. "He'd already had a great day, you remember, and when he comes up to bat against Goose Gossage, with two men on and first base open, you know they're going to put him on. But Gossage has a different idea. Dick Williams"—Williams was the Padres skipper—"is waving four fingers, but Goose just stands there. Dick goes out to talk to him, and Sparky is yelling out to Kirk, 'They don't want to walk you!' He can't *believe* it—nobody can. But Goose wins the argument somehow, and Gibson hits the ball into the upper deck there at Tiger Stadium, and comes around and jumps up and down on home plate about six times in that wild, wild scene. Maybe it's not as big as Gibson's pinch-hit shot against Eckersley out at Dodger Stadium, but this is the one I think of first. It was the one lively thing in that whole Series, except for the cab catching fire outside the stadium."

"Does batting practice count?" Ringolsby asked. "Just this once? O.K., then there's Pete Incaviglia's first at-bat of the year at Pompano, in '86. Pete's late getting to camp—he's a rookie, and most of us have never seen him—and on his first turn in the cage his manager, Bobby Valentine, is throwing B.P. First swing, Pete knocks the ball on a line down the right-field line and through the wooden fence out there. Not exactly a home run, but it sure had that feel. The wall was rotten, it turned out, and all that spring the visiting players and writers kept stopping by and looking at the place, and picking more pieces out, for souvenirs. By the end of the month, you could put your head through the hole. It had become a legend."

By the way, Dan Shaughnessy, of the Boston *Globe,* believes that the Gibson homer against Dennis Eckersley would be universally ranked as the game's greatest if it had happened in the last game of a World Series instead of the first. "It also came on a Saturday night," he said to me. "The worst time in the world for deadlines, and everybody had to rewrite. I had a whole piece done about how the Dodgers were only the latest in a succession of National League fraud teams in the Series, and all that, but I hadn't pushed the button yet, so I was able to kill it. That home run came along after 'The Natural' had been playing around the country, you know, so the wounded Kirk Gibson gimping up to the plate was like Roy Hobbs come to life. It still feels like a miracle."

Baseball memories leap over decades at a single bound, and long-flown afternoons return without effort, often in the heroic present tense. The flight feels easy if you're talking to Jim Kaat, who is an announcer for CBS these days but looks very much the way he did when he was the No. 1 starter for the Twins, a couple of decades ago—ochre-freckled, tall and intense, with farmer cheekbones and a high, thick chest.

"I'm pitching against the Yankees, up at the Stadium," Kaat said to me in Port St. Lucie. "This is in 1967, the year we lost the pennant to the Red Sox on the very last day, but this game was way earlier. I've got the Yankees beat, 1–0, two out in the ninth, and Mantle's the hitter. The count goes to three and one. I thought about pitching carefully and maybe putting him on, but Elston Howard was on deck, and he was always more dangerous for me than Mantle. Well, I challenged Mickey. You remember in the old Stadium it was still four hundred and fifty-seven feet to the auxiliary scoreboard in left field? That's where he hit it. The game was tied now, and we got rained out in the tenth. We came back a month later, and, ironically, I was the pitcher in the makeup game, against Steve Barber, and I lost, 1–0. When you lose a pennant by one game, you pick out moments to do over, and I always go back to Mantle. That one pitch..."

The prime first-in-a-career home run in the books... happened at the Polo Grounds—a modest clout by Hoyt Wilhelm, the Hall of Fame knuckleballer, against the Braves on his very first major-league at-bat, in 1952. It has probably remained clear in Wilhelm's memory, since he went on to pitch in a thousand and sixty-nine more games—a total unmatched by any pitcher to date—and never hit another. But it's probably safe to say that every major-leaguer keeps a firm hold, in memory, on his maiden downtowner. Al Rosen, the Giants' general manager, told me that his had come on Opening Day in 1950, in Cleveland, when he had just taken over as the starting third baseman for the Tribe. His distinguished predecessor at the corner, Ken Keltner, had been released the week before, so Rosen was aware that he was under considerable scrutiny from the home-town fans. (The Indians, I feel forced to explain, were a baseball power in those days, having won a pennant two years before and finished third in '49.) In the eighth inning, with his team down by two runs, Rosen got around on a waste pitch thrown by the Tigers starter, Freddy Hutchinson, and put it into the seats. Hutchinson, a celebrated sorehead of his time, followed Rosen around the bases, shouting imprecations. "When I crossed the plate, he was still right behind me," Rosen said. "'You hear me, don't you, you bush bastard?' he yelled, and I said, 'Yes, Mr. Hutchinson, I hear you,' and I went back to the bench and sat down. Quite a feeling." Rosen, it might be noted, upset some other pitchers that season, when he went on to whack thirty-six more dingers—a record for rookies in the American League that stood for thirty-seven years.

Another day, another Giant. Will Clark, asked for the first home run that came to mind, gave me a burning stare (he looks this way all the time) and said, "Easy. My first at-bat in the big leagues.

Opening Day—April 8, 1986, in Houston. One out, one-and-one count. Third pitch, first inning, Nolan Ryan. My mom and dad were in the stands. Solo shot—center field. Not a bad way to enter the big leagues."

"Wow!" I said. "Can you think of any other homers you've hit?"

"Sure," Clark said. "A bunch of them—only, you said one. Right?"

"Right," I said. "Yup. Thanks."

Bill Rigney is more of a long talker. When he was an infielder for the New York Giants, he roomed with the Big Cat, Johnny Mize, on the road, and he still cheerfully claims to be a co-holder of the "Most Home Runs, Roommates" record—one stat not to be found in the books. Mize, a beefy first baseman, smacked fifty-one in 1947, while Rig, who is built (in his phrase) more like a 2-iron, crashed through with seventeen; it was a career year in this category for them both.

At dinner one night in Scottsdale, Rigney regaled me with accounts of several Harmon Killebrew blasts (Rig was Killebrew's manager on the Twins in the early seventies), including one in Cleveland on a day when the Indians' Sudden Sam McDowell seemed to have the visitors in hand in the ninth, with a one-run lead. "We've got a man on second, Harmon is the batter, and Oliva's on deck," Rigney said. "Alvin Dark, their manager, calls time and runs out to the mound and says something to Sam. Then he runs back, and before he gets his foot back in the dugout Killebrew hits it over the center-field fence. You know, I keep meaning to ask Alvin what it was he said out there."

A day or two later, Rig came up to me at the ballpark in Phoenix (he is the senior baseball adviser to the Athletics) and asked if I wanted to hear about a minor-league home run he'd just recalled.

"Are you in this story?" I asked.

"How'd you guess?" he said.

It was in the American Association in 1955. Rigney, a young player-manager—he was thirty-seven years old—had the Minneapolis Millers in first place, riding an eight-game winning streak. The Toledo Mud Hens were leading in this tilt, however, when the Millers put a couple of men on in the ninth, causing the Toledo manager to opt for a change of pitchers. The man out of the bullpen, it turned out, was Monk Meyer, a right-hander whom Rigney had batted against more than once in the majors, when Meyer pitched for the Phillies. "I'm coaching third base," Rigney told me. "But I come walking back to the dugout while he's warming up. We had a couple of left-handed pinch-hitters, and each one is looking at me, thinking, Is it me? Is it *him*? But I say, 'I'll handle this one myself, boys,' and I take a bat and go out there. We had this very short right-field fence there at the old Nicollet Park, and—well, the very first pitch, I hit it out. Which meant our ninth win, and we go on to win eight more in a row, seventeen straight. When I got to home plate, there was quite a crowd, you know, but in all that noise I heard our second-string catcher say, 'Well, now we've seen *everything*.'"

Last-ever homers stay in mind, too, and the one we should find room for here was Babe Ruth's, which he knocked on Saturday, May 25, 1935, against the Pittsburgh Pirates, eight days before he hung up his spikes for good. Ruth was forty years old by this time and, worn and embittered, had gone off to play for the Boston Braves. Nothing worked out for him there except this one afternoon, when he hit a single and three home runs. The third—Ruth's farewell and his famous No. 714—flew over the double-decked stands in right field and out of the park, a feat never previously accomplished at Forbes Field. I have written about this shot before, I believe, and probably will again. It is his greatest. (I have not overlooked Ruth's called-shot home run in the World Series of 1932, but the burden of evidence—most of all, the evidence of game stories written at

Wrigley Field that day—suggests that Ruth, instead of gesturing to the place he would hit the ball, actually held up one *and* then two outstretched fingers to the Cubs pitcher, Charlie Root, in accompaniment with the first and second called strikes during that raucous at-bat. Then he hit the next delivery into the center-field stands. It was a brash and brilliant deed, but probably not quite the legend that almost immediately sprang into being—and that the Babe was smart enough never to deny.)

My own boyhood memories of the Babe include several home runs, but none of them of truly Brobdingnagian proportions. Indeed, they most resembled lofty fly balls that simply declined to come down and, eventually running out of field room, fell among the straw-hatted gents in the right-field stands or the bleachers. (Sometimes in those days you'd see the businessmen-fans still coming into the Stadium in the fourth or fifth inning, with the *World-Telegram* or the *Sun* tucked under their arms; games started at three-fifteen in the afternoon back then, and moved along briskly enough to get everyone home in plenty of time for supper.)

Hank Aaron, who surpassed Ruth's lifetime total in 1974 and went on to establish the present summit of seven hundred and fifty-five home runs, was more celebrated for his consistency and his persevering power than for awesome distant shots; he also holds the record marks for lifetime runs batted in and extra-base hits. Although he was capable of the occasional scary poke, as Roger Craig had observed that day at the Polo Grounds, Aaron's wristy, late swing tended to impart backspin to the ball, which made for line drives rather than the towering rainmakers that characterized the work of Mantle, Killebrew, and Frank Howard, to name but a few. Photos of these thick, granitic figures at the apex of their upbound swings all show a planted, columnar front leg, with every other part of the body pulling back violently against the hawser line of the bat and the now departed ball; that deep-dug front leg and the heaving, upraised arms make them look like anchor men on a tug-of-war team. Ted Williams, in his classic text, "The Science of Hitting," extolls a slight upswing in midstroke, because it increases the area of solid contact with the pitched ball. Tony Kubek, talking with me up at Yankee Stadium not long ago (he does the Yankee games on local cable television now), made the same point about swinging up and *through* the ball as a means of imparting topspin, which results in a drive that seems to bite through the air, almost accelerating upward as it heads away and perhaps out. "That phrase 'a quick bat' means nothing, you know," he said. "But a bat that swings through the ball and *looks as if it stays in contact* is what does the trick. You saw that with Mantle all the time. It sounds impossible, but after he hit one you had the feeling that the ball and the bat had been together forever, there in the middle of the swing. Hank Aaron was the other way. Most of his homers stayed low, because of his style—low and long. Which tells something about the kind of power he had."

Hank Aaron's No. 715—the homer that broke the known-by-heart Ruthian lifetime record total that had stood for almost four decades—was hit in the fourth inning of a Braves home game on April 8th, 1974 (Al Downing, the Dodger left-hander, was the hittee), and what struck me about it, aside from its glory, was the fact that the outfield at Atlanta Fulton County Stadium had already been primped up with a memorial decoration, painted on the grass, celebrating the event in advance. Hank's total had stood at seven hundred and thirteen at the end of play in 1973, when he had wafted forty homers all told, so a very early date with the record books the following spring was a certainty. Aaron hit the tying blow on April 4th, at Cincinnati, and the Braves then played two more road games in Cincinnati, while the Braves front office held its breath, in the horrid thought that the grand deed might be committed out there, far from the panting sellout home-town hordes. When the famous ball did go out—I was watching at home, along with the rest of America—play was stopped for eleven minutes, for speeches and photos and tears down by home plate: a separately sponsored pause in mid-game that startled me more than the historic dinger itself. The P.R.-enhanced record-breaking event, a staple of modern sports, had been born, and we have seen its like often since then, I'm sorry to say—most recently when Rickey Henderson broke Lou Brock's lifetime stolen-base record out in Oakland, earlier this month. Records are part of the game, to be sure, but to me these All-Time ceremonials feel as flat and as tacky as Mother's Day.

(A very different variety of home run might also be mentioned here, in passing—the Never Was. One well-known former big-leaguer told me in some detail about a home run of his that I found sufficiently interesting to make me write it up for this piece. The only thing wrong with it, a regretful fact checker later discovered, was that it never happened—a soaring deed that went from legend to myth in midair.) ...

Theme: Sox Socks.

Time & Place: 9 A.M., Winter Haven, Fl.

Characters: Mahogany-toned Red Sox alumni, here as spring coaches, happy as quahogs.

Johnny Pesky (*he is seventy-one, still with an infielder's narrow frame and alert gaze*): "When I came up as a rookie in '42, Ted Williams was already there. They put me batting ahead of him in the lineup, and sometimes in a close game he'd say, 'Get on, Johnny, and I'll hit one off this guy.' Then he'd *do* it. I know he hit one like that off Hank Borowy, in Yankee Stadium, and one against Allie Reynolds—two that come to mind. Nobody else would say anything like that. Unusual man."

Frank Malzone (*twelve years at third base, twenty years of scouting; sixty-one years old*): "The one I hit in the All-Star Game in 1959, off Don Drysdale. Third or fourth inning—something like that. It was at the old Coliseum, in L.A. Rocky Colavito and Yogi Berra also hit home runs for the American League in that game. Three home runs, all by Italians."

Carl Yastrzemski (*the one and only*): "Of my own? I guess the one I hit that tied up the game in Detroit, a couple of weeks before the end in 1967. There was one out in the top of the ninth, and we were in that tough, tough pennant race."

I remembered the moment. This was the same wild September in the American League that Jim Kaat had talked about—a scramble that ended with the Red Sox edging out the Twins and the Tigers on the final Sunday. Down the stretch, Yaz had carried the Sox with one of the great sustained bursts of individual slugging that the game has seen—a performance that won him a Most Valuable Player award later that year. Standing behind me up in the Tiger Stadium press box was Clif Keane, a wry longtime beat writer with the *Globe,* and as we watched Yaz step up to bat in that ninth-inning crisis he growled, "Go on, prove you're the M.V.P. Prove it to *me.* Hit a homer." Yaz hit the homer.

As might be expected, I won't be able to find room here for more than a handful of the game's all-time homers, or anything like all the great sluggers who hit them. Mike Schmidt and Frank Robinson aren't here, as they should be, and Willie Stargell surely deserves a further and more fervent accolade; I meant to cite Dick Allen and Ralph Kiner, too, of course. Nor will I find space to say what I'd wish to about sterling current practitioners like Eddie Murray, Andre Dawson, Dewey Evans, Jack Clark, and the others. As it has turned out, some of the friends and players I bothered with my questions must be left out, for lack of room, and their favorite downtowners along with them. Here, in any case, are the premier home-run hitters—the lifetime leaders—and their totals:

Hank Aaron	755	Reggie Jackson	563
Babe Ruth	714	Mike Schmidt	548
Willie Mays	660	Mickey Mantle	536
Frank Robinson	586	Jimmy Foxx	534
Harmon Killebrew	573	Ted Williams	521

Willie Mays, sole proprietor of the six-hundred level in this distinguished edifice, still looked loose when he once again came to Scottsdale for the spring semester as some kind of coach for the Giants. (One Giants official, asked by a visiting TV reporter for Mays' job description, said, "Willie's work here is to be Willie Mays.") Some mornings, you could hear Mays' boyish, high-voiced, jabbering way of talking even before you got through the tunnel into the clubhouse, and you'd find him in there perhaps autographing boxes of team baseballs at a table while he agitated with the clubhouse man and anybody else around. Each day, he wore a faded pink polo shirt with "Say Hey" over the breast. He looked his age—he just turned sixty—but you could still see the thick muscles under the now softer skin of his forearms. He was a little impatient when I asked him to remember a home run for me—I hadn't stopped to think what sort of catalogue selection this would entail—but then he said, "Home run against Claude Raymond, in the Astrodome. Somebody was on first, and it tied the game. Jim Davenport won it for us in the eleventh or twelfth inning. Raymond threw me thirteen fastballs, and I fouled them off. The ball went over the fence in left-center field. What *year*? You'd have to look that up. Ask Claude Raymond—he probably knows it better than I do. That was the only dramatic type of home run I ever hit."

Tracking this one down took a while, but the trip was worth it. Lon Simmons, a handsome, deep-voiced veteran California broadcaster, vividly remembered the confrontation and its result, and said he thought that the blow had been Mays' six-hundredth roundtripper. Not quite, it turned out. No. 600, on September 22, 1969, was in fact a game-winning pinch-hit job, down in San Diego, when Mays batted for George Foster and hit one out against a rookie pitcher named Mike Corkins.

"Why'd it have to be me?" Corkins said disconsolately to his manager, Preston Gomez, after the game. (I found the tale in Charles Einstein's book "Willie's Time.")

"Son," Gomez said gently, "there've been five hundred and ninety-nine before you."

I continued the quest over the telephone once I got home, helped immeasurably by a bulldog Giants media person at Candlestick Park. "What about this one?" she said, evidently consulting some thick Book of Willie out there by the Bay. "August 29, 1965— a three-run homer against Jack Fisher, of the Mets, in the ninth inning. It was Willie's seventeenth of the month."

"Sorry," I said. "It's got to be in Houston."

"Hmmm. Well— Oop, how about June 13, 1967? Mays failed as a pinch-hitter in the sixth inning, in Houston, but stayed in the game and won it with a grand slam against Barry Latman. It was his first slam since '62."

"Wrong pitcher," I said. "It *sounds* exciting, but who are we to say?"

There was another pause, and then she had it. The homer, Willie's No. 501, had indeed tied up the game, just as Mays told me, in the Astrodome on September 14, 1965—a fearsome month in the National League, I recalled, when the Giants had fought off two or three closely pursuing clubs, only to fall to the Dodgers near the end.

Mays, going for the fences in the ninth, had become "embroiled in a prolonged battle with reliever Claude Raymond," my faraway researcher read aloud, and had fouled off four pitches before "sending the ball soaring four hundred feet over the center-field fence." Davenport's pinch-hit single then won the game, in the twelfth.

Four foul balls? I went to Claude Raymond, just as Willie had told me to in the first place. Possibly the only Quebec-born right-hander yet to attain the majors (Denis Boucher, a *habitant* rookie twirler with the Blue Jays, throws left and *bats* right), Raymond had wound up his career, predictably enough, with the Montreal Expos in 1971, and had then stayed on as a color commentator for that club. I called him at home, and he remembered the moment at once.

"I threw Mays thirteen straight fastballs," he said, even before I could ask. "And he fouled off thirteen. Jay Alou was the base runner on first, and Mays was up there to hit a home run. All those fouls were nicks or little ticks back to the screen—nothing close to a base hit. Then I threw one more, a little inside, and Willie bailed out but opened up on the ball at the same time, the way only he could do, and it went out. I remember Paul Richards, our general manager, came up to me afterward and said how happy he was I'd gone fast-ball all the way. He said it was a great duel."

I told Raymond that Mays had described it as the only dramatic home run of his career.

"Well, it's a great compliment," Raymond said, in his pleasing North Gaul tones. "You can thank him for me."

Willie was right about the thirteen fouls, after all, but perhaps we can quarrel with him just the same. David Bush covers the Athletics for the San Francisco *Chronicle*, and when I asked him to remember a homer for me he came up with a long standoff game he'd listened to at home, on the radio, back when he was a freshman at U. Cal, in 1963: "That game matched up Juan Marichal, of the Giants, against Warren Spahn, and it went on interminably," Bush said. "No score after nine innings, no score after twelve. Both the starting pitchers stayed in there. I was a Giants fan, of course, but by this time I was rooting for Spahn, because of who he was and because he was just about at the end of his career. Willie beat him, 1–0, with a homer in the bottom of the fifteenth. I didn't see it, but I still feel as if I *almost* saw it. It was that kind of a hit."

David's story reminded me of something, and when I got home I dug out my files of the *SABR Bulletin,* a useful newsletter published for members of the Society for American Baseball Research. There, in the February, 1991, issue, I reconfirmed the news: Willie Mays is the only major-league ballplayer to have hit a home run in every inning from the first through the sixteenth; moreover, he leads all comers with twenty-two lifetime extra-inning home runs. (Jack Clark is second, with seventeen.) Too bad none of them were dramatic.

The longest home run I've ever seen—the longest, easily—was a 1975 spring-training space vehicle launched by Dave Kingman, of the Mets, against the Yankees' Catfish Hunter one night at Fort Lauderdale. Everyone who was there still remembers the moment and talks about it happily when the subject comes up. Both principals had joined a Gotham club that winter—Hunter coming over from the World Champion Oakland A's, and Kingman from the Giants—and there was a sizable media horde on hand when Kingman got around on an offspeed Hunter delivery in the first inning. The ball went over the left-field fence about three palm trees high (or so I described it in this space, a bit later). Mickey Mantle, on hand that evening as a Yankee batting coach, said that he'd never seen a longer blow, and Yankee manager Bill Virdon, reminding us that there was another full diamond out there beyond the main field, ventured that the ball had been a simultaneous homer here and double next door.

Others among my collection of grand-master dingers sometimes waver in clarity or relative merit, I've noticed, but Reggie Jackson's third homer of the night against the Dodgers in the final game of the 1977 World Series has not lost its lustre. As most of us surely remember, he whacked the three in consecutive at-bats, each against a different pitcher and each on the very first pitch. The feat still seems unimaginable, but that third home run would have been special even as a solitaire. It came against the Dodger knuckleballer Charlie Hough, and landed deep in the uninhabited sector of the center-field bleachers (the black "batter's eye" background), where it bounced around in celebratory fashion—an enormous shot. Fran Healy, a teammate of Reggie's on that club, keeps that homer at the top of his own lifetime chart. "The thing people don't know about Reggie is that he was a great knuckleball hitter," he told me. "I don't know how you can do that, because that pitch has no pattern, you know, but Reggie always knew how to handle it, somehow. *Oh*, was that ball hit!"

Like other long-term baseball writers, I have had a firsthand view of many of the other celebrated late-season and post-season home runs of the past three decades, but, in common with every sports fan, I have noticed that their very celebrity—in particular, their numbingly repeated reappearances in video-clip on my home screen—eventually drains them of meaning and emotion. Carlton Fisk's twelfth-inning shot in Game Six of the 1975 World Series now feels like Jimmy Stewart's tearful late homecoming in "It's a Wonderful Life"; and similar fabulous blows, such as Kirk Gibson's previously cited game winner in the 1988 Series, Dave Henderson's stunner against the Angels in the '86 American League playoff, and Bucky Dent's little sailer into the screen at Fenway Park which destroyed the Red Sox in a one-game playoff in '78, are in danger of similar Hallmarking. Only a deliberate effort of memory and imagination—a private revisiting of the scene, so to speak—can sometimes bring them back into view for an instant or two.

The blurring of these thrilling moments because of overexposure is a shame, but there is probably no help for it. Hollywood historians still bemoan the loss of hundreds of early movie classics that fell to dust because they were shot on unstable nitrate film, but I have sometimes perversely wished that our sports footage could suffer the same fate, so that we might again learn to rely on memory as a depository for our most precious games. One night at Yankee Stadium last month, when the White Sox were in town, I asked Carlton Fisk whether that ceaselessly replayed scene of his gyrations along the first-base line as he watched his Game Six homer go up and out on that long-ago night had not come to replace his own memories of the moment, and he said, "You know, I'll bet you I haven't viewed it more than four or five times, for just that reason. I turn it off or go out of the room whenever it comes along, because I want to keep it fresh in my head. I try not to talk about it or to answer questions about it, either. I want to keep hold of the memory of what it felt like, as opposed to what it looks like on the screen. Maybe there'll come a time later on when I can be relaxed and think about it again on my own, but right now it's best to keep it enclosed."

Meantime, he said, he can dwell on a homer he smacked on August 17th last year—to set a new all-time record for all White Sox hitters, and simultaneously break Johnny Bench's record for most home runs by a catcher. Making a *new* memory may be the best trick of all.

Monsters still await us. On April 17, 1953, Mickey Mantle, batting right-handed, drilled a Chuck Stobbs pitch over the loudspeaker that stood above a high wall in dead center field at Griffith Stadium, in Washington, and out of the park. Later that day, the Yankee P.R. man, Red Patterson, went in search of the ball and claimed to have found its owner, a small boy, who pointed out the landing place, five hundred and sixty-five feet away from home plate. Beat writers of the day, knowing Patterson as a keen appreciator of a good headline, were skeptical (Patterson had forehandedly brought along a fresh ball and a few bucks to swap for the memento when the lad conveniently turned up), but no matter: the tape-measure homer had been born. Some sourball in the press box that famous afternoon complained that a breeze had been blowing out, helping Mantle's shot along, but Clark Griffith, the patriarch Senator owner, said, "Hell, the wind has been blowing out here for fifty years, and nobody ever did *that* before!"

Mantle, in any case, accounted for some other fabled flights during his eighteen years up in the Bronx. Some old teammates mention a homer that struck the Gem Razor billboard on top of the right-field bleachers, which barely averted its arrival on the El-station platform just beyond, but there's general agreement that his explosive, steeply rising drive against Bill Fischer, a right-handed pitcher with the Royals, on May 22, 1963, surpassed all. That home run, a solo shot, struck the green filigree-work just below the third-deck roof in right field (this was before the Stadium suffered its character-destroying modernization in the mid-seventies, when the upper roof and its frieze were taken down), and its height and distance, as depicted next to a thick, dotted flight path painted over a tabloid photograph of the day, are precise: three hundred and seventy-four feet out, a hundred and eight feet and one inch up. (I think I can almost remember this vivid pictograph on the back page of forty or fifty motion-trembling copies of the *News* in my car on the Lexington Avenue Express the next morning.) Two eyewitnesses told me about it this year. Tony La Russa, a teammate of Fischer's on the Royals back then, said, "We'd been agitating the heck out of him just before he crunched it. Eddie Lopat was our manager, and he was real upset. It made this loud noise"—he popped his hands together—"when it hit up there, and then we got real quiet. Nobody else I saw ever hit a ball like that."

Tony Kubek, a Yankee teammate, was sitting closer but had an imperfect view of the event. "We all jumped off the bench to watch it go," he said. "But it was hit so hard that the ball had bounced back down onto the grass before we could get to the top step of the dugout. Bang and it was over. I don't know if that was Mickey's longest ever, but it was the hardest-hit."

Kubek told me that he had been talking with some members of the Toronto Blue Jays a couple of years ago, just after their first baseman, Fred McGriff, mashed a long homer into the upper reaches of the Stadium. They seemed to think it was an all-timer, but Kubek told them to imagine a ball hit ten or twenty rows farther back and then up to the level of the present light tower out there: that was the Mantle shot. They doubted him, so the next day he stopped by the Yankee offices and found the old photograph and took it down to the clubhouse, where it changed some minds. "'Oh!' they said," Kubek reported. "'Ohhhh!'"

Modern-day long home runs lack the misty aura of these decades-gone parabolas, but the ball, it seems certain, is flying as far as it ever did. Jose Canseco, the Athletics' gargantuan cruncher, hit a homer against the Blue Jays in the 1989 American League playoffs which landed in the fifth, and topmost, level of the vast SkyDome—an area to this day unvisited by any other baseball. Someone later estimated the landing site at eleven stories above the field. Even at that, Canseco himself, along with some other witnesses, has expressed a preference for a grand slam he struck against Frank Wills last May, in the same stadium, which caromed off the protective front glass of Windows on SkyDome, the third-level restaurant in dead center field. Kit Stier, who covers the Athletics for the Oakland *Tribune,* subsequently hiked out to interview some of the startled dinner patrons there, who told him that the ball, if undeflected, would have continued untouched into the kitchens. (Pleased by the buoyancy of indoor Toronto air, Josey later suggested that he wouldn't mind a trade or a free-agency deal someday that would permit him to bash for the Blue Jays; then he heard about the Canadian tax laws and changed his mind.) I was reminded about three or four other Canseco blasts in the course of my interviews (including a dead-center-field World Series slam I saw at Dodger Stadium, which was dimmed by the Kirk Gibson all-timer in the same game), but this was a pattern I had already come to recognize. Great home-run hitters—Mays, Mantle, Kingman, Killebrew, and the rest—have often seemed to be in competition with themselves most of all.

Bo Jackson's predilection for strikeouts and a passing uncertainty with fly balls had so far kept him from being considered a major-league player of the first rank, but when he really connected with a pitch all that was forgotten. His monument may turn out to be the second-inning home run he lofted against Oil Can Boyd in Fenway Park on July 16, 1988. The ball left the yard just to the right of the center-field flagpole and struck close to the top of a wall up there that runs well above the upper bleachers, at the same level as the screening atop the Green Monster. Conservative Red Sox observers put the point of impact sixty-two feet up and better than four hundred feet out. Lou Gorman, the Boston general manager, believes that *another* Bo-vs.-Can home run, smacked the following spring in the Royals' Florida park at Baseball City, may have flown even farther, but an absence of any surrounding architecture makes computation difficult.

Gorman told me that he also had a vivid recollection of a flyer set sail by Boog Powell, the massive old Orioles doorstop, that glanced off the back edge of the right-field roof at the old Comiskey Park, beyond the light towers, and off into the outer darkness; native runners sent in search of the pill said they'd found it three blocks away. These *National Geographic* trackdowns are entertaining but historically dubious, since local topography and the excitability of witnesses come into play. Joe Morgan, the Red Sox manager, recalled for me a wind-aided dinger hit a few seasons ago by a Pawtucket outfielder of his, Sam Bowen, that landed beyond the left-field wall (this was in Toledo)—a paced-off five hundred and seventy-three feet away. He feels confident about the distance, he said, because he dispatched two idle pitchers of his in search of the souvenir, who came back and told him that the arriving missile had startled (and just missed) the second baseman of a Little League nine at play out there. Well, maybe.

This need of ours for the longest-ever, out-of-the-election-district home run seems to arise from a curious inner uncertainty; we need constant statistical reassurance that the latest wonder, on the field or on the tube, equals or exceeds anything from the past before we can accord it a full measure of awe and delight. Many ballparks now offer the fans and the media a computer-assisted insta-stat announcing an extended, hit-the-ground distance of each home run even when it has failed to leave the park: a fraud, inasmuch as one ingredient of the trigonometry will always be a pure guess about the ball's angle of flight on departure or ricochet. This particular numbers game may have had its origin with the Twins, whose P.R. people were approached one day in 1961 by a math instructor at Stillwater State Prison, in Minnesota, with the request that he be permitted to make some measurements of their then current yard, Metropolitan Stadium. Thus armed, he soon returned with a chart of the premises which set forth the distances from home plate to every fair-ball seat in the park. "Harmon Killebrew was with us back then," Twins media director Tom Mee told me, "and everybody loved those numbers."

What I enjoy is the landmark landing sites and measurements *within* a park—a painted seat or a star-shaped decal with the slugger's initials inside—which a number of teams have dedicated, in the manner of a historical society immortalizing a local battlefield. Sitting in the stands before the game and picking out these faraway wonders is a kick. Tim McCarver, the passionate Mets and CBS game announcer, tipped me off that the star up in right field at Veterans Stadium which marks a 1971 Willie Stargell blast against Jim Bunning is not absolutely accurate. "It was a hanging slider—I should know, because I was the catcher who called the pitch," McCarver said. "And it went way out there and suddenly disappeared through an entranceway in the top deck. No noise, no carom or bouncing around—it was just *gulped*. When they came to put up one of their commemorative stars, they could only stick it by that exit. They had no idea how far the ball actually went."

Leaving over-all home-run distances unmeasured encourages legend and simultaneously preserves science, I submit. The boomed line drive that caroms off some unoccupied top-deck seat with no previous apparent droop or sag to its flight path is particularly thrilling, because it looks as if it would continue onward and upward forever; I still recall a pulled Joe DiMaggio home run like that, into the left-field upper deck at Yankee Stadium. The laws of physics, however, decree that once a missile begins to lose its propulsive force it quickly reverts to gravitational free-fall: almost a straight downward path. As a young fan, I used to observe this phenomenon prettily demonstrated in the laboratory of the Polo Grounds, which had a frighteningly proximate right-field wall, two hundred and fifty-seven feet down the line, with an overhanging upper deck just above. Again and again, you'd see a right fielder jam his back up against the wall, put up his hands, and catch a fly ball that looked like a flowerpot nudged off a fire escape above his head. Next time, he'd stare up, stick up his mitt, and, open-mouthed, catch nothing: a home run, usually by Mel Ott.

Tim McCarver also reminded me about Darryl Strawberry's thunderous blow against Ken Dayley at Busch Stadium in 1985. The game, on the last Tuesday of the season, was the first of a critical three that the visiting Mets had to sweep in order to stay alive in their division, and the two starters, John Tudor and the Mets' Ron Darling, had pitched a double shutout through the regular distance before being relieved. The Strawberry homer, in the top of the eleventh, bounced off the scoreboard clock, high up in right center: the sudden stroke of a mighty bell, one felt. (The Mets won the next night as well, behind Doc Gooden, but went down in the third game and were eliminated.) "Busch was never a home-run stadium," McCarver said, "but Straw could small-up any park." (Strawberry, who has departed Shea Stadium and its derisive "Darr-ylll!" catcalls to play for the Dodgers, entered this season with two hundred and fifty-two lifetime home runs; his one hundred and seventy-one over the past five years is the best among all active sluggers.)

The longest homer ever hit at Busch, Tim McCarver went on, was Willie McCovey's against Alvin Jackson in 1966, the park's first year. "There's no doubt in my mind about this," he said. "I called that pitch, too. It was as if McCovey had hit it off a tee. It caromed off the upper part of the scoreboard and bounced back onto the field. It was longer than Straw's homer, by *far.*"

McCarver was a highly regarded major-league catcher for twenty-one years, mostly with the Cardinals and the Phillies, before he moved up behind the mike, and though he was not known as a slugger, I was pretty sure he had a favorite home run of his own tucked away somewhere, and I asked for it. "Tenth inning of the fifth game of the World Series in 1964," he said, like a slide lecturer punching up the south portal at Chartres. "A three-and-two sinker by Pete Mikkelsen that didn't sink. We had two men on, up at Yankee Stadium, and it won the game. I remember the pitch, but I don't remember going around the bases. I was twenty-two years old, and very impressionable."

McCarver, I noticed, had delivered McCovey's name a little oddly, and I seemed to detect the same tone whenever that name came up in conversations. A *hush.* Lon Simmons recalled a McCovey two-run shot against Steve Blass at Pittsburgh's Three Rivers Stadium on the last day of the 1966 season. "It was a line drive over the center-field wall, and it went on *forever,*" he said. "But of course I'd seen him do the same thing with that sweeping stroke of his, years before, when he hit one against Jim Maloney in the old Cincinnati ballpark, over that moon-deck in right field. Only a couple of balls had ever been hit up there before."

Fran Healy, who had been a young teammate of McCovey's on the Giants in the early seventies, told me that Sparky Anderson, then the manager of the Cincinnati Big Red Machine, hated to pitch to Stretch under any circumstances. "There was a game against them in their park one day when we had a runner on third with no outs, so they had to play their infield in, with McCovey up at bat," Fran said. "I looked out, and they were all standing sort of sidewise, to make less of a target. Later on, one of them said they should be drawing combat pay, because of those line drives of his. McCovey was the only hitter I can remember that had whole teams in awe of him."

A PRETTY GOOD DAY
IN THE LIFE OF A
RESEARCH SCIENTIST

Daniel Paisner's book, *Ball,* from which this extract is taken, uses the de-
vice of following the ball itself, made in Turrialba, Costa Rica, for fifty
cents–worth of tanned cowhide over a tightly wound mass of string and
rubber. On September 27, 1998, Mark McGwire hit it down the left-field
line for his seventieth home run of the season and eclipsed Roger Maris's
long-standing record. The book goes on to describe what subsequently
happened to the ball—caught by a young man named Phil Ozersky, kept
in a bulletproof Plexiglas box, and eventually sold for three million dollars to a comic-book tycoon who had already bought McGwire's 1st,
63rd, 67th, 68th, and 69th home-run balls. He called the 70th "the Big
Boy." The section that follows deals only with the Big Boy's journey into
the left-field seats.

⊘

A S DILEMMAS GO, this one's not much: Mark McGwire, last
game of the season, at 68 home runs and counting, or the going-
nowhere-fast St. Louis Rams facing the going-nowhere-just-yet Arizona Cardinals, in town for the first time since the team quit their
long-suffering supporters for the sweetheart leases of Phoenix. For a
baseball fan, it is no contest. Even for a football fan, it's a toss-up.

The conflict didn't exactly sneak up on Philip Ozersky, a twenty-
six-year-old research scientist earning $29,000 as a finisher in the

genetics lab of the Genome Sequencing Center on the Washington University campus. His colleagues had arranged for these tickets months earlier, long before McGwire shattered the home run record, and long before Rams season ticket holders were inclined to check the football schedule. The idea was to get the people from work together for an end-of-summer office party, with husbands and wives and significant others helping to fill the hundred or so bleacher and standing-room seats in the private Batting Cage party box in the left field stands. Ozersky, a big time baseball fan, was all for it. His former boss, Nancy Miller, arranged for the seats back in May (at $45 per), and she settled on the final game by default. There weren't many dates still available and the last game seemed fine, even though the Cardinals weren't likely to be in the hunt for much.

Ozersky shares his season seats to the Rams with his father, Herbert, a retired site analyst for a pharmaceutical company; his brother, David, a computer analyst, and his sister-in-law, Kristen, also have tickets, and they usually drive out to the stadium together. Between them, it's not like they couldn't find someone to take the extra ticket. In weighing which game to attend, Ozersky didn't pay much attention to whether McGwire would hit one out and set a new record. Mostly he was thinking how he and these end-of-summer lab outings at Busch had a history. Last year, he met his girlfriend Amanda Abbott in the same Batting Cage party box, so there was a little bit of a good luck thing in his thinking as well.

This game hasn't even started yet, and already he's ahead. He's here with Abbott, and a group of people have arrived early to watch batting practice and get started on the free beers—one of the bonus features of the Batting Cage party box. Ozersky, a one-time high school defensive lineman with a hangdog expression, a hands-in-pockets demeanor, and a birthmark around his left eye that leaves people wondering what happened to the other guy, is not even thinking what it would take for a ball to find its way through the giant break in the front wall of the box, opening out to a gorgeous view of the field. Most times, he goes to a game, he checks out his seats, he does a little figuring on his chances of catching a foul ball, or a home run, depending. He's been going to games all his life, a couple hundred by his count, and he's never come close. Well, once, during the 1996 Division Series against the Padres, he got his hands on a ball tossed into the bleachers by Brian Jordan, but it bounced out of his reach, and he tended not to count that one anyway because it wasn't a game ball. It was just a ball.

Here, boxed into this room, he doesn't even process his chances. It's not an impossibility, mind you, but the ball would have to come in low, at an angle, and the likelihood of a ball being hit that hard, that far, at just that right angle wasn't worth considering. However, at the very moment of Ozersky's not considering, Ron Gant sends a batting practice pitch over the left field fence and directly through the open wall of the room. Man! Ozersky keeps his eyes on the ball as it arcs toward him, but he doesn't move for it. The ball clambers up the room's portable metal bleachers and comes to rest a couple yards from where Ozersky sits. He's the first to spot it, primarily because the few people in the room aren't paying full attention. It's just batting practice, after all, and the ball comes to rest beneath the seat of Laura Courtney, a colleague in the finishing lab with what Ozersky guesses is only a passing interest in baseball.

So what does Ozersky do? He picks up the ball and hands it to Courtney. She'd have had it, easy, if she'd thought to look, and he gives it to her like this sort of thing happens every day.

For home plate umpire Richard Rieker, finishing up his fifth season in the bigs, it is a day to not screw up. After six months on the road, not seeing his family, not getting any time off more than a couple days running, not always knowing what city it is outside your hotel window, it is like a whole bag of Fridays bunched into one. It is the last day of the season, and he's thinking, *Let's bring it on. Let's get it over with and get home.*

Rieker had known for a couple days he'd be working the plate for this final game; he'd seen that was how the rotation was headed, but he didn't give it much thought. There's only so much you can pay attention to the rotation, this time of year. His main concern, when he thinks about it at all, is for the game to go smoothly. That's what people don't realize about umpiring. When you're behind the plate, or even when you're out on the bases, the thing is to call the game without incident, and in a game like this that would be especially so. History is fine, home run records are fine, but the key is for everything to come out the way it's meant. Keep your name out of the papers. You don't want to be remembered as the guy who screwed things up.

Normally, two clubs under .500, no sweat, you're playing out the string. A game like this, you'll usually see a lot of rookies, up from the minors to show what they can do, so for them it's everything. There are whole careers at stake, even though the season is shot. But here Rieker knows the baseball world will be watching. Heck, it's almost bigger than baseball, this McGwire assault. It's front-page news, all over the planet. In some ways, it's bigger than baseball needs, if such a thing is possible. See, baseball itself had plenty going on. There were, what, four National League series that meant something that final weekend. You had the Cubs, the Giants, and the Mets all going for the wild card. Going into the weekend you also had the Padres and the Astros playing for home field advantage. How often does that happen, last couple days of the season, so much on the line?

But mostly, Rieker knows, there is McGwire. It's the biggest thing he'd ever seen in baseball, this home run race. Five years is not an especially long term of service for a big league umpire, but he'd logged another dozen in the minors. He'd seen a lot of ball, and he can tell you how big this thing was. He'd drive around his neighborhood in St. Louis and see a local church with its sign out front, talking about when services were that week, when they were having their annual fish fry, and then, at the bottom, it said, "God bless you, Mark." That's how much McGwire means to the people in St. Louis, how much he means to baseball. It's bigger than sports. People who don't know a thing about the game know about McGwire. His appeal cuts across economic lines, racial lines, religious lines, every line you could imagine. You can't turn on the radio and *not* come across his name. The last thing Rieker wants is to get in the way of any of that. An umpire's job is to maintain a perfect environment for the players.

People tend to shine over events in their minds. They forget. They forget the game in Milwaukee, just last week, fifth inning, McGwire hits a rope off pitcher Rod Henderson toward the seats in left center and some fan reaches over the railing to grab the ball and umpire Bob Davidson rules it a double. Okay, so they remember the game, Rieker supposes, but they don't think what it means from the umpire's perspective. It doesn't register that way. Happens all the time, an ump maybe misses a call, but never under this kind of microscope. McGwire's rounding the bases and Davidson actually has to send him back to second, and the crowd starts booing like crazy. The press starts calling it the 65½ home run ball. They said he should have had 66, and then Sosa went and hit his 66th and jumped out ahead. The folks around here were just about ready to string up Bob Davidson, they were so upset about the call. For a beat or two, that's how it looked, at least until McGwire hit a couple more and surged ahead, and even then there was talk of an asterisk.

Rieker had seen all the replays, and there wasn't one that showed that Davidson missed the call. There was even a shot, clear as day, front page of *USA Today*, showed the ball in the fan's glove, way over the yellow line of the fence. It was a double fence, two and a half feet separating the fans from the field of play, but a grown man, leaning over, his glove arm outstretched, he can reach over two and a half feet like nothing at all. Try it sometime and you'll see.

What happened, Rieker theorizes, was that this whole home run thing had gotten into people's guts from day one. You had a season's worth of buildup, and the fans started to see things with their hearts and not with their eyes. They wanted it to be a home run, so that's what they saw. The sportscasters, too. They've got their own emotions getting in the way, same as the fans. They're thinking about ratings, or whatever it is those people think about. Plus, you never really get the right camera angle. The only people in that ballpark who had the right angle on that call were the second base umpire and the center fielder, Grissom. They're the only ones looking straight on at the ball, and Grissom himself had come out and said Davidson made the right call.

Then there's the game he had worked about a month before, August 29 in St. Louis, Cards against the Braves, when Sam Holbrook had to toss McGwire for arguing a called third strike, and the fans were about ready to run Holbrook out of town. Can you imagine? To have to take the bat out of a guy's hands when he's chasing down a record big as this? If you want to know the truth, to Rieker's thinking, his colleague was more patient than Rieker would have been. He gave McGwire at least three warnings. Rieker himself will give a guy one warning, and if he keeps it up then he's gone. But Holbrook finally had to toss him, LaRussa and third base coach Rene Lachemann too, and the fans, they just went crazy. They threw so much garbage down onto the field it looked for a while like the Cards might have to forfeit the game. Rieker had his wife and children at the ballpark that day, and it was so bad he had the security people take them down from their seats and set them up in the umpire's room for the rest of the game.

No, it wasn't a good day to be an umpire that day against the Braves, not in St. Louis, and the last thing Rieker wanted, going into this final game, was a repeat of that kind of situation. Folks don't realize, all he has to do is call McGwire out on strikes, and if somehow Sammy Sosa winds up winning the home run race, Rieker can look out his window the next morning and find a cross burning on his front lawn. Right here in St. Louis. And God forbid he has to toss McGwire. He doesn't even want to think about that.

Rieker has enough to worry about, calling the game, and on top of that, he has to keep his "traders" straight with the ball boy, "Urkel." The system they've come up with for authenticating the balls means Rieker has to make sure he puts the correct ball in play, the one that corresponds to the chart the Major League Baseball security people are keeping over in the owner's box, behind the plate. They've got the balls marked, in sequence, and then they've got another marking on it you can only see with a special light. The numbers, though, those you can see, and McGwire will come up, the ball boy will run out four new balls, and Rieker will have to place them in order in the ball bags at his hips. He works with two ballbags, so what he'll do is empty the bags of all the ordinary balls and give them back to the ball boy. Then, he'll hold out the lowest-numbered ball for the pitcher, and put the highest-numbered ball in his left ball bag. He'll put the others in the bag on his right hip, and if McGwire fouls one off, or if the pitcher doesn't like the look of the ball he's been given, Rieker can just reach into his right bag and have a 50-50 chance on picking the next one.

He tries to commit the routine to the place in his memory where he won't have to think about it. He works through all the ways he might screw up, and he comes up nearly empty. About the only way he can think of is if McGwire hits a long foul, right down the line, just outside the foul pole, and then, the very next pitch, he hits one in almost exactly the same spot, just inside the foul pole for a home run. If he somehow puts the wrong ball into play, that's the one hole in the system. There'd be two balls out there, in virtually the same section, and it's possible someone could question which was the home run ball and which was the foul ball. It's possible the same guy could come up with both balls, and then where would we be? It isn't likely to happen, but for Rieker it is the ultimate nightmare.

Middle of the third, two outs, bases empty. Cardinals ball boy Kevin Corbin, a twenty-year-old junior at St. Louis University, puts the game on pause.

Really.

He's been doing this, last month or so, every time McGwire bats at home, and he doesn't think he'll ever lose the thrill he feels in running out these special balls to the home plate umpire. He remembers the first time—September 4, beginning of a weekend series with the Reds, the day before McGwire hit his 60th. Ever since, he's worked these moments so many times in his head that when they come around in the lineup he can almost do what he needs to do without thinking about it.

What he needs to do is this: run over to the owner's box behind home plate, where Major League Baseball's Al Williams and Linda Pantell are sitting in the aisle on folding chairs snatched from the locker room. Corbin collects from them four numbered balls, in sequence, and stops to check the stamped numbers on the balls. He has to hand the balls to the umps in order, so he puts the two lowest numbered balls in his right hand, the two highest in his left hand, and runs them out to Mr. Rieker behind home plate. Some of the umps want the balls lowest to highest, some want them highest to lowest, and this is the best way he can think to keep them straight.

After each at bat, Corbin reclaims the balls and returns them to Pantell. If it's a ground out to end the inning, he'll get the ball from the other team's first baseman. If the Cardinals are still up, and the ball is returned to the pitcher, the home plate umpire will signal for it, and Corbin'll run out and make the switch. On the way back to the owner's box, he'll look at the balls and see if they can be used again, next time up. Usually, with McGwire, he hits the balls so hard they don't come back. Either it leaves the field of play, a home run or a foul ball, or it's scuffed so badly it's out of the rotation. However it goes, it's the end of the ball.

Corbin's been a ball boy for five seasons, longer than most. It's a job he was lucky to land, back in high school, and he's not giving it up any time soon. He doesn't even mind that they all call him Urkel. First time it happened, his first year with the club, the Pirates were in town, and they had the television tuned to that show, *Family Matters*. He walked in to the visitors' clubhouse, the Pirates looked at Corbin, then they looked at the television, then the name stuck. Corbin himself can see the resemblance, although the two don't dress alike. The resemblance ends there. Now it's gotten so they all know him as Urkel. The umps, the clubhouse guys, the players. Even some of the visiting players remember him by name, one road trip to the next, and he answers to it, same way he answers to Kevin. It's all part of the same ride.

This season, most of all, it's been something he'll never forget. He tells people he has the best seat in the house, to one of the best shows in baseball history. He runs out those special balls and takes his usual post, on a stool about one hundred feet behind home plate, and then he just sits and watches, like everyone else. It's like being on the inside of a dream, looking out. He can't really describe it. He told a friend of his one time that it was like a kind of heaven. He and Tim Forneris, the guy who caught number 62, they talk about this. They even talked about it before McGwire broke the record, and he remembers Tim saying if he caught one of these balls he would definitely give it back, so he was good to his word. It gets to

Corbin, at the end of the day, how connected he is to something as big as this, how close. Sometimes, McGwire'll round the bases, and Corbin'll step to home plate to switch balls with the ump, and he'll have a chance to give McGwire one of those high-fives. He's in on the celebration. He's even been in the newspaper, a couple times, and he's always on television.

No sir, he wouldn't trade seats with anyone.

Kerry Woodson sees it coming, the whole way.

There's a *crack*, and then a kind of *whoosh*, and then everyone in section 282 is on their feet, certain the ball is heading in their direction. That's how it gets, out here in these home run seats. It's a tricky angle. The ball's hit, and your stomach drops. If you're an outfielder, Woodson supposes, this is something you get used to, but if you're a fan, all the way out here, every fly ball looks like it's got your name on it.

This one, in Woodson's case, does. He reaches up and makes the grab, and his first thought, amazingly, is for McGwire. He qualifies it with a word like *amazingly* because people have since told him that their first thoughts would have centered around what the ball was worth, but Woodson's not thinking about money. He's twenty-two, freshly graduated from Southwest Missouri State, a marketing representative for his father's auto body store, and money is just not the most important thing in a situation like this. Going happily crazy and pumping his fists are the most important things. Also, thinking what an accomplishment like 69 home runs means for a guy like McGwire, and for the game of baseball. It's Ruthian. That's the word that comes to mind. It's positively Ruthian.

His second thought, also amazingly, is for Steve Ryan, the Chicago-based memorabilia dealer who teamed with New York speculators Mark Lewis and Scott Goodman to place to $1 million bounty on the last home run ball of the season. He qualifies his thinking here because just last week, on a visit to Chicago, Woodson took in a game at Wrigley and sat behind Ryan in the bleachers. Woodson mentioned that he was planning to attend the last game of the season at Busch, and Ryan told him to keep him in mind, in case he got his hands on a McGwire home run ball. He even gave the kid his business card. You never know, he said.

Naturally, the $1 million flashes through his mind—not just the amount, but the extraordinary coincidence. He starts to think maybe it was preordained, him coming up with the ball. There's a *Time* magazine reporter sitting in his section, and all game long he's been talking about the money, and soon enough Woodson's thoughts are completely routed in this direction. He's hurriedly escorted from his seat by members of Kevin Hallinan's extraction team, and as he goes, he starts to think, there's no way Felipe Alou is even gonna pitch to McGwire, rest of the game. Woodson begins to believe this so deeply, he almost wills it so. There's no way Alou is gonna let this guy beat him deep, two times in the same game, two games in a row. Not with everything Woodson's heard about Alou, how competitive he is.

He's thinking, Steve Ryan, get your $1 million ready.

Seventh inning, four or five beers in, last call.

When Philip Ozersky is not thinking about McGwire's 69th, which was incredible, or Gant's batting practice home run, which was unbelievable, he's thinking about the beer. That's pretty much the best thing about this party box, on a game-in, game-out basis. You can't always count on baseball history, and you can't always count on catching batting practice home runs, but you can count on plenty of food and drink.

It's not any kind of luxury box, this room. There are metal bleachers, a couple faded pictures dotting the spare walls, squeezed mustard packs flattened to the poured-concrete floor. There's a shot of the 1967 world championship Cardinals team, a picture of Ozzie

Smith, a portrait of Red Schoendienst. Really, there's not much in the way of decoration, or direct sunlight, but when the beer flows this freely no one's complaining. No one's doing much of anything. In fact, when McGwire hauls his Bunyan-like forearms out to the plate for what will likely be his last at-bat of the season, no one is doing much of anything but watching. It gets that way, when McGwire hits—basically all the time, but lately most of all. You could be loading up on beers before they shut you off, but you'll set them down and stop to look at what will happen next, because when Mark McGwire comes to bat almost anything can happen next, and of all the things that could possibly happen next your being shut out of your last couple drafts does not tally too high on your list when weighed against most other game-related outcomes.

Still, some of Ozersky's colleagues mill about the beer stand, and some wander back to the sixteen-wheeler-sized opening atop the BJC Health Services sign with a beer in each hand, or maybe a beer and a hot dog, and they stand, riveted. People have been doing this all season. Even in batting practice, McGwire's opponents stop to watch him hit, their mouths dropped to where you could fit a baseball inside. Each turn at bat is like a scene from that old television show *Bewitched,* where Elizabeth Montgomery twinkles her nose and freeze-frames the rest of the room so that she can work her magic undetected; only here the rest of the room is Busch Stadium, and the 46,110 fans in paid attendance don't need any kind of witchcraft. They've fixed on whatever next piece of magic there might be, on their own. They are dressed mostly in Cardinal red, and they are ready for anything, and everything, all at once.

Ozersky, at least, has his hands free, and when McGwire finally sends his threshold-establishing home run toward the left field fence, the young research scientist instinctively rises to meet it. In the rising, he gets that thrilling stomach drop even major league outfielders admit to feeling when they see the ball coming their way. It is a sensation anyone who has played any kind of ball knows firsthand—that delicious, purposeful moment, tinged with fear, during which the game takes every conceivable turn in your head. It's a feeling that almost leaves a taste in your mouth. Ozersky recognizes that taste, and his heart quickens in response. His stomach's in his throat, and he's thinking, *Here it comes, here it comes, here it comes.*

A guy like Ozersky, he's always prided himself on his drive. His athletic ability, he'll admit, is right in the middle of the curve, he's never been the best at anything, but he'll run a mile to make a play. He still plays intramural softball, football, and even co-ed basketball, and the people he plays with know this about him, and it's important to Ozersky that they know this about him. He'll never fulfill the highlight-reel fantasies of his childhood, but he doesn't care if he ends up on the ground, hurt, as long as he makes the play. He's not jumping into any pool, not knowing if there's any water in it, but that doesn't mean he's not going to hurt himself, playing all out like he does, all the time.

Here, the ball reaches the small room like it has someplace else to be. It ricochets off the back wall, about twenty feet in, and Ozersky is quick enough to feel thankful he didn't try to bare-hand it and that it didn't hit him in the head. Some guy actually does reach his hand in the way of the ball, he'll see it later on the replays, and the ball changes direction a little bit, but not so much that most people notice. Ozersky notices, but at first he thinks maybe the ball hit the handrail, maybe it came in kind of low. Then he turns along with everyone else and follows its path to the wall. The people scattered among those metal bleachers turn their heads mighty quick. *Zip,* the ball whooshes past, and their heads dart as if they are all seated center court at a tennis match.

For a ball that had left Mark McGwire's bat less than five seconds earlier, Ozersky has had an enormous amount of time to think things through. Others in the box will report the same thing—that these next moments play out on a too-slow speed, all around—but it is Ozersky who uses his next moments to advantage. When the others turn to the wall, thinking perhaps the ball will have imbedded itself in the concrete, Ozersky thinks to play the carom. He works the angles in his head. He makes a quarter turn and thinks, *Okay, where's it going?* He reacts like a pool shark, and then he shifts to poker. Without really thinking about it, it occurs to him that the eyes of his colleagues will be the tell, and he quickly scans the room for someone who might have seen something or felt the breeze of the caromed ball as it bounced off the wall in front of them. What he can't see himself he can perhaps pick up on, from someone else. He inventories his friends and colleagues for a contrary expression, and he finally, miraculously spots one—on the metal bleachers, back a bit toward the wall. In an instant, he susses that what this person is looking at is slightly different than what everyone else is looking at. There might as well be a sign over this guy's head, the way his expression stands out from everyone else's. There's definitely something else going on in this person's sightline, and Ozersky follows the gaze to the floor, and there it is: Mark McGwire's 70th home run ball, resting wondrously beneath one of the thin metal slats of bleacher.

If he is anything else, as an athlete, Phil Ozersky is a football player. He may be a huge baseball *fan*, but the only game he ever truly had was football. In high school, he played offensive guard and defensive tackle, even though he was somewhat small for those positions. On the other side of the line, they were 250 pounds, 280, but Ozersky outplayed them at 180. He played every down with the kind of fearless abandon that wins football games—the same fearless abandon, it turns out, that comes in handy chasing down errant home run balls. He dives toward the ball—actually dives, the way you might have seen Ozzie Smith move to his left to grab a low liner up the middle. He doesn't care about the metal bleachers in his path, the dislocated shoulder he's nursing. He just goes for it, and on his way he has time to think how in football it's rarely the first person on a loose ball who winds up with it. They're usually trying to run with the ball or advance it in some way, or they're trying too hard and can't find the handle. Invariably, they make some kind of mistake, and the ball bounces away and into some other set of surer hands. He actually has time to think about this, as he leaves his feet and hurtles himself in the direction of the metal slats to retrieve the ball, and when he lands with a thud on his hurt shoulder, it's still foremost in his mind. He hits his elbow, hard, against the edge of one of the metal footrests but manages to reach his hand underneath the bleachers and swallow the ball in his grip. The phrase that occurs to him is *encompassing* the ball. As he does so, he notices another colleague from the lab, a young man named Jason Kramer, splayed out in a similarly awkward and reckless position, coming up just short in his reach: one beat ahead and two inches short. Ozersky considers that if there were another inch to Jason Kramer's wingspan, he might have encompassed the ball ahead of him. Ozersky looks into Kramer's eyes and gets back what he can best describe as delirium. Ozersky's own expression seems to want to explode in disbelief. He's not sure if he's speaking, or if maybe his thoughts are simply careening about in his head, but what he's thinking, and what he's thinking about saying, is *Oh, my God. Oh, my God. Oh, my God.* Over and over.

What strikes home plate umpire Rieker is the sheer velocity with which the ball leaves the park. He works close to the ground, on his knees, much lower than most guys tend to work the plate, and by the time he's shot to his feet the ball is gone.

To Rieker, it looks at first like McGwire lashes a screaming line drive back to the third baseman, only it's a line drive that somehow keeps screaming all the way to the fence. It's not clear it'll go the distance when it's hit; it's more likely it will bore a hole through the left field wall, but it just keeps going, climbing. He wonders if maybe there was some rise to it, if such a thing is possible. Anyway, it's like a bullet, is how it is, and Rieker has to think that part of what propels that bullet is all the pressure that's been heaped on Mark McGwire, all season long. When you're in the zone like that, when there's commotion all around and you're able somehow to make it fall away, it all adds up. It's got to come out somewhere, that pressure.

From this moment on, he'll be known as the ump behind the plate when McGwire hit his milestone 70th home run, but what Rieker takes away will come down to this one image of himself, hurrying to rise from his crouch before the ball clears the fence. It's like a race, him against the ball. He'll remember the game itself, and the crowd. He'll remember the grace of Mark McGwire and Sammy Sosa, the class. He'll remember the reporters and the flashbulbs. He'll remember the butterflies he felt, seven innings back, at calling a good game. But mostly he'll remember the raw power of this final swing, the hurry the ball is in. The race, as McGwire uncoiled, to have to uncoil himself in the same time it took for the ball to leave the park. To his dying day, he'll hear the number 70, and this is what he'll remember.

HOT TO TROT WITH NO PLACE TO GO

Rick Reilly's often acerbic, always clever columns have delighted readers of *Sports Illustrated* for over fifteen years. He once listed the main targets of his jibes—cheerleaders, hunters, baseball, the NBA, the BCS, the INS, the IOC, the NCAA, college jocks, pro jocks, Detroit, France, Little League, and the twentieth century—but then went on to list ninety-nine (by my count) things he loves about sport in a nonstop sentence that runs on for two pages... "the penalty box and starting blocks and 'Rock chalk, Jayhawk!' and NFL Films spirals and eye black and ear holes and slobbermouth tackles and multimillionaires piling on each other with glee and dignified CEOs sitting behind huge mahogany desks wearing Slippery Rock boxers and how the diamond explodes on you coming out of a stadium tunnel and long walks to the green with your putter and crossover dribbles so quick a mountain lion would gasp and broken bats and salt-stained hats and Minnesota Fats and Wrigley ivy and Fenway monsters and every blade at Augusta..." ad almost infinitum.

Y OU KNOW WHY KIDS don't play baseball anymore? Because they took down the fences.

It's the era of the dread multiuse field. Every kid's diamond now has to share its centerfield with three other fields and a tai chi class. This way, come spring and fall, the park can be turned into (cough, hack, spit) soccer fields.

What fun is baseball without a fence? Without a fence you can't hit a real home run, and without a real home run you can't do the **home run trot,** which is one of the last truly American joys.

I love the **home run trot.** The longer, the better. Did you see Rickey Henderson's **home run trot** the other night in Baltimore? You could've washed and waxed a 1973 Plymouth Barracuda in the time it took him to get around the bases. Henderson turns a home run into an HBO special. First, he pulls at his jersey. Then he slaps his helmet. Twice. Then he hip-hops in the box a few times, and, finally, he takes off on his epic journey, going so wide around first and third that he nearly steps in both dugouts. Generally, Henderson gets around the bases just a hair faster than a man laying sod.

Pete Rose used to fly around the bases as though he had a pot of soup boiling over somewhere. Occasionally he'd touch a bag, but he wasn't a stickler about it. Frank Robinson told him, "Kid, you better leave those homers to those of us who can act them out."

Mickey Mantle always ran with his head down in shame, as if he were eight years old and had just put one through a stained glass window. Babe Ruth ran with little mincing steps, as though he were trying not to step on cracks. Dave Parker used to trot with fingers pointed like pistols.

Right now is a great time to be alive if you're hot for trots, on account of sluggers are hitting home runs every three minutes. Mark McGwire is on pace to hit 311 this year. McGwire has a very humble trot, but he does the coolest thing before he starts: The instant he connects, he flips the bat away, end over end, like a toothpick, as if to say, "Well, there's no use having that around anymore."

Just the idea of the trot is wonderful. Here a man is being allowed to gallivant from one base to the next—real estate that is fraught with peril and angst in every other moment of the game—at his leisure! As he does this, the fielders have to just stand there, hands on hips, and watch, clench-jawed, as he mocks them with his lazy left turns.

You could retype Shakespeare's sonnets into Sanskrit in the time it takes Barry Bonds to get around, yet he's still faster than Oscar Gamble was. One day Ken Griffey Sr. was in the New York Yankees' clubhouse in Minnesota when teammate Gamble smashed one out. Griffey dashed out of the clubhouse, around a corner and down a tunnel, figuring he'd get to home plate just as Gamble was crossing it. Except when Griffey got to the top step of the dugout, Gamble was still waiting for the bat boy to come get his bat. Why rush?

Great trotters are men of courage because they know they might get an earful of cowhide next time up. Yet they carry on. Jeffrey (Hackman) Leonard let his left arm hang limp and leaned toward the pitcher as he ran, like some disabled Cessna. Reggie Jackson would pose long enough to strike a decent oil painting.

The trot is part of the game's very fabric. Remember the look on the face of the death-threatened Hank Aaron when the two fans caught up to him between second and third on number 715? Remember Jimmy Piersall going around backward on his 100th? Do you realize the greatest **home run trot** ever was done on one leg— Kirk Gibson's, after his heroic pinch-hit 1988 Series shocker against the Oakland A's?

Look, baseball is a game of simple pleasures. I coach a team in the Catholic Youth League, and when one of my kids slams a huge one, he doesn't get the glory of a trot. He sprints madly around the bases in case the kid in left has somehow grown a catapult for a right arm and can throw him out from some lady's purse on Field Number 14.

Please, Mr. Parks and Rec Director, if you love baseball, fence us in. Home runs and childhood are over way too soon.

ACKNOWLEDGMENTS

• •

I am, of course, very grateful to those writers who agreed to have their work appear here. There are others: Bill Francis of the Baseball Hall of Fame at Cooperstown was especially helpful. His associates there and many members of the Baseball Writers Association of America contributed to the poll of dramatic home runs. A number of books were especially useful for research, in particular Donald Honig's *Baseball America*. My gratitude to *Sports Illustrated* for the original framework of the "Home-Run Chronology" which has been edited and much added to. Don Johnson, the editor of *Aethlon: The Journal of Sport Literature*, was as helpful as he could be in the search for poems on the home run, which, alas, poets have not been moved to write about. My thanks to Tom Moffett for compiling the contributor notes and, finally, my thanks to André Bernard and Margie Rogers of Harcourt.

CONTRIBUTORS

ROGER ANGELL's first collection of baseball essays, *The Summer Game,* was published in 1972. His other books include *Season Ticket: A Baseball Companion* and *Once More Around the Park: A Baseball Reader.* He has worked at *The New Yorker* since 1956 and is the editor of *Nothing But You: Love Stories from the New Yorker.*

GREGORY CORSO was a seminal poet of the Beat Generation. His books include *Gasoline, Long Live Man,* and, most recently, *Mindfield: New and Selected Poems.* He won the Jean Stein Award for Poetry from the American Academy of Arts and Letters. He died in January, 2001.

ROBERT W. CREAMER is a distinguished sportswriter and baseball historian. A founding writer for *Sports Illustrated,* he was a senior editor at the magazine from the late 1950s until 1985. His books include *Babe: The Legend Comes to Life* and *Stengel: His Life and Times.*

DON DeLILLO is the author of eleven novels, including *White Noise, End Zone, Libra,* and *Mao II,* and has won the National Book Award and the PEN/Faulkner Award for Fiction. He is a member of the American Academy of Arts and Letters.

PAUL GALLICO's thirteen-year stint as a sportswriter included being knocked unconscious after boxing one round with Jack

Dempsey and ended with the publication, in 1938, of *A Farewell to Sport*. In the years until his death in 1976, Gallico wrote prolifically, publishing numerous screenplays, children's books, and popular novels, including *The Snow Goose* and *The Poseidon Adventure*. He received an Academy Award nomination in 1942 for the screenplay for *Pride of the Yankees*.

ROBERT HAMBLIN is a professor of English and the director of the Center for Faulkner Studies at Southeast Missouri State University. He is the author of several collections of poetry and the book *Win or Win: A Season with Ron Shumate*. He is the poetry editor of *Aethlon: The Journal of Sport Literature*.

GARRISON KEILLOR is the author of eleven books, including *Lake Wobegon Days* and *The Book of Guys*. He has hosted the Minnesota Public Radio program *A Prairie Home Companion* since its first broadcast in 1974.

BERNARD MALAMUD is the author of seven novels including *The Assistant* and *The Fixer*, for which he was awarded the Pulitzer Prize. His short fiction has been collected in *The Complete Stories*. He died in 1986.

SADAHARU OH holds the world record for home runs, hitting 868 in his twenty-two seasons with Tokyo's Yomiuri Giants. He is the author, with David Falkner, of the autobiography *Sadaharu Oh: A Zen Way of Baseball*.

DANIEL PAISNER has collaborated on several bestsellers with, among others, George Pataki and Edward I. Koch. He is the author of a novel, *Obit*.

ROBERT PETERSON is a former newspaper editor who has written several books on sports, including *Cages to Jump Shots: Pro Basketball's Early Years* and *Pigskin: The Early Years of Pro Football.*

GEORGE PLIMPTON is the editor of *The Paris Review.* His writings on sports include *Out of My League, Paper Lion, Shadow Box,* and the novel, *The Curious Case of Sidd Finch.* His most recent book is *Pet Peeves or Whatever Happened to Dr. Rawff?*

RICK REILLY is in his sixteenth year as a senior writer for *Sports Illustrated* and is the author of the weekly column, "Life of Reilly." In addition to co-authoring books with Marv Albert, Wayne Gretzky, and Charles Barkely, Reilly has written the sports-related novels, *Missing Links* and *Slo-Mo!: My Untrue Story.* He has been voted National Sportswriter of the Year six times.

GRANTLAND RICE became one of America's most prominent sportswriters, reporting on baseball, college football, and golf for the *New York Tribune* (later the *New York Herald Tribune*) during the early part of the twentieth century. In later years he covered sports in both film and radio broadcasts, remaining an active reporter until his death in 1954. His writings include *The Duffer's Handbook of Golf* and *The Tumult and the Shouting: My Life in Sports.*

RED SMITH is widely considered America's most celebrated sportswriter. His "Views of Sport" column was syndicated by the *New York Herald Tribune* from 1945 to 1967 followed by "Sports of the Times," appearing in the *New York Times* from 1971 until Smith's death in 1982. The recipient of numerous awards for sportswriting, Smith was awarded the Pulitzer Prize for Commentary. His writings have been collected in several volumes, most recently, *The Red Smith Reader.*

RICK TELANDER is the lead sports columnist for the *Chicago Sun-Times* and a Chicago-based contributor to *ESPN the Magazine*. He is the author of five books, including *Heaven Is a Playground* and *The Hundred-Yard Lie*. In his nearly seventeen years at *Sports Illustrated*, he wrote over 270 articles and three dozen cover stories.

JOHN UPDIKE is the author of over twenty novels, including the *Rabbit Angstrom* tetralogy, *In the Beauty of the Lilies*, and, most recently, *Gertrude and Claudius*. Among his numerous collections of short stories, poetry, essays, and criticism, is *Golf Dreams: Writings on Golf*. He has been awarded the National Book Award and the Pulitzer Prize for Fiction and is a member of the American Academy of Arts and Letters.